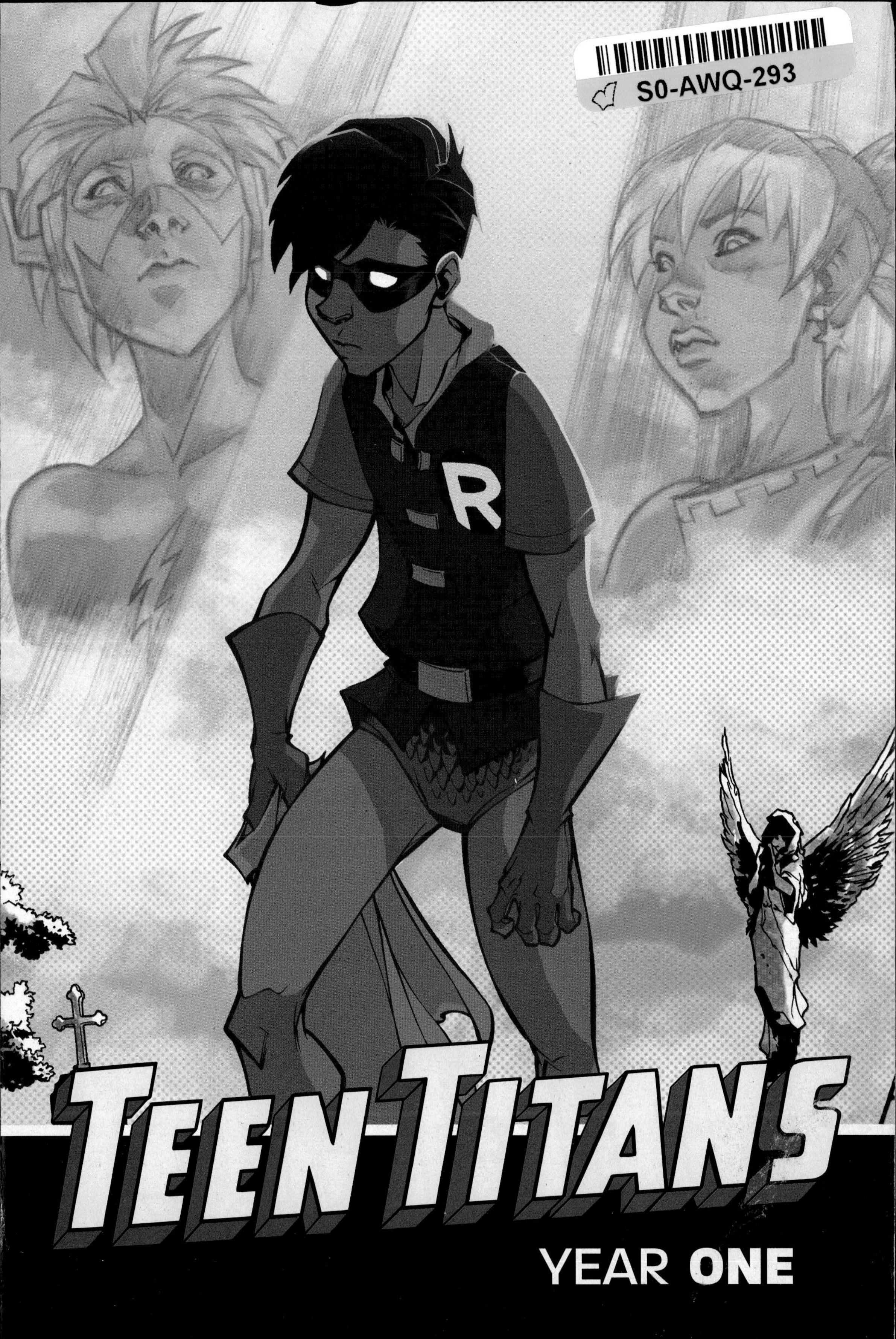
TEEN TITANS
YEAR ONE

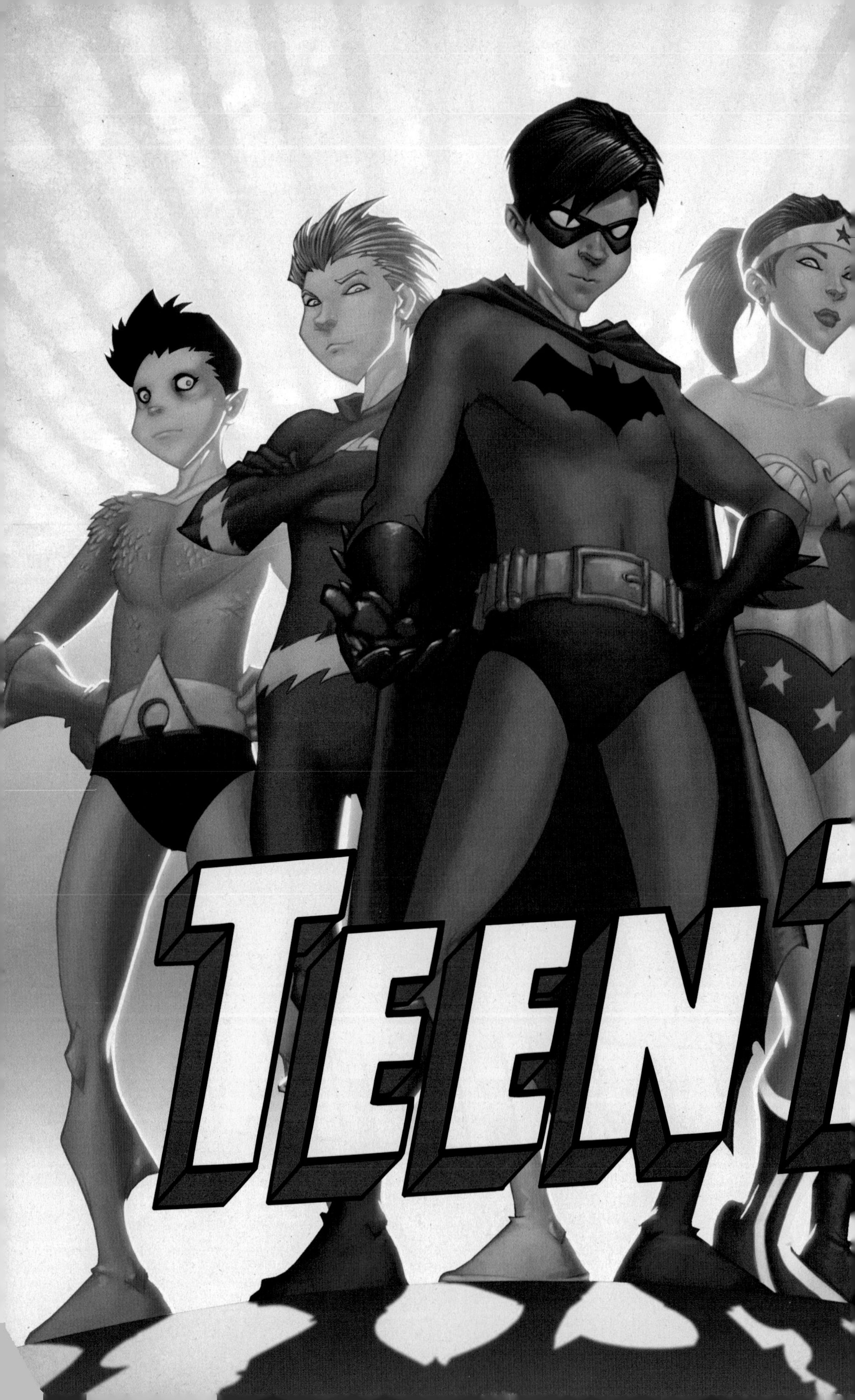
TEEN

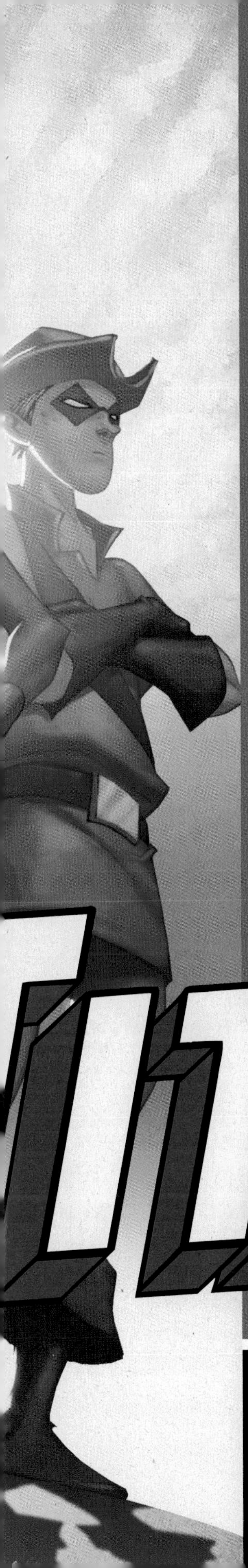

Written by
AMY WOLFRAM

Penciled by
KARL KERSCHL

Inked by
SERGE LAPOINTE

Colored by
STEPH PERU
JOHN RAUCH

Lettered by
NICK J. NAPOLITANO

Series & collection cover art by
KARL KERSHL &
SERGE LAPOINTE

TITANS

YEAR **ONE**

TEEN TITANS: YEAR ONE

Published by DC Comics. Compilation and all new material Copyright © 2016 DC Comics. All Rights Reserved. Originally published in single magazine form in TEEN TITANS: YEAR ONE 1-6. Copyright © 2008 DC Comics. All Rights Reserved. All characters, their distinctive likenesses and related elements featured in this publication are trademarks of DC Comics. The stories, characters and incidents featured in this publication are entirely fictional. DC Comics does not read or accept unsolicited submissions of ideas, stories or artwork.

DC Comics, 2900 West Alameda Ave., Burbank, CA 91505
Printed by Solisco Printers, Scott, QC, Canada. 11/18/16. First Printing.
ISBN: 978-1-4012-6724-7

Library of Congress Cataloging-in-Publication Data is available.

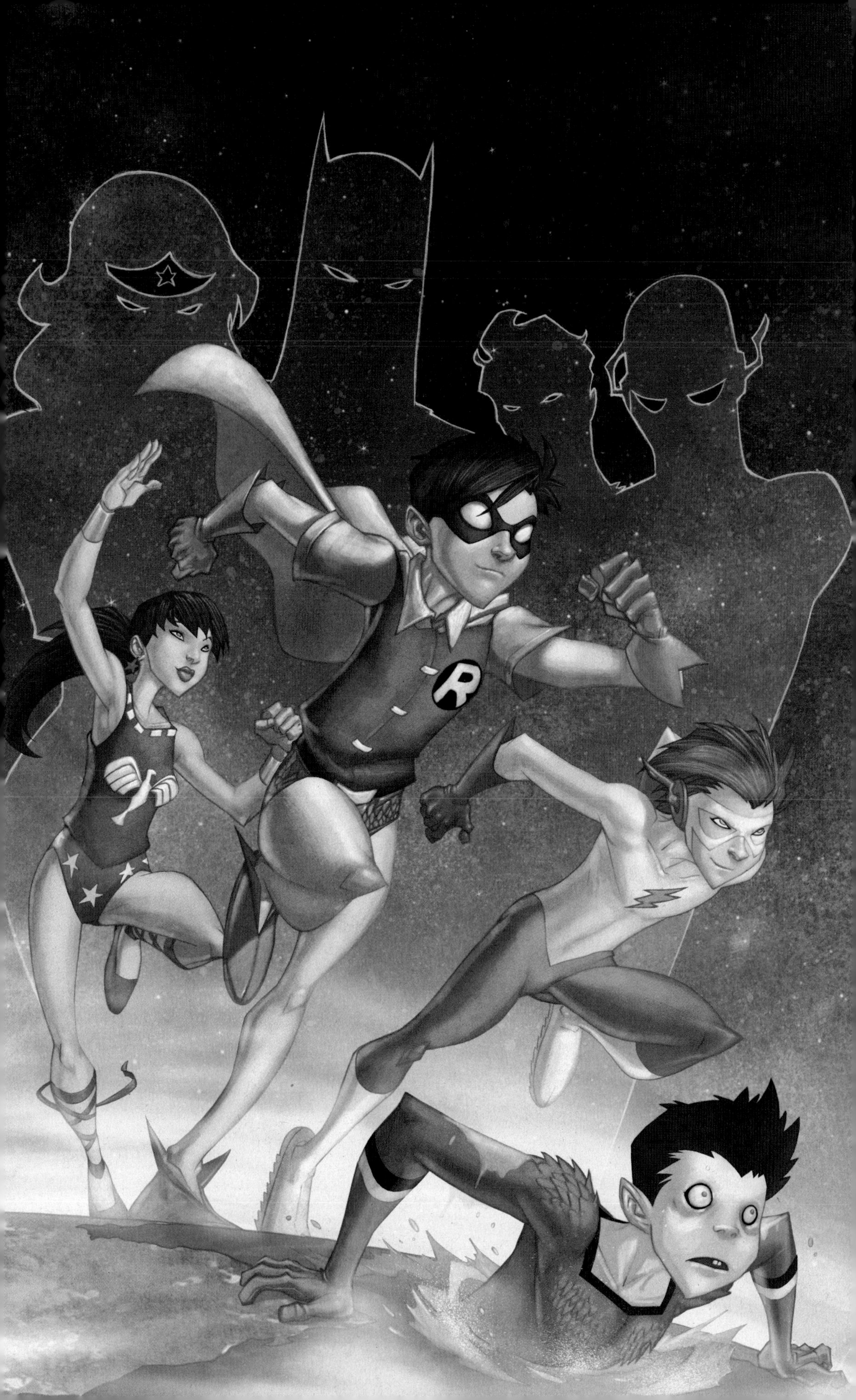

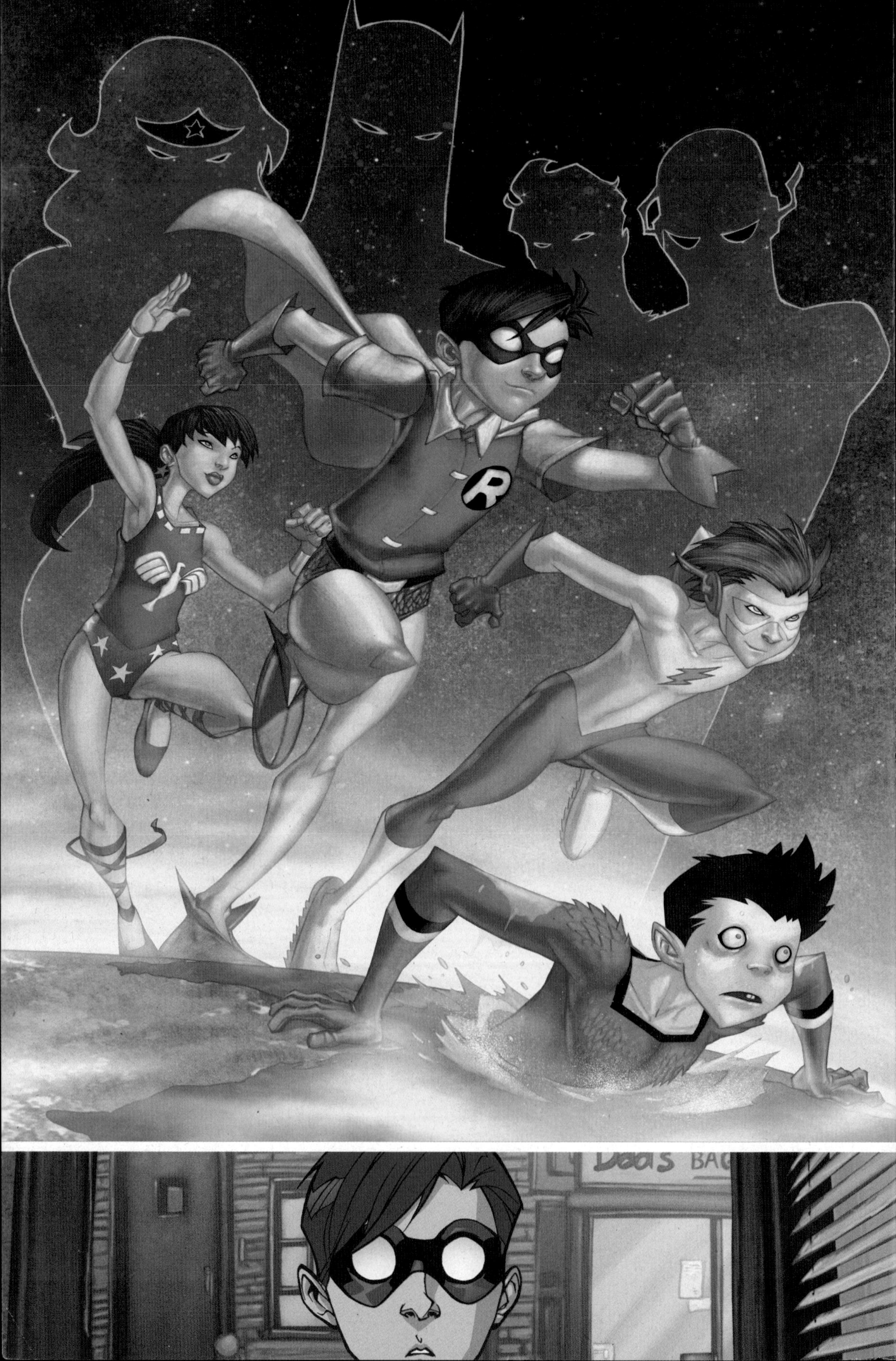

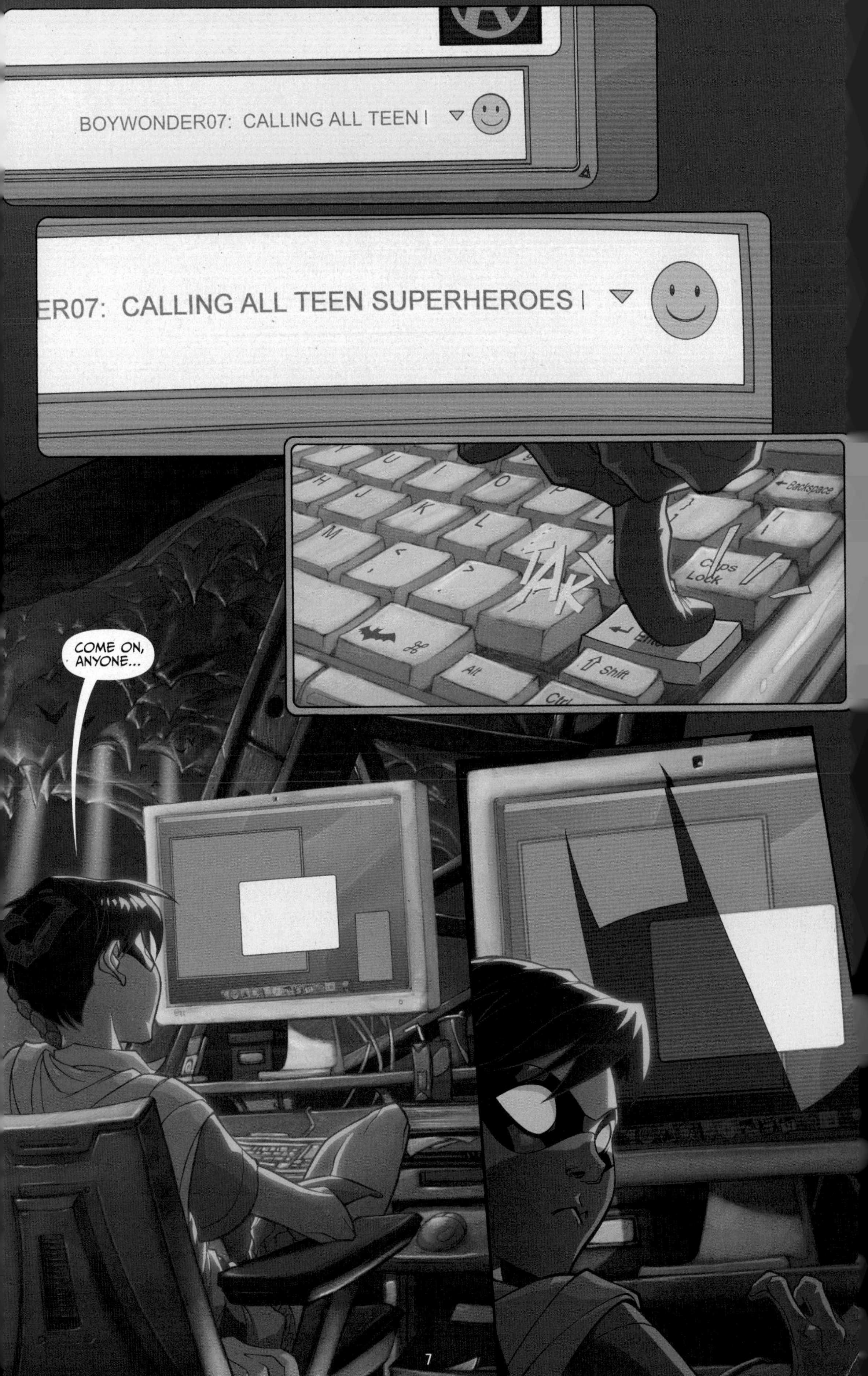
BOYWONDER07: CALLING ALL TEEN
ER07: CALLING ALL TEEN SUPERHEROES
TAK
COME ON, ANYONE...

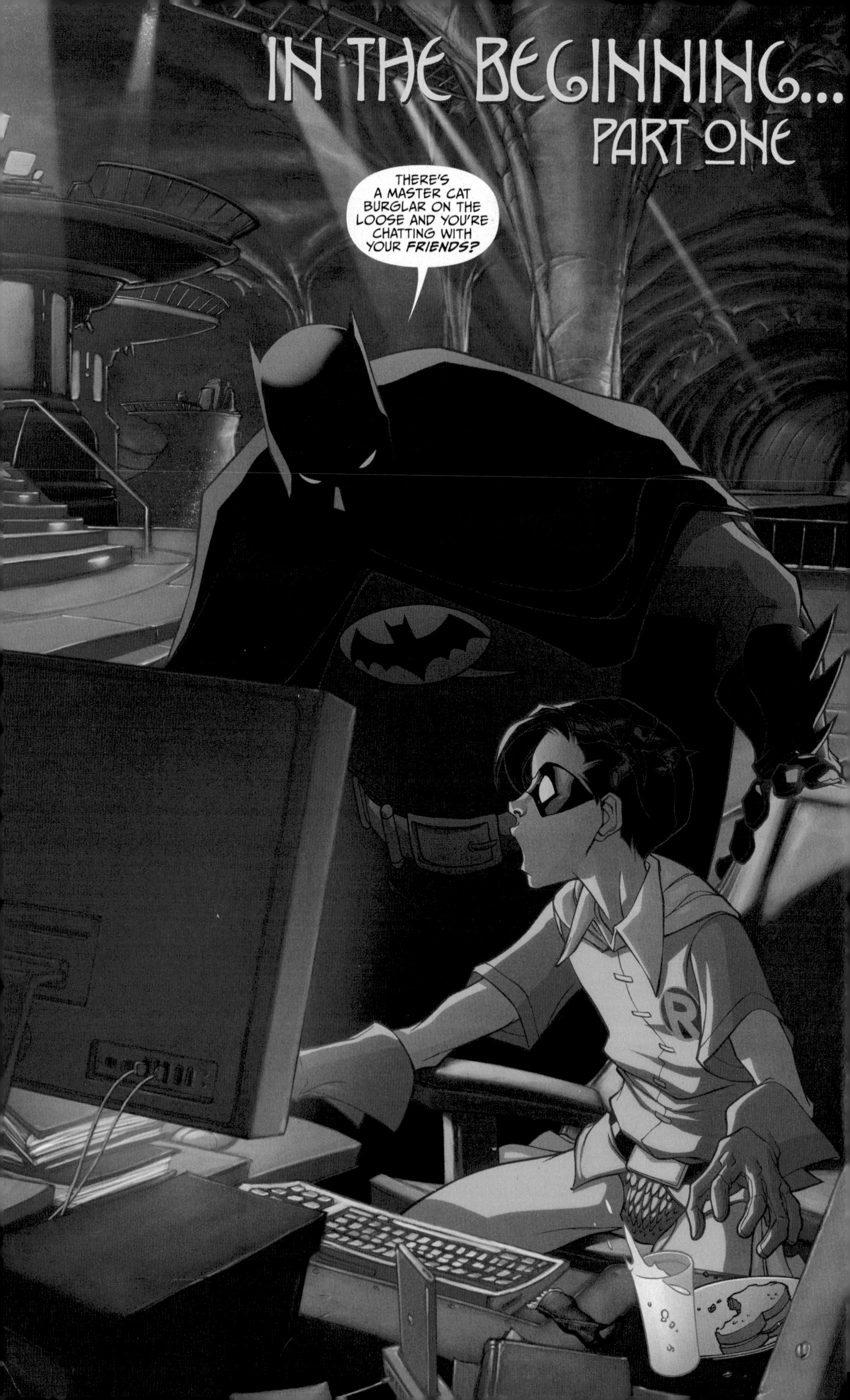
IN THE BEGINNING...
PART ONE
THERE'S A MASTER CAT BURGLAR ON THE LOOSE AND YOU'RE CHATTING WITH YOUR FRIENDS?

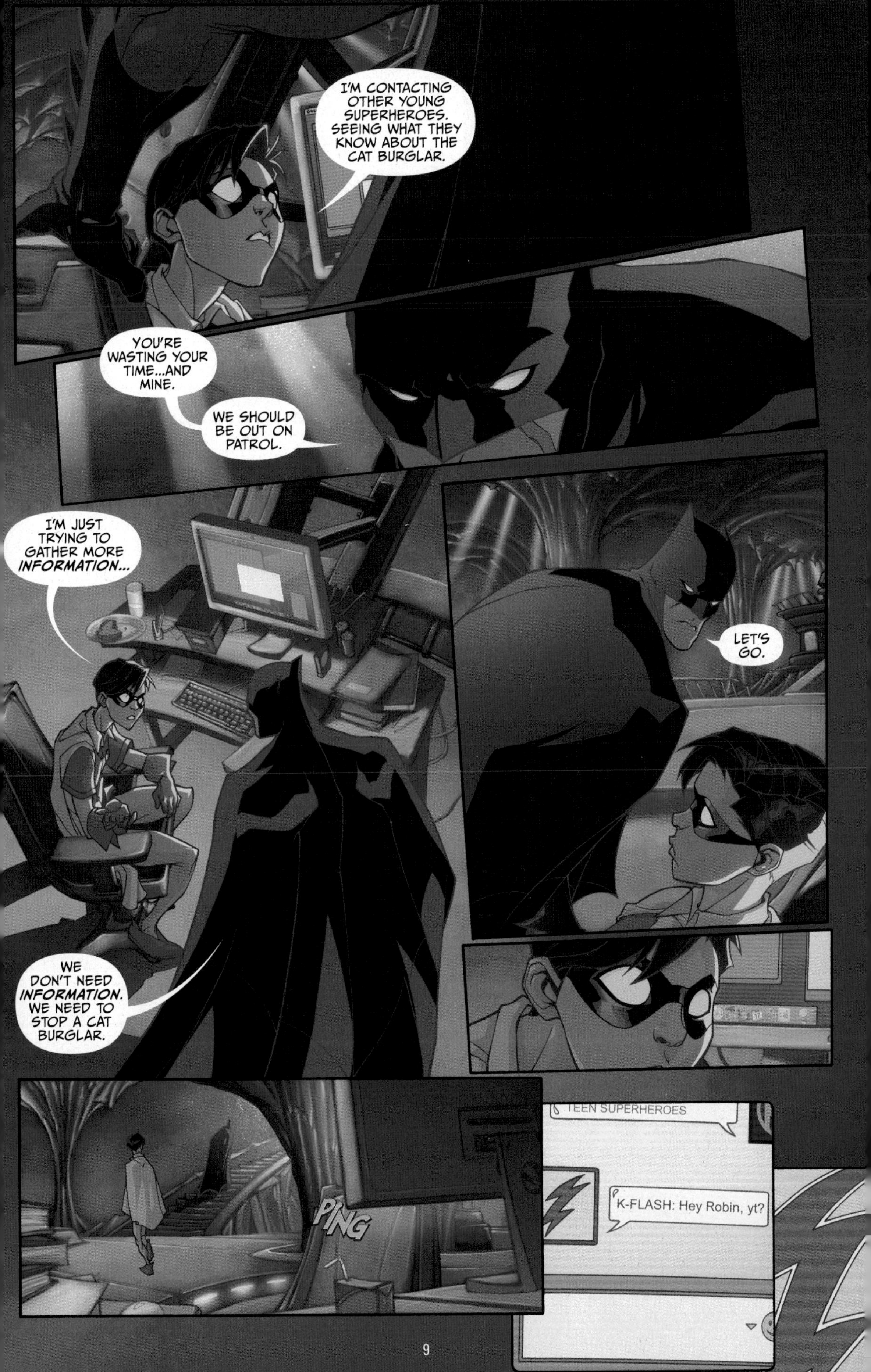
I'M CONTACTING OTHER YOUNG SUPERHEROES. SEEING WHAT THEY KNOW ABOUT THE CAT BURGLAR.
YOU'RE WASTING YOUR TIME...AND MINE.
WE SHOULD BE OUT ON PATROL.
I'M JUST TRYING TO GATHER MORE *INFORMATION*...
WE DON'T NEED *INFORMATION*. WE NEED TO STOP A CAT BURGLAR.
LET'S GO.
PING
TEEN SUPERHEROES
K-FLASH: Hey Robin, yt?

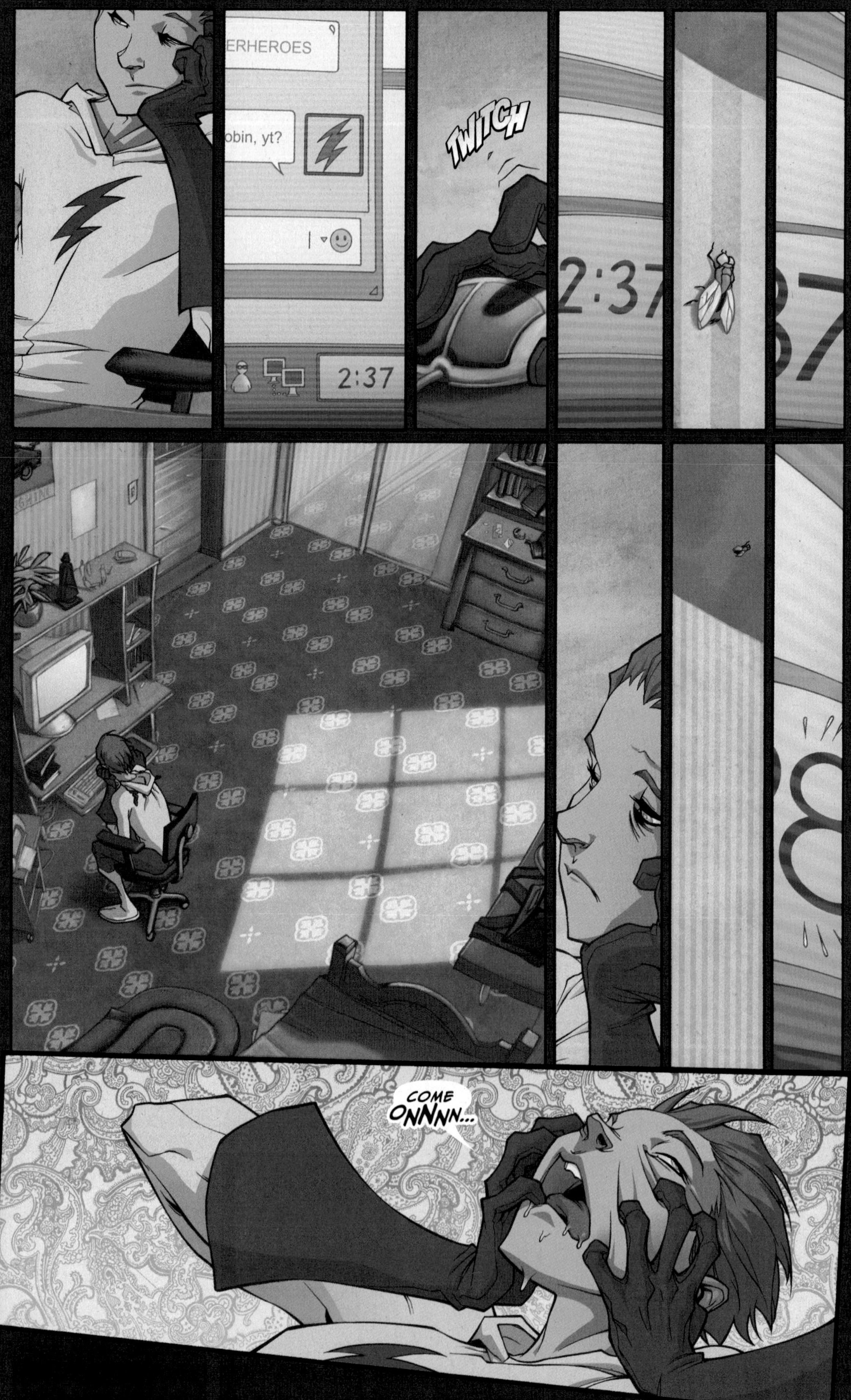
ERHEROES
obin, yt?
2:37
TWITCH
2:37
37
COME ONNNN...

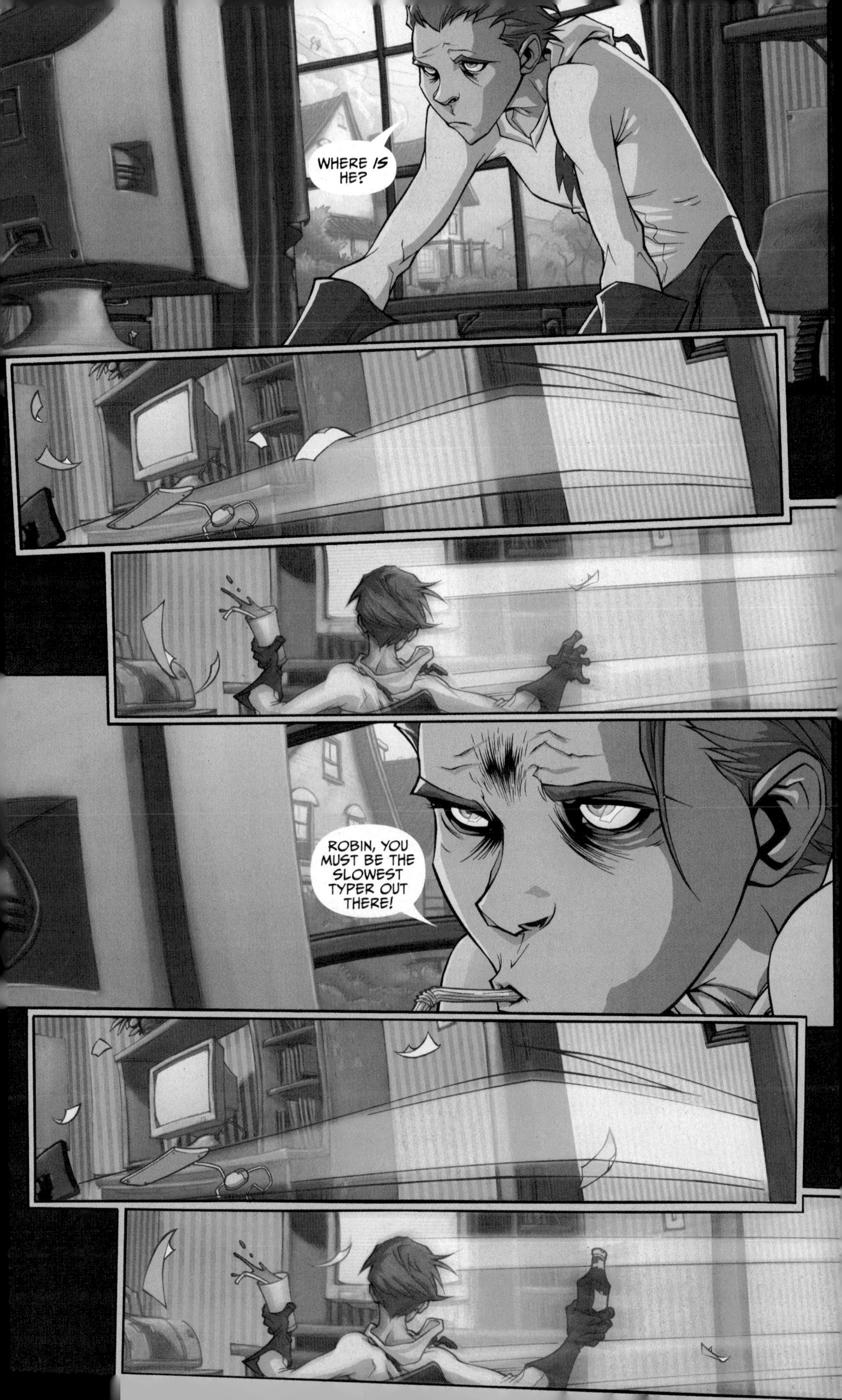
WHERE IS HE?
ROBIN, YOU MUST BE THE SLOWEST TYPER OUT THERE!

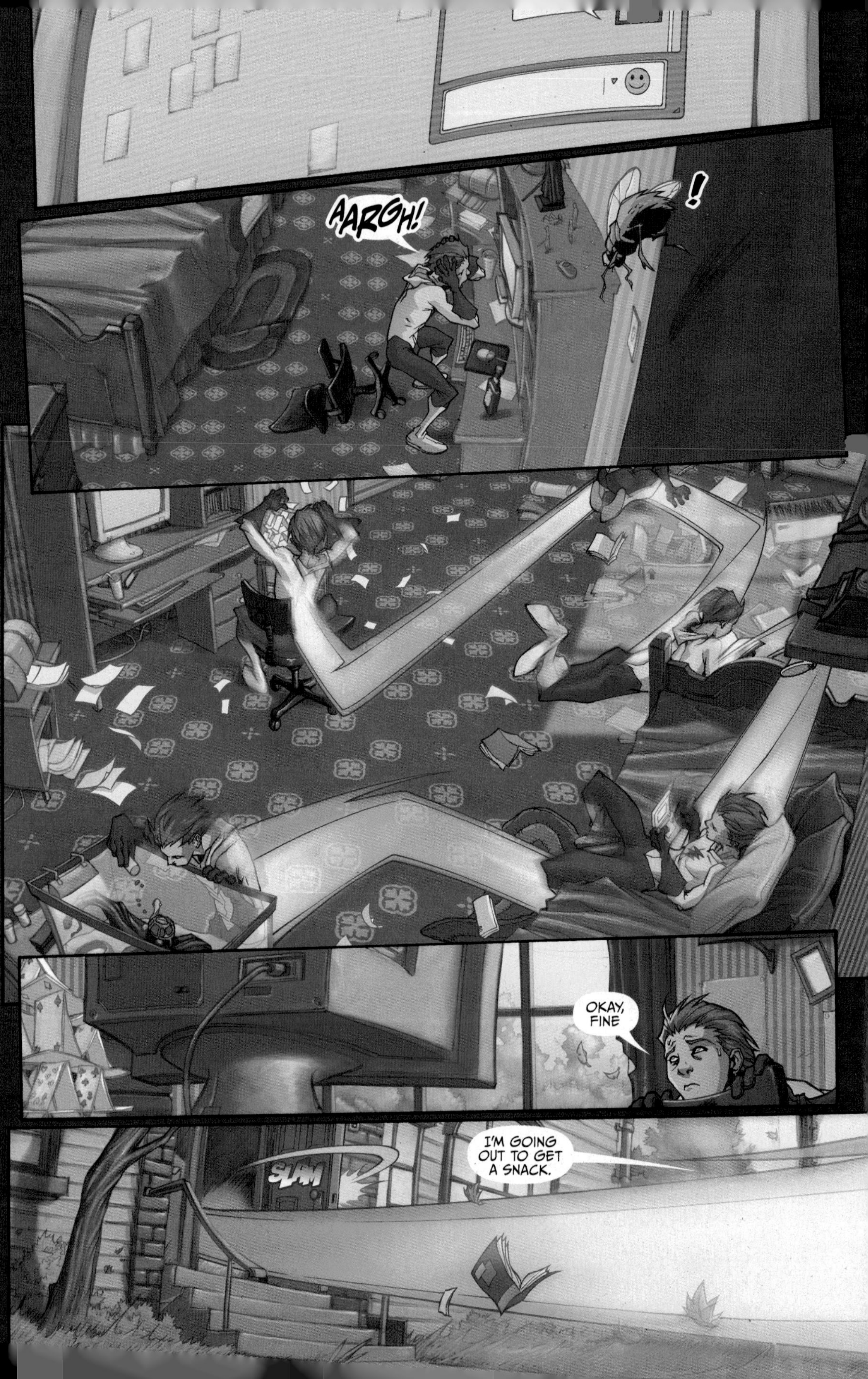
AARGH!
!
OKAY, FINE
SLAM
I'M GOING OUT TO GET A SNACK.

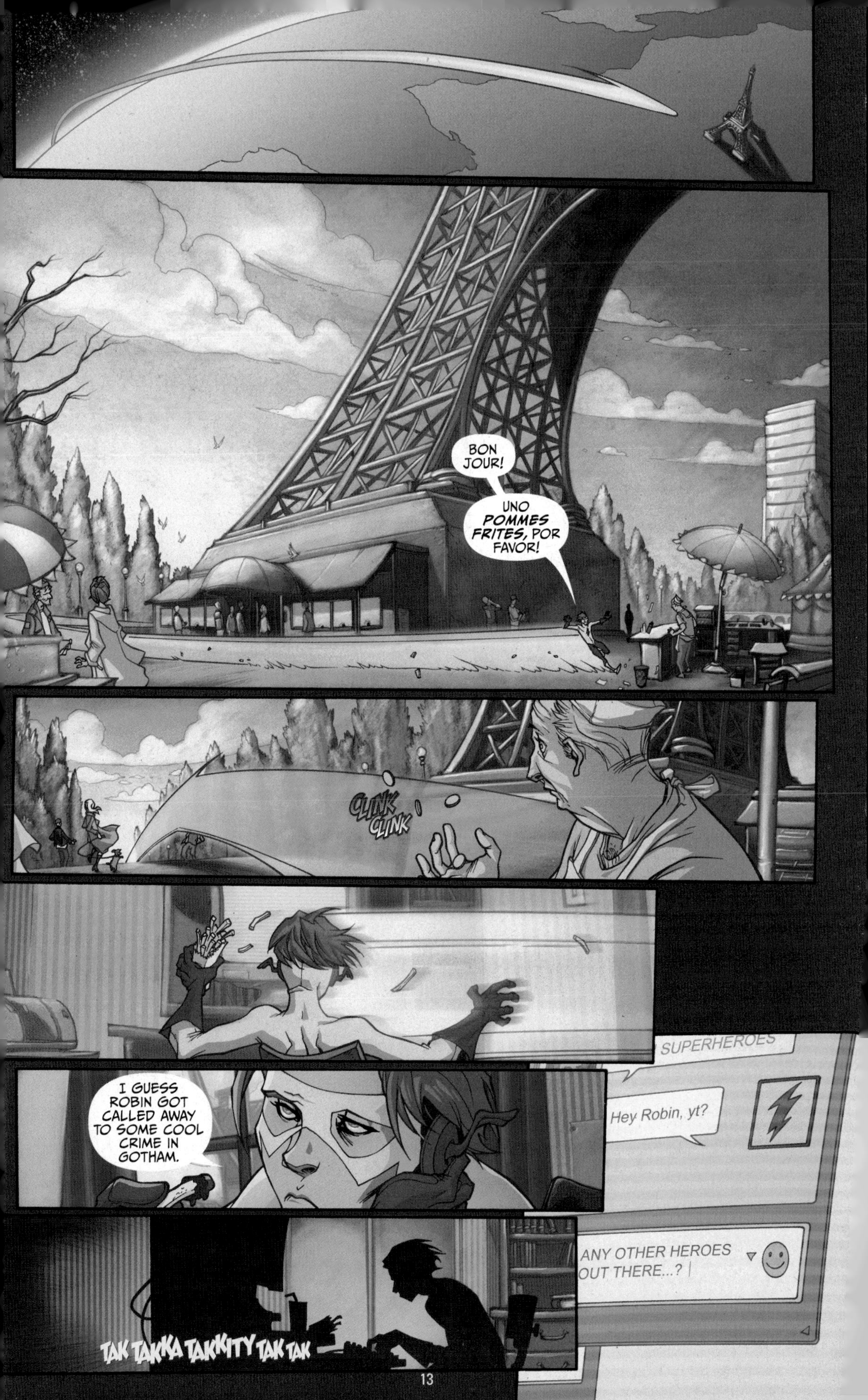
BON JOUR!
UNO POMMES FRITES, POR FAVOR!
CLINK CLINK
SUPERHEROES
Hey Robin, yt?
I GUESS ROBIN GOT CALLED AWAY TO SOME COOL CRIME IN GOTHAM.
ANY OTHER HEROES OUT THERE...?
TAK TAKKA TAKKITY TAK TAK

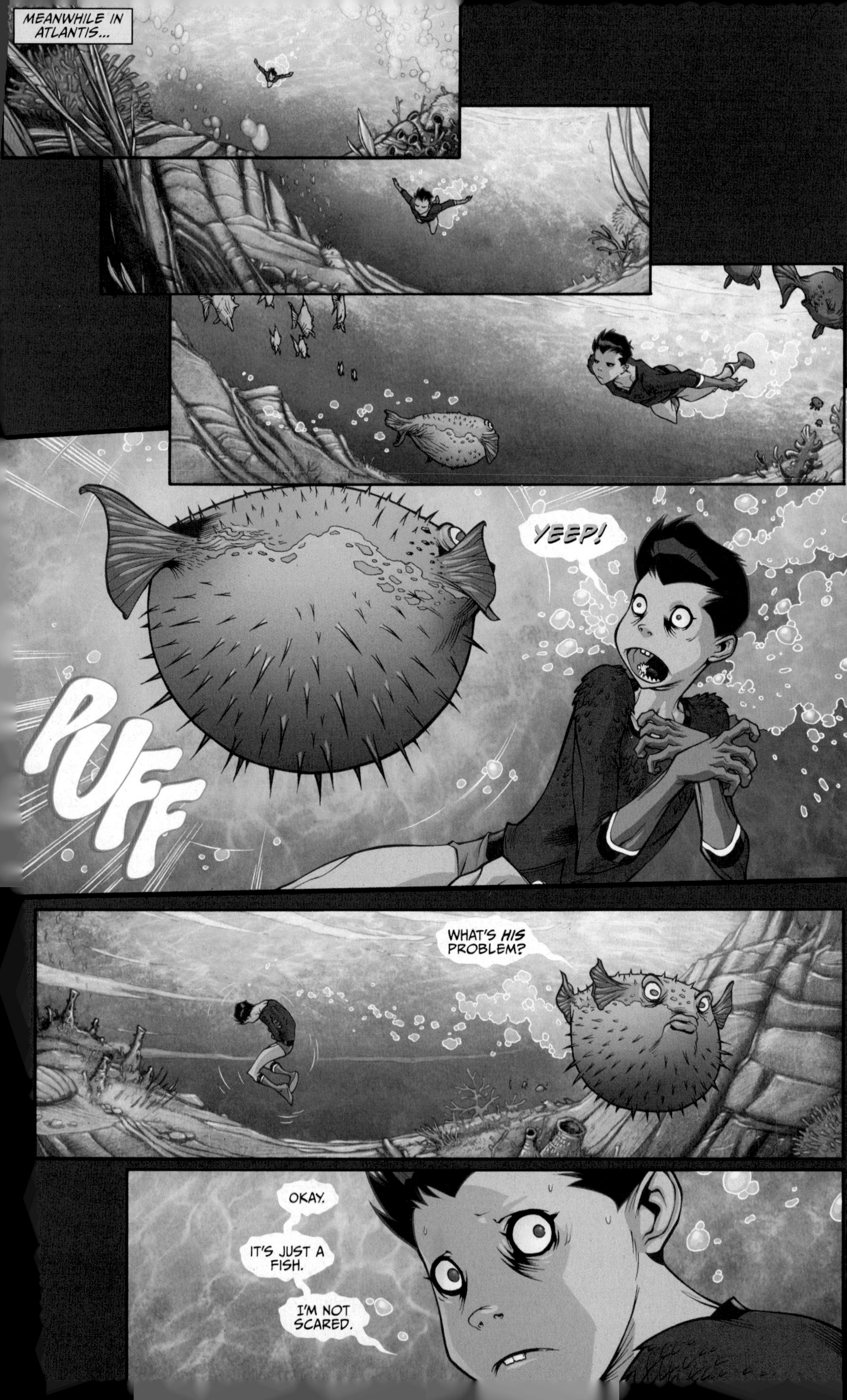
MEANWHILE IN ATLANTIS...
YEEP!
PUFF
WHAT'S HIS PROBLEM?
OKAY.
IT'S JUST A FISH.
I'M NOT SCARED.

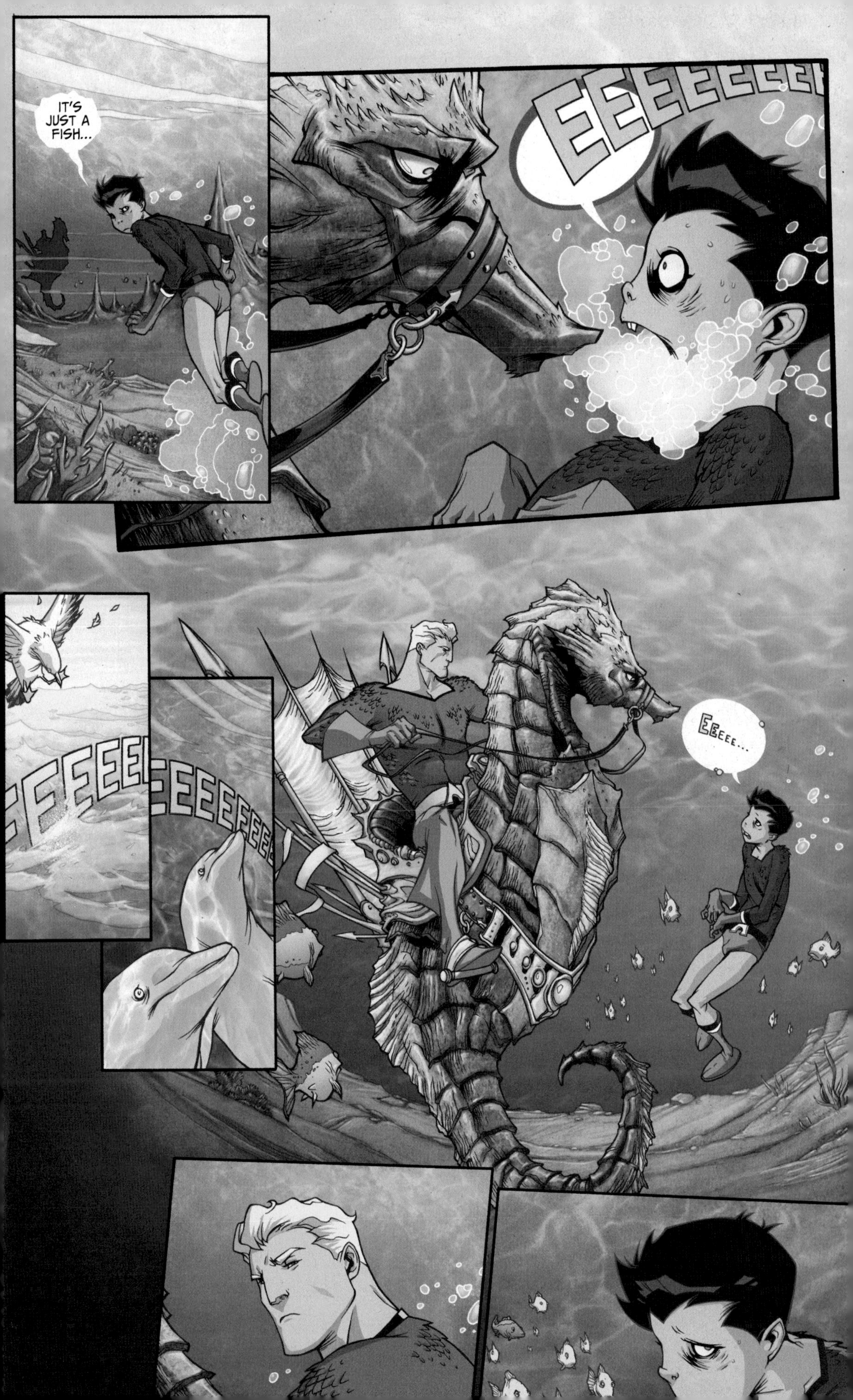
IT'S JUST A FISH...
EEEEEEEE
Eeeee...

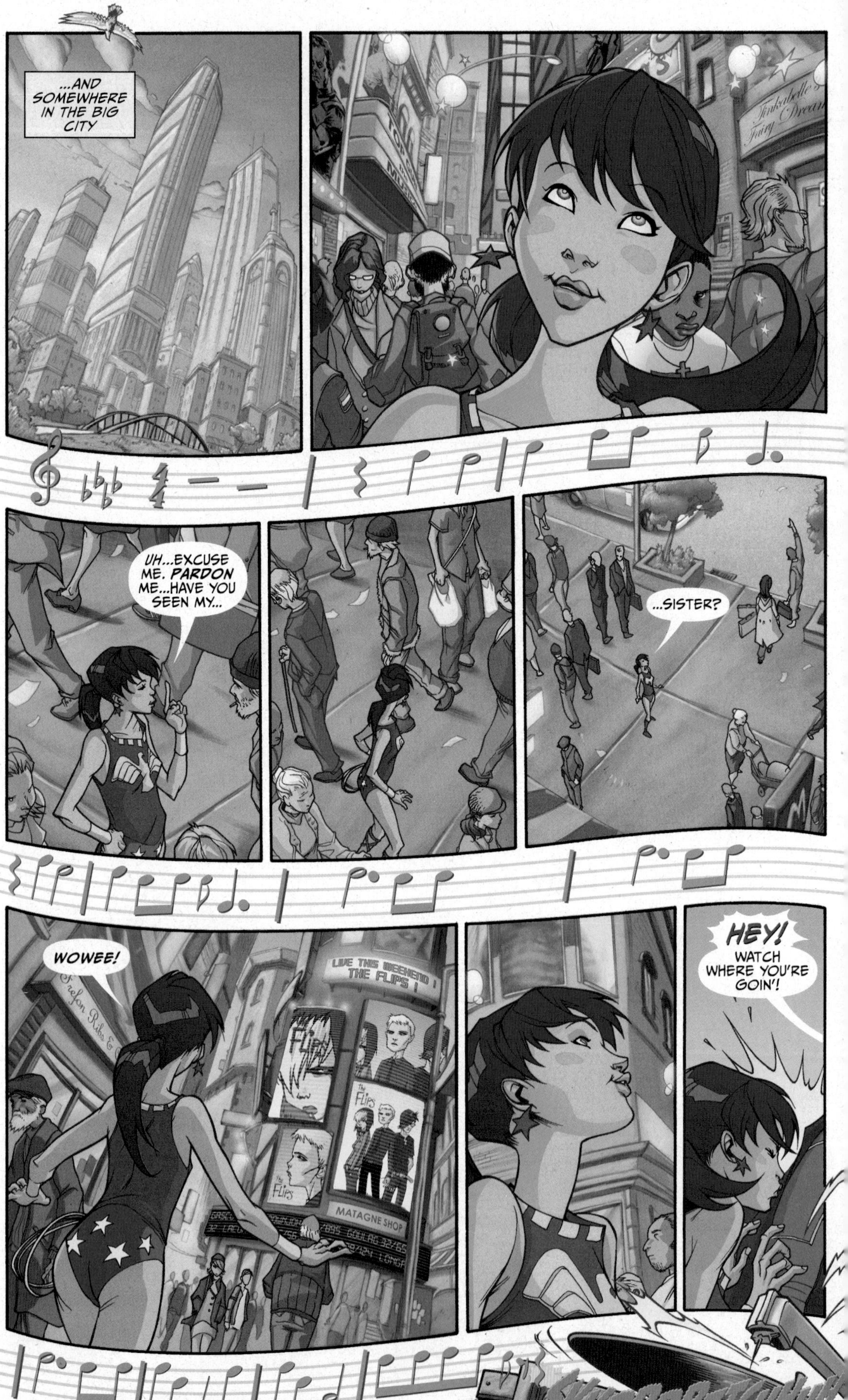
...AND SOMEWHERE IN THE BIG CITY
UH...EXCUSE ME. PARDON ME...HAVE YOU SEEN MY...
...SISTER?
WOWEE!
LIVE THIS WEEKEND THE FLIPS!
MATAGNE SHOP
HEY! WATCH WHERE YOU'RE GOIN'!

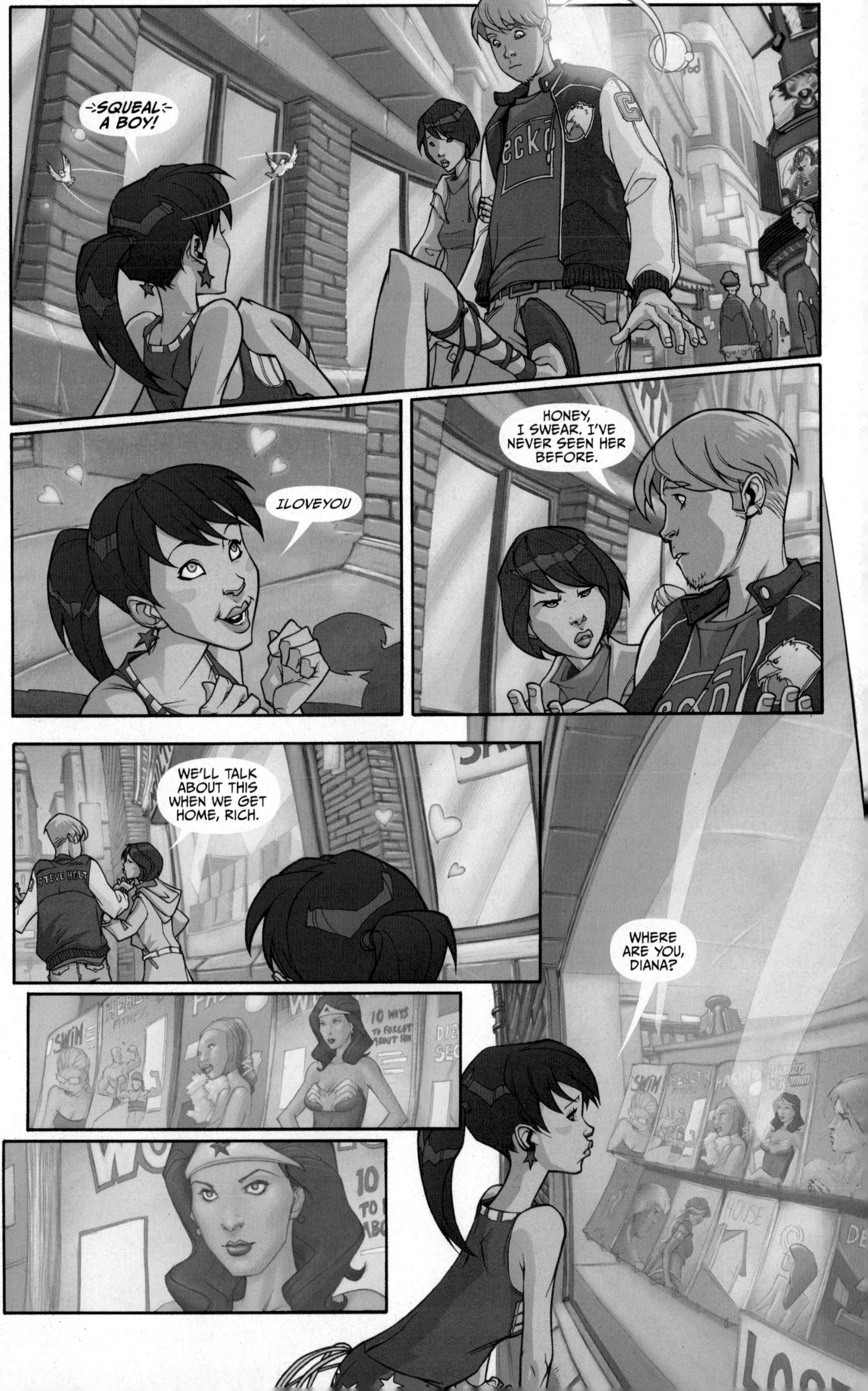
SQUEAL
A BOY!
ILOVEYOU
HONEY, I SWEAR. I'VE NEVER SEEN HER BEFORE.
WE'LL TALK ABOUT THIS WHEN WE GET HOME, RICH.
STEVE HOLT
10 WAYS TO FORGET ABOUT HIM
WHERE ARE YOU, DIANA?

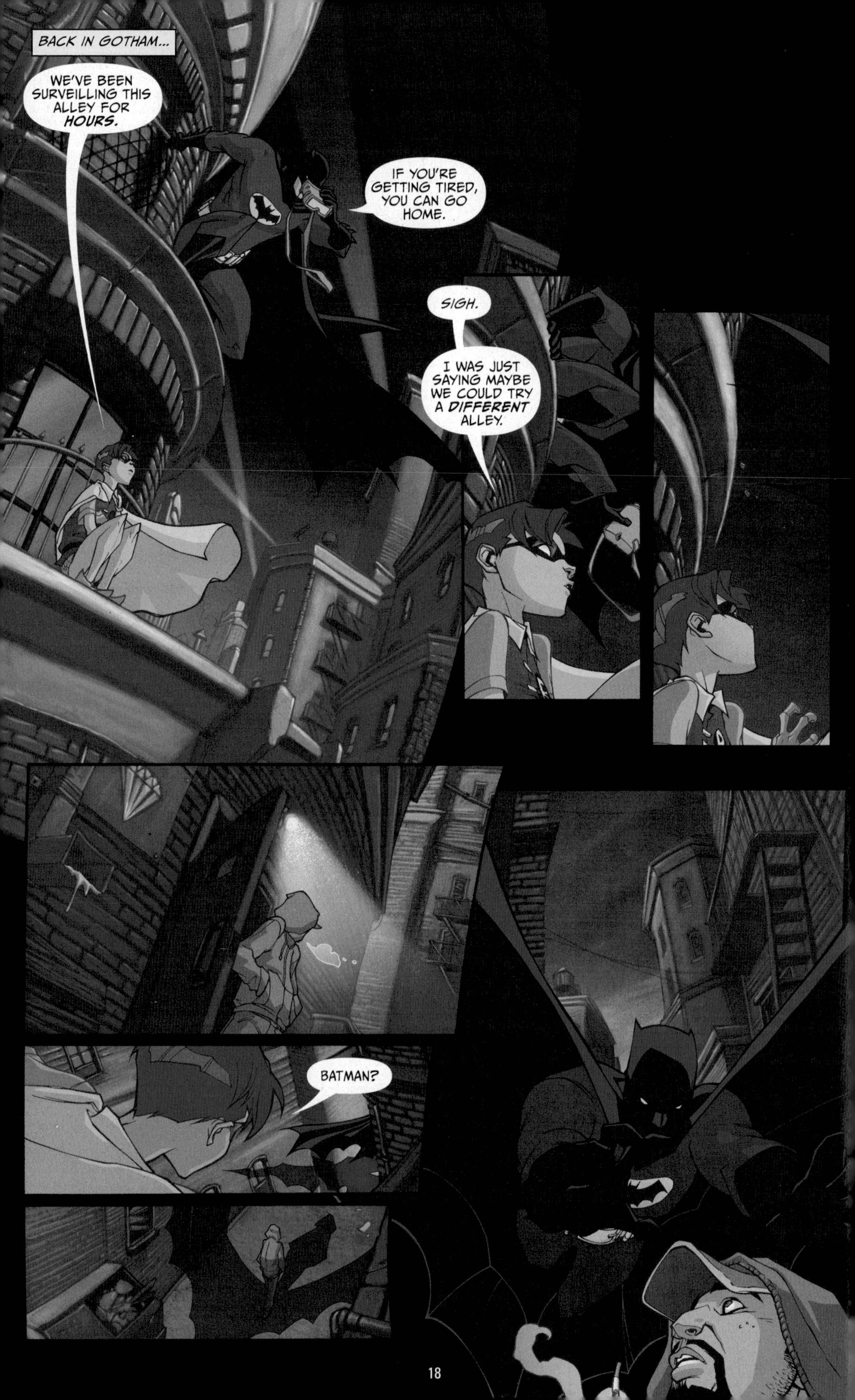
BACK IN GOTHAM...
WE'VE BEEN SURVEILLING THIS ALLEY FOR HOURS.
IF YOU'RE GETTING TIRED, YOU CAN GO HOME.
SIGH.
I WAS JUST SAYING MAYBE WE COULD TRY A DIFFERENT ALLEY.
BATMAN?

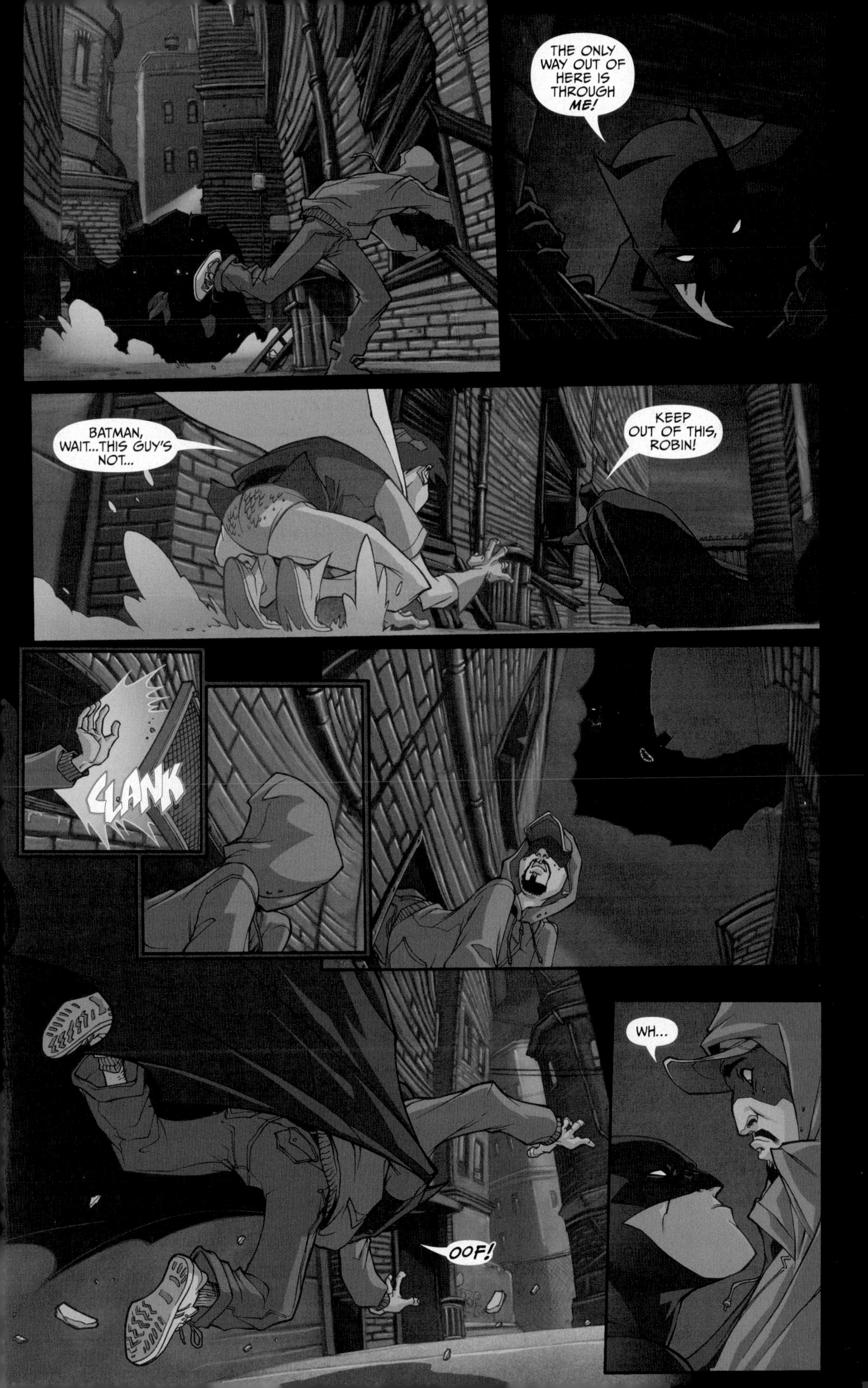

THE ONLY WAY OUT OF HERE IS THROUGH *ME!*
BATMAN, WAIT...THIS GUY'S NOT...
KEEP OUT OF THIS, ROBIN!
CLANK
OOF!
WH...

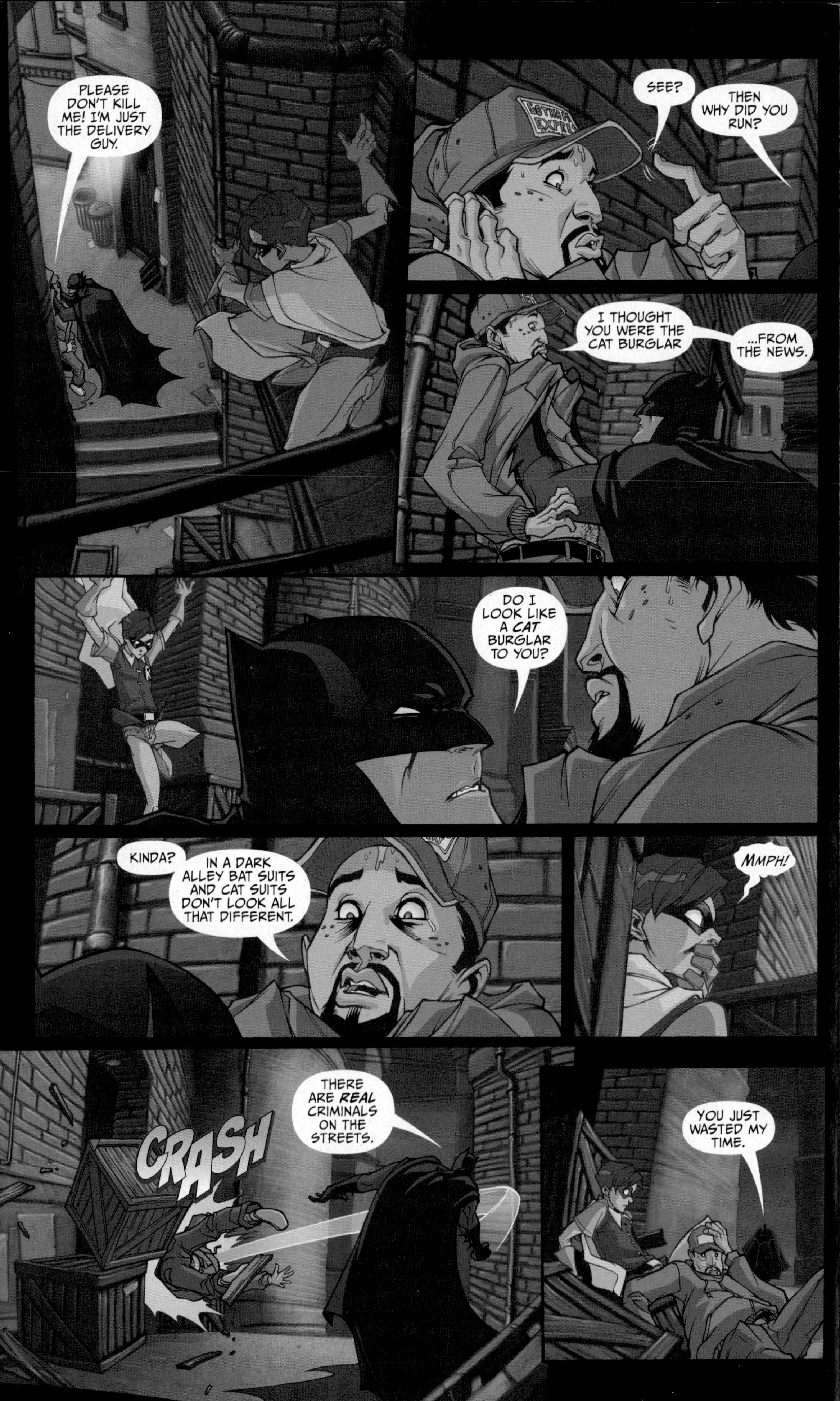
PLEASE DON'T KILL ME! I'M JUST THE DELIVERY GUY.
SEE?
THEN WHY DID YOU RUN?
I THOUGHT YOU WERE THE CAT BURGLAR
...FROM THE NEWS.
DO I LOOK LIKE A CAT BURGLAR TO YOU?
KINDA?
IN A DARK ALLEY BAT SUITS AND CAT SUITS DON'T LOOK ALL THAT DIFFERENT.
MMPH!
CRASH
THERE ARE REAL CRIMINALS ON THE STREETS.
YOU JUST WASTED MY TIME.

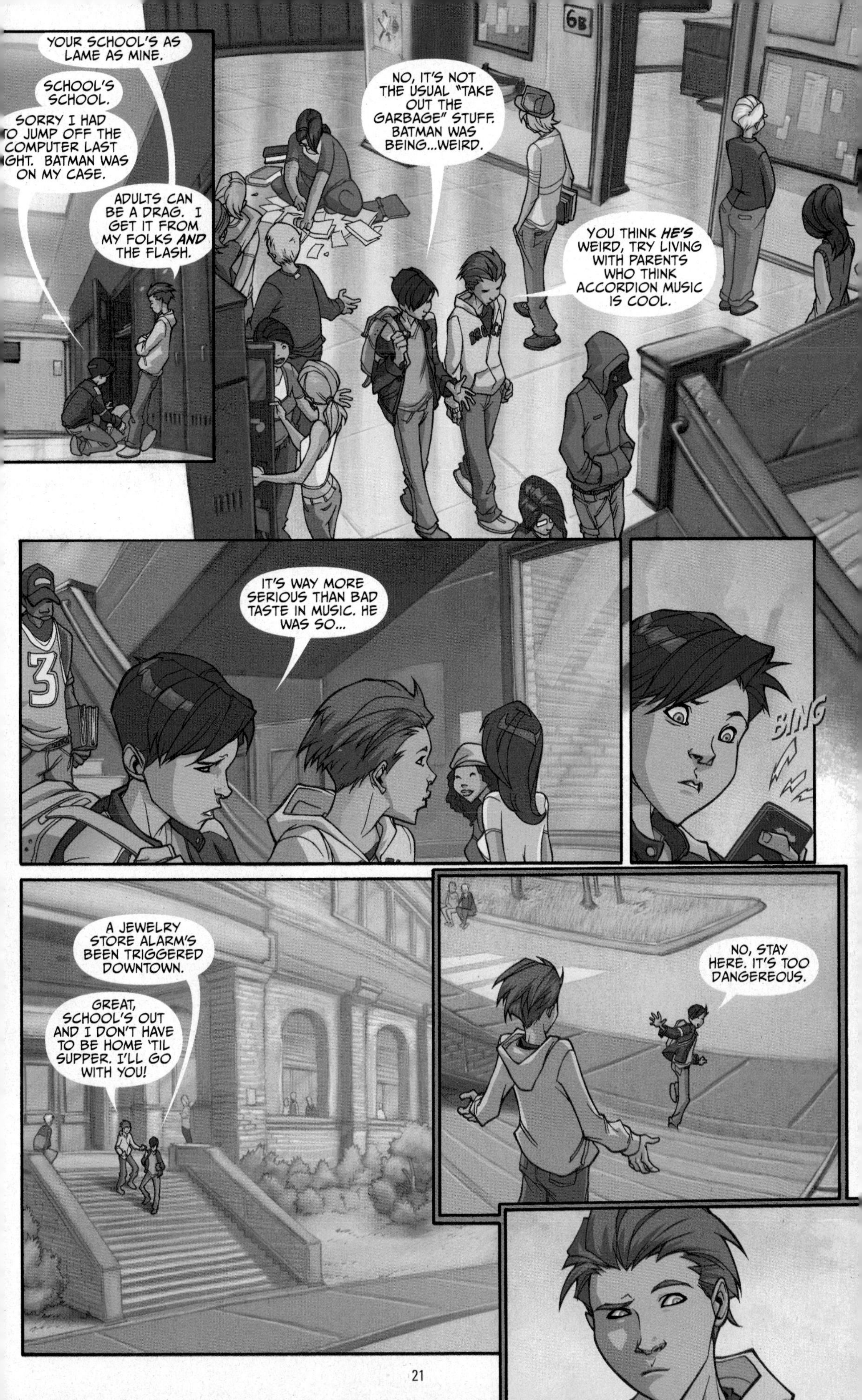
YOUR SCHOOL'S AS LAME AS MINE.
SCHOOL'S SCHOOL.
SORRY I HAD TO JUMP OFF THE COMPUTER LAST NIGHT. BATMAN WAS ON MY CASE.
ADULTS CAN BE A DRAG. I GET IT FROM MY FOLKS AND THE FLASH.
NO, IT'S NOT THE USUAL "TAKE OUT THE GARBAGE" STUFF. BATMAN WAS BEING...WEIRD.
YOU THINK HE'S WEIRD, TRY LIVING WITH PARENTS WHO THINK ACCORDION MUSIC IS COOL.
IT'S WAY MORE SERIOUS THAN BAD TASTE IN MUSIC. HE WAS SO...
BING
A JEWELRY STORE ALARM'S BEEN TRIGGERED DOWNTOWN.
GREAT, SCHOOL'S OUT AND I DON'T HAVE TO BE HOME 'TIL SUPPER. I'LL GO WITH YOU!
NO, STAY HERE. IT'S TOO DANGEREOUS.

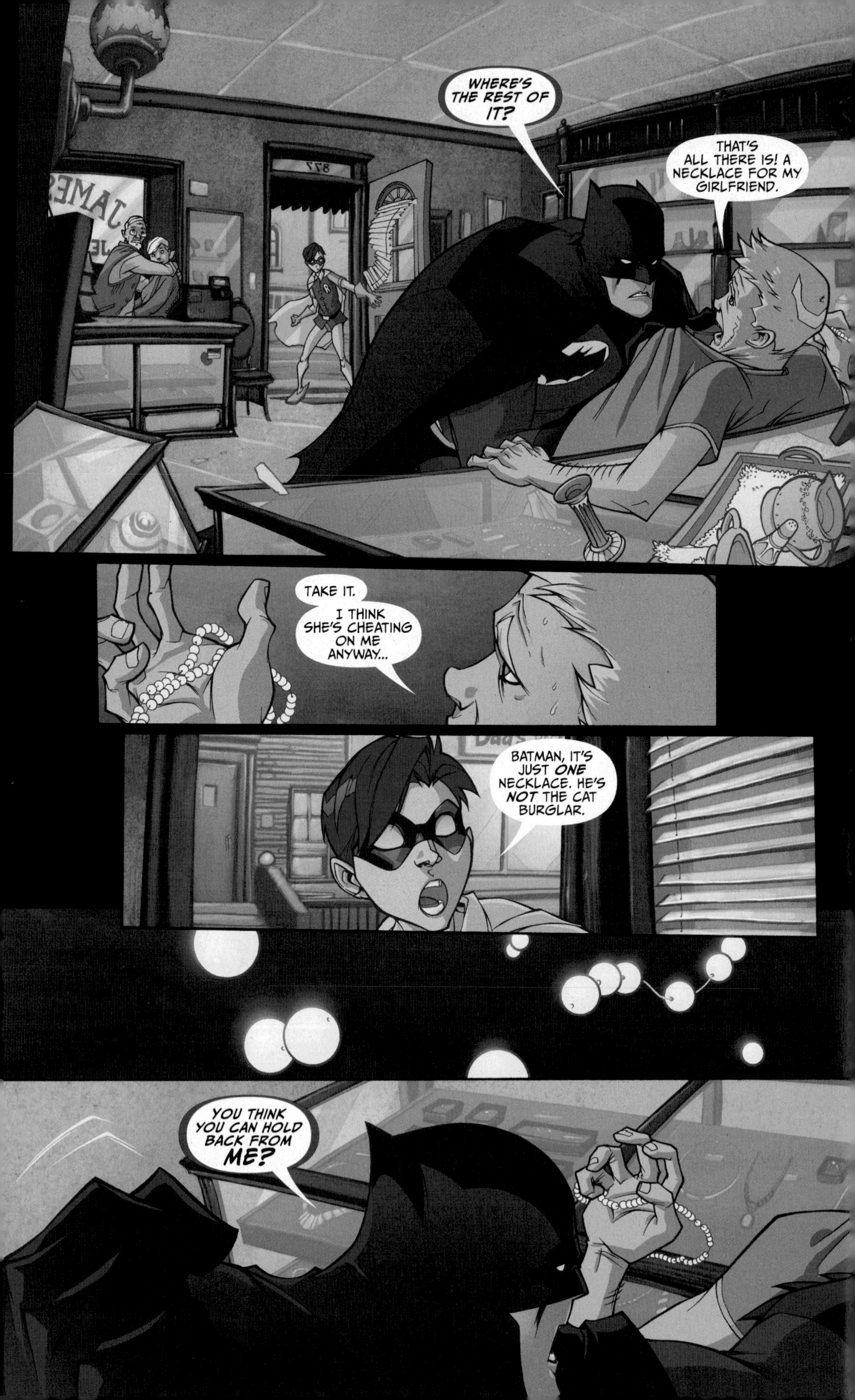
WHERE'S THE REST OF IT?
THAT'S ALL THERE IS! A NECKLACE FOR MY GIRLFRIEND.
TAKE IT.
I THINK SHE'S CHEATING ON ME ANYWAY...
BATMAN, IT'S JUST ONE NECKLACE. HE'S NOT THE CAT BURGLAR.
YOU THINK YOU CAN HOLD BACK FROM ME?

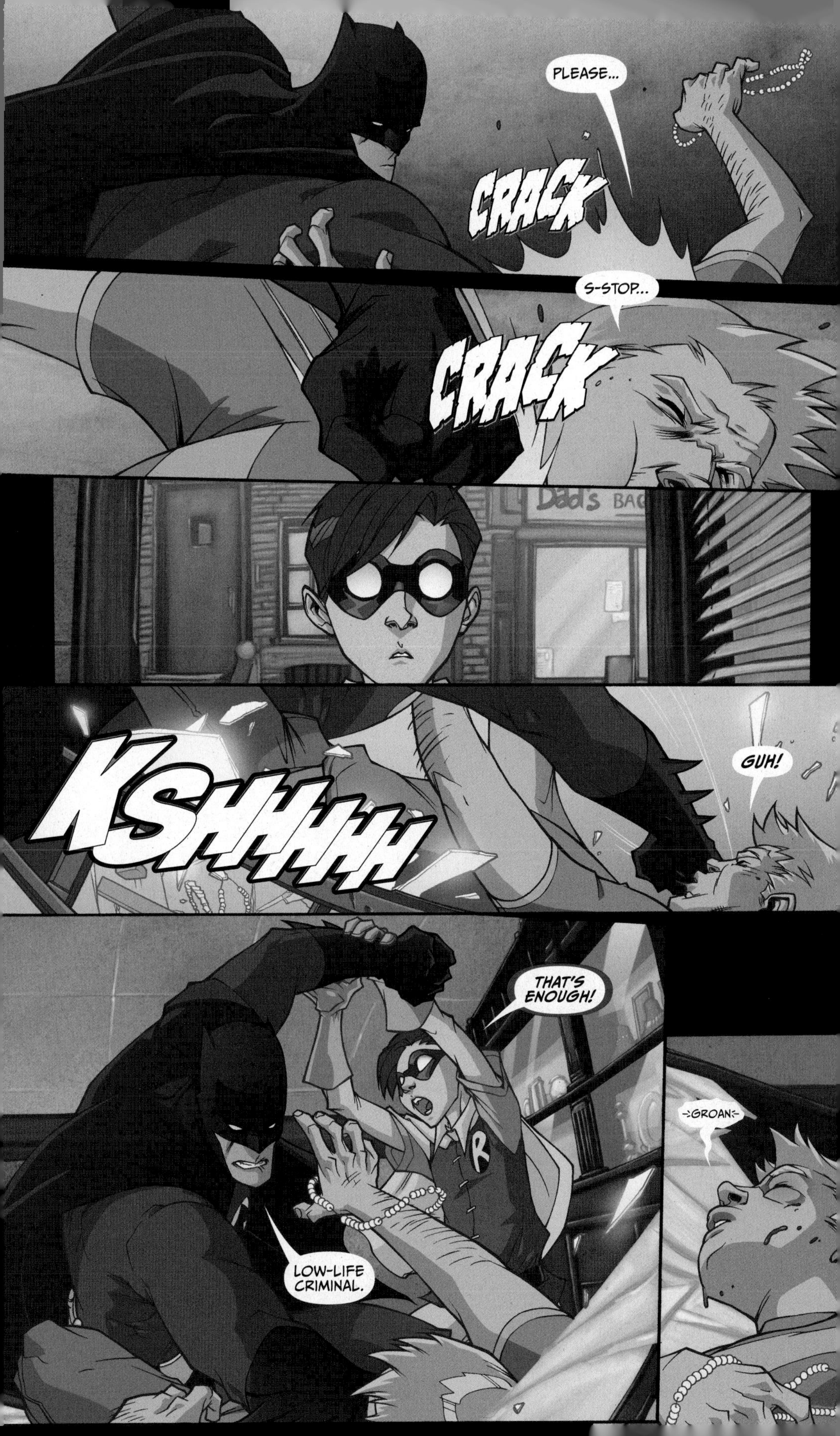
PLEASE...
CRACK
S-STOP...
CRACK
Dad's BAG
KSHHHHH
GUH!
THAT'S ENOUGH!
LOW-LIFE CRIMINAL.
-GROAN-

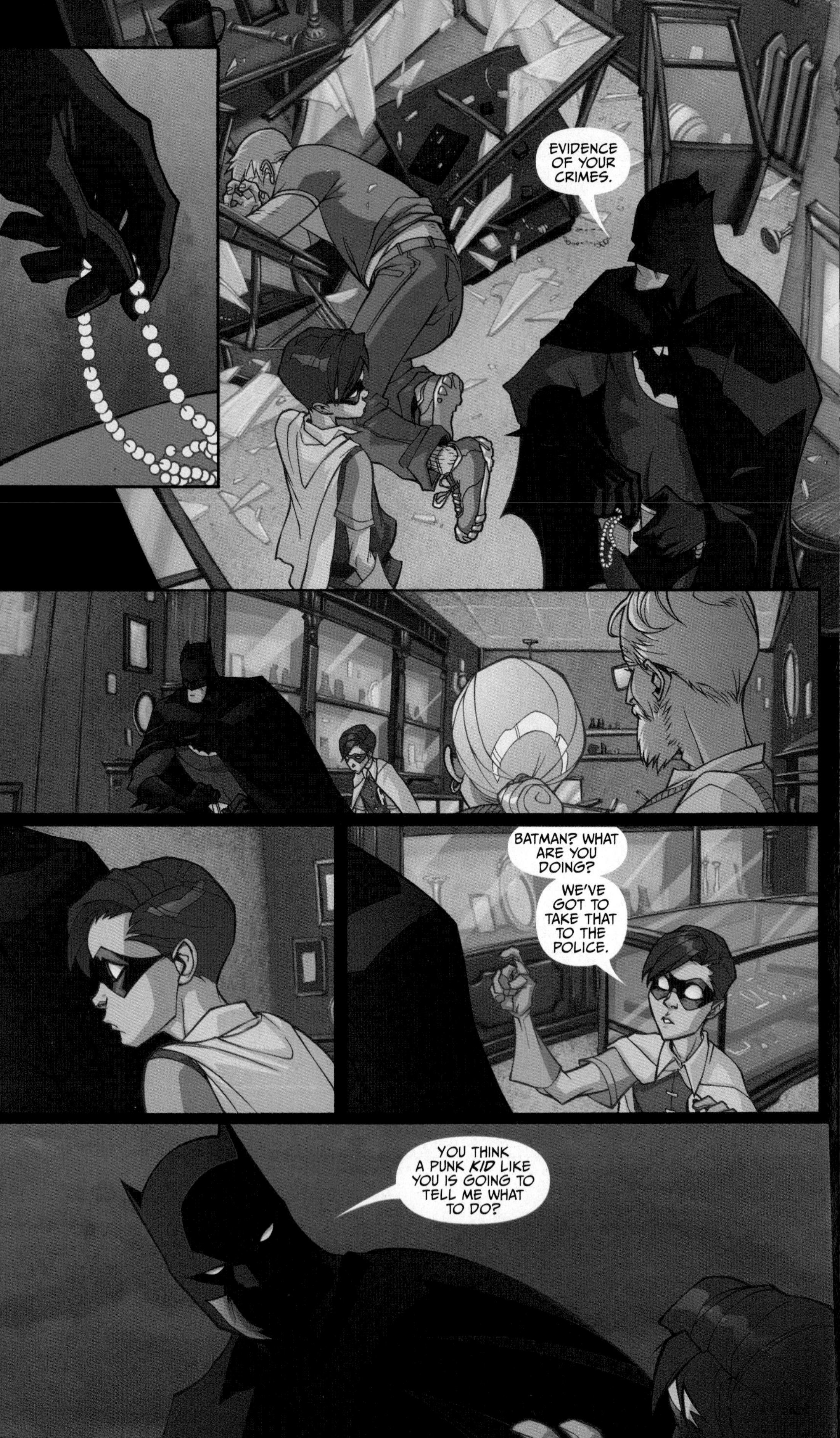
EVIDENCE OF YOUR CRIMES.
BATMAN? WHAT ARE YOU DOING?
WE'VE GOT TO TAKE THAT TO THE POLICE.
YOU THINK A PUNK *KID* LIKE YOU IS GOING TO TELL ME WHAT TO DO?

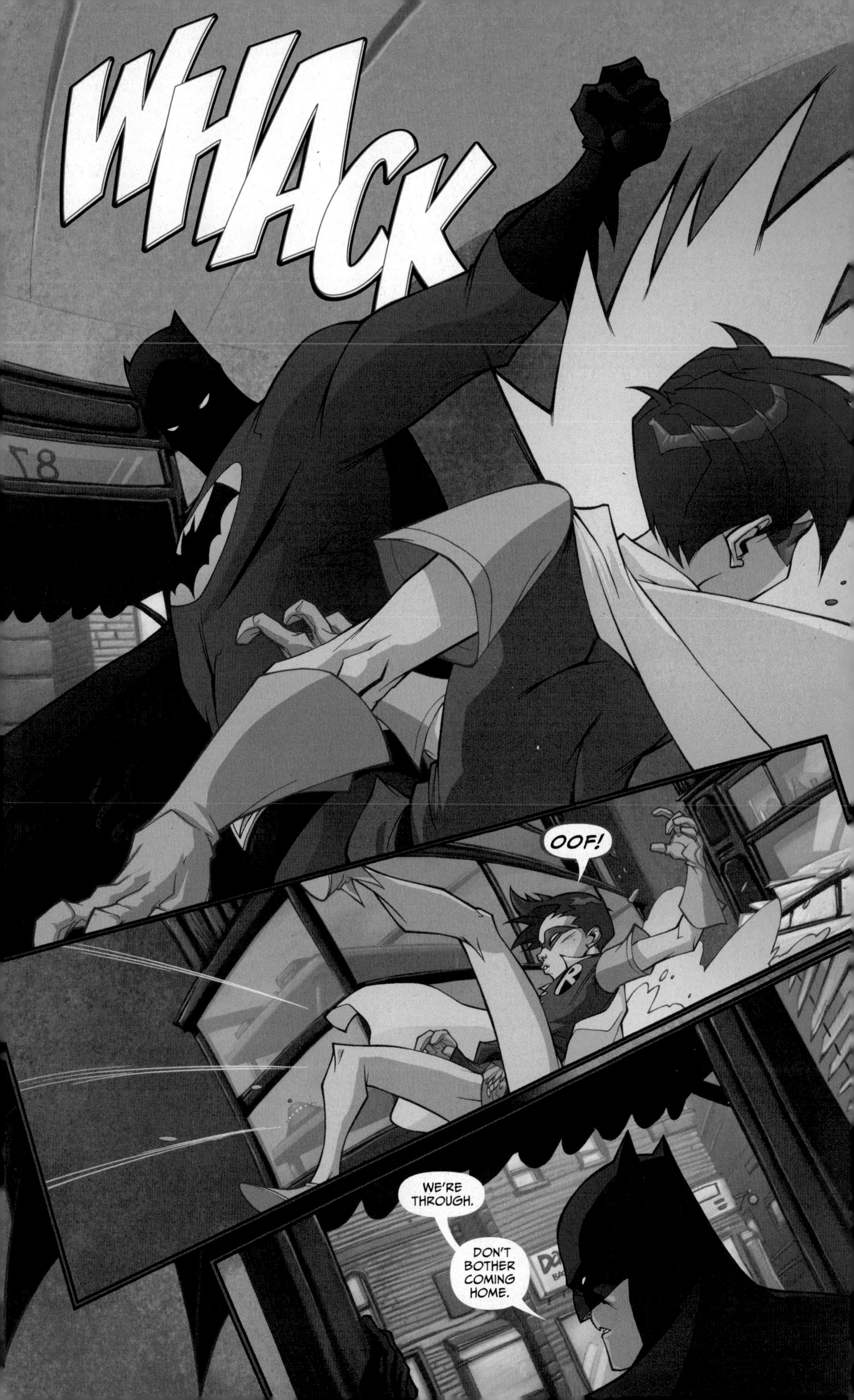
WHACK
OOF!
WE'RE THROUGH.
DON'T BOTHER COMING HOME.

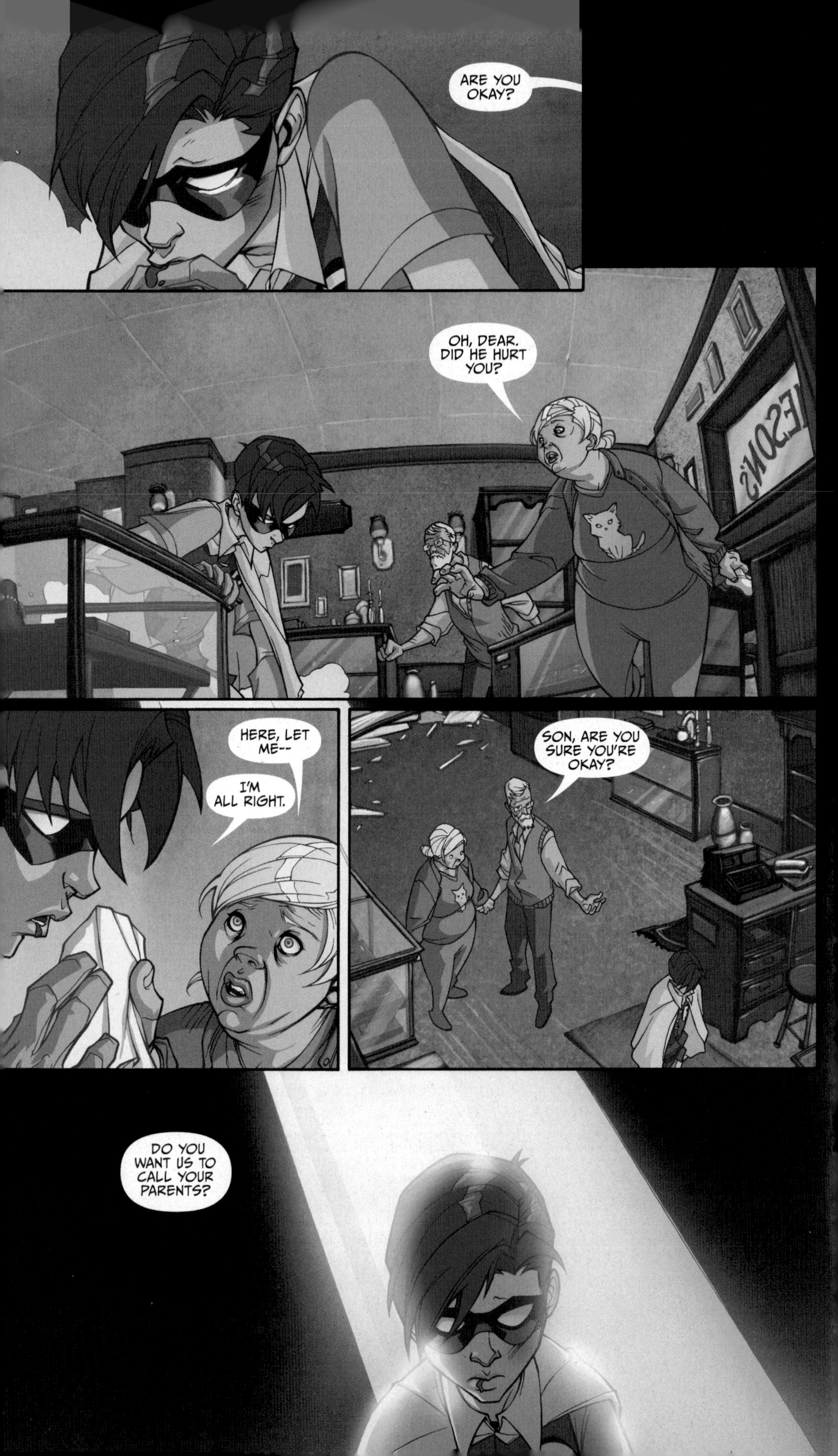
ARE YOU OKAY?
OH, DEAR. DID HE HURT YOU?
HERE, LET ME--
I'M ALL RIGHT.
SON, ARE YOU SURE YOU'RE OKAY?
DO YOU WANT US TO CALL YOUR PARENTS?

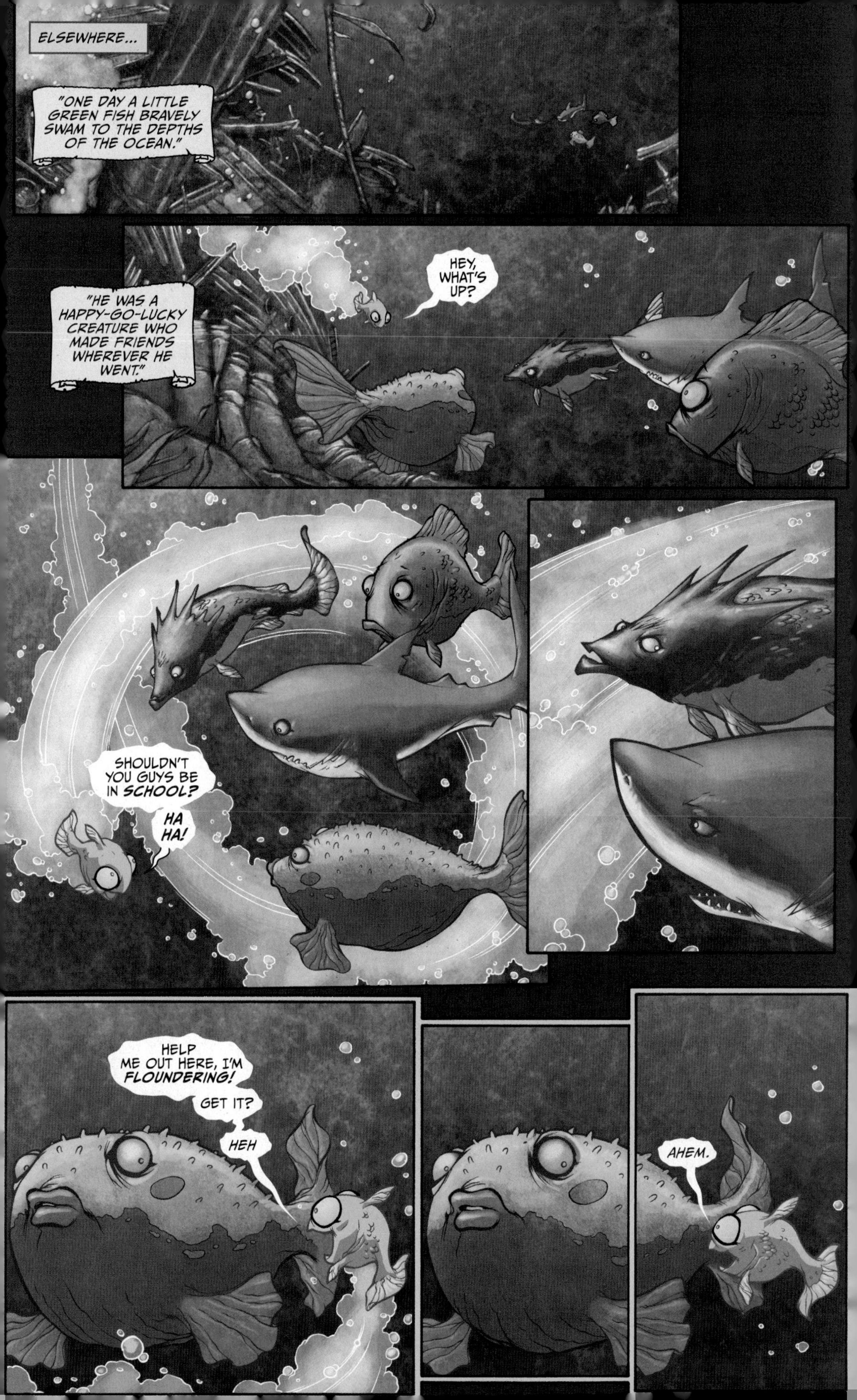
ELSEWHERE...
"ONE DAY A LITTLE GREEN FISH BRAVELY SWAM TO THE DEPTHS OF THE OCEAN."
"HE WAS A HAPPY-GO-LUCKY CREATURE WHO MADE FRIENDS WHEREVER HE WENT."
HEY, WHAT'S UP?
SHOULDN'T YOU GUYS BE IN SCHOOL?
HA HA!
HELP ME OUT HERE, I'M FLOUNDERING!
GET IT?
HEH
AHEM.

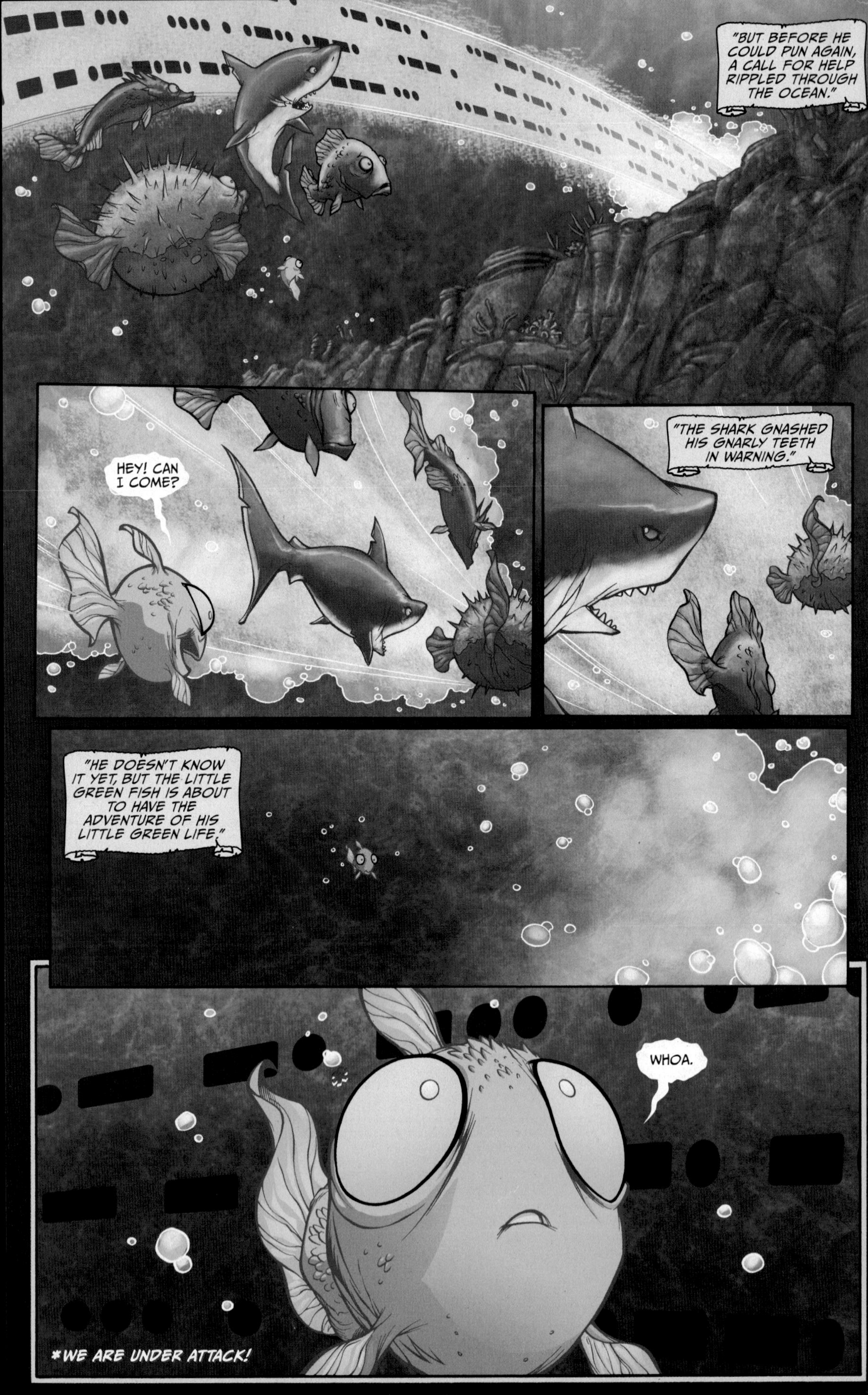
"BUT BEFORE HE COULD PUN AGAIN, A CALL FOR HELP RIPPLED THROUGH THE OCEAN."
HEY! CAN I COME?
"THE SHARK GNASHED HIS GNARLY TEETH IN WARNING."
"HE DOESN'T KNOW IT YET, BUT THE LITTLE GREEN FISH IS ABOUT TO HAVE THE ADVENTURE OF HIS LITTLE GREEN LIFE."
WHOA.
*WE ARE UNDER ATTACK!

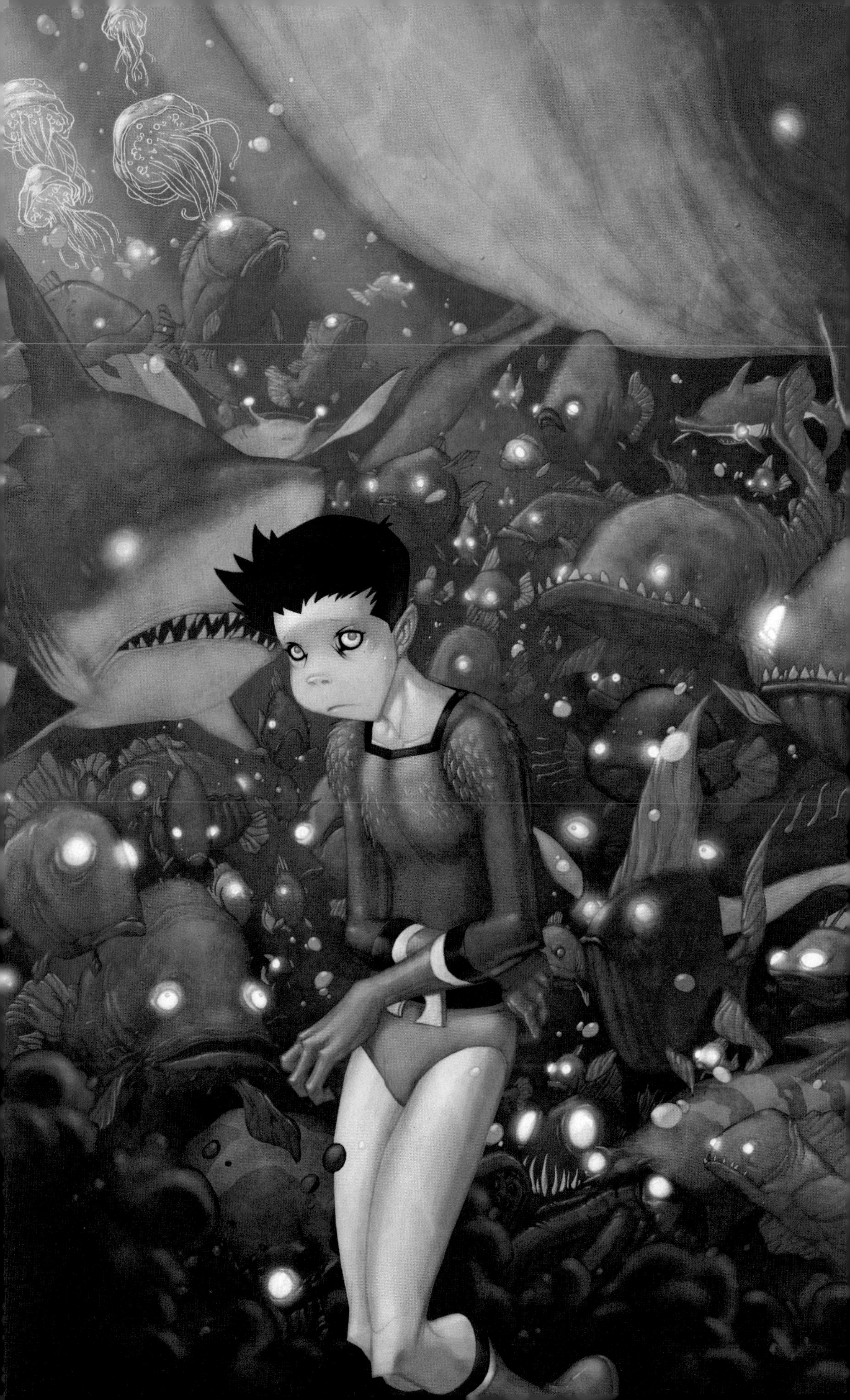

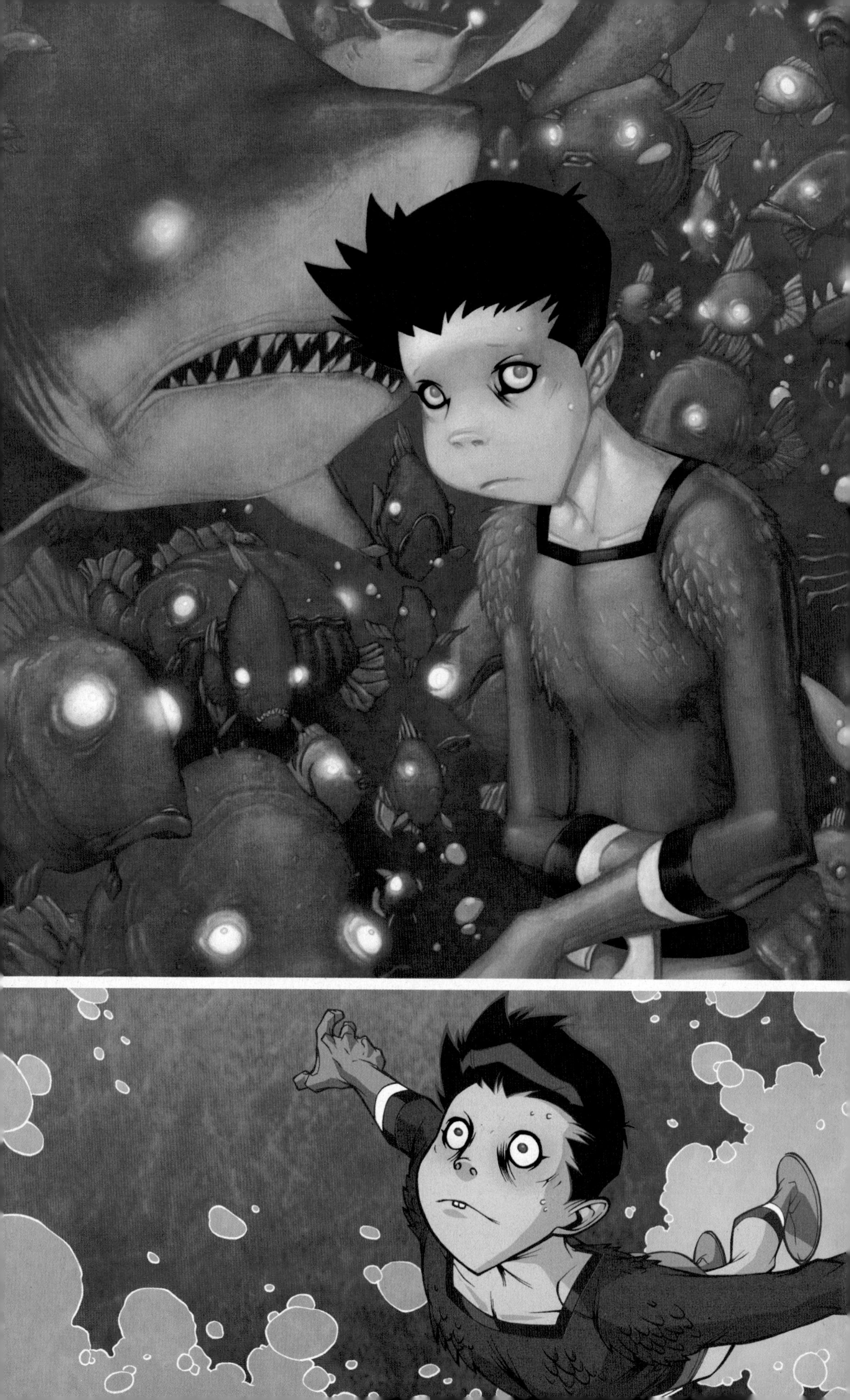

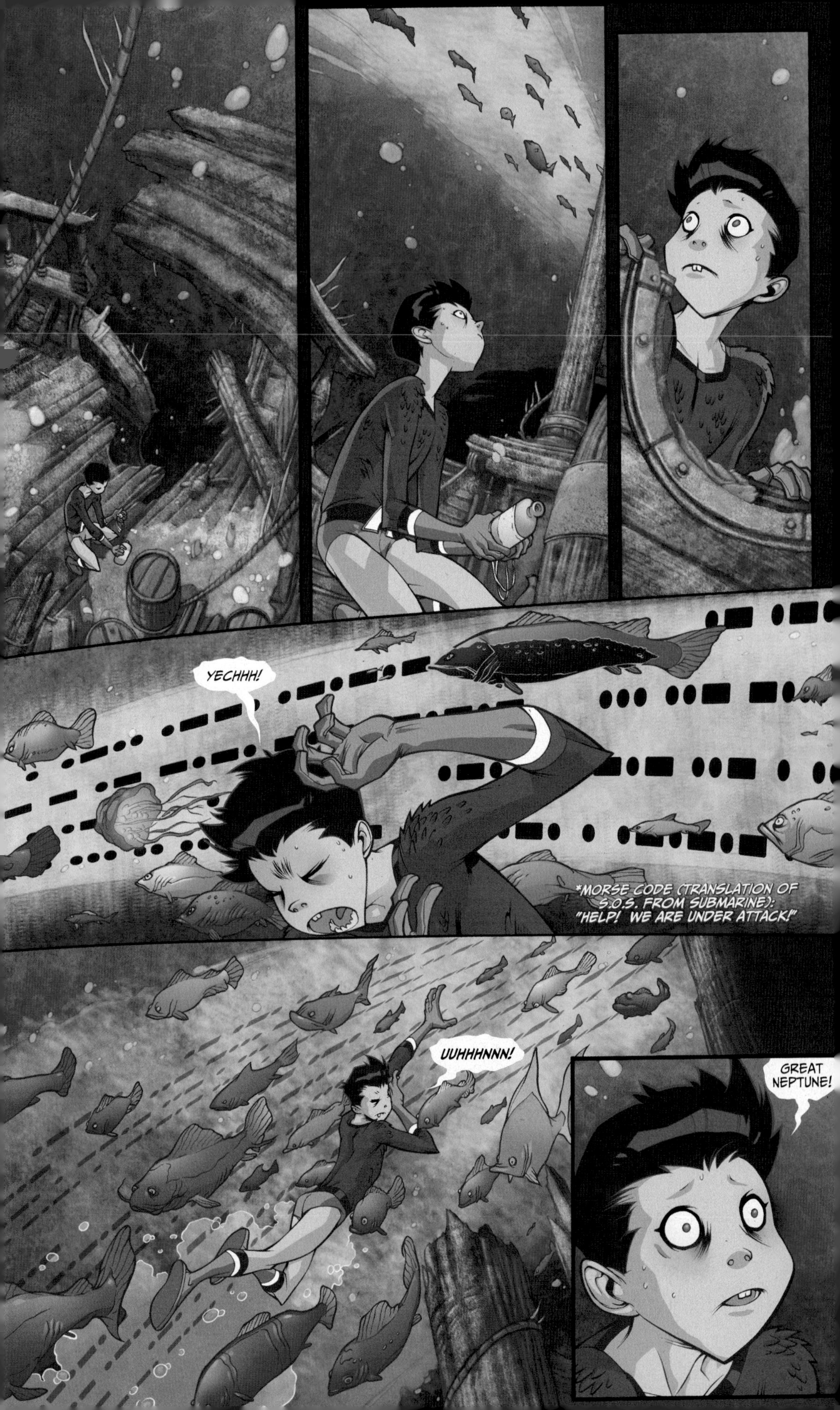
YECHHH!
*MORSE CODE (TRANSLATION OF S.O.S. FROM SUBMARINE): "HELP! WE ARE UNDER ATTACK!"
UUHHHNNN!
GREAT NEPTUNE!

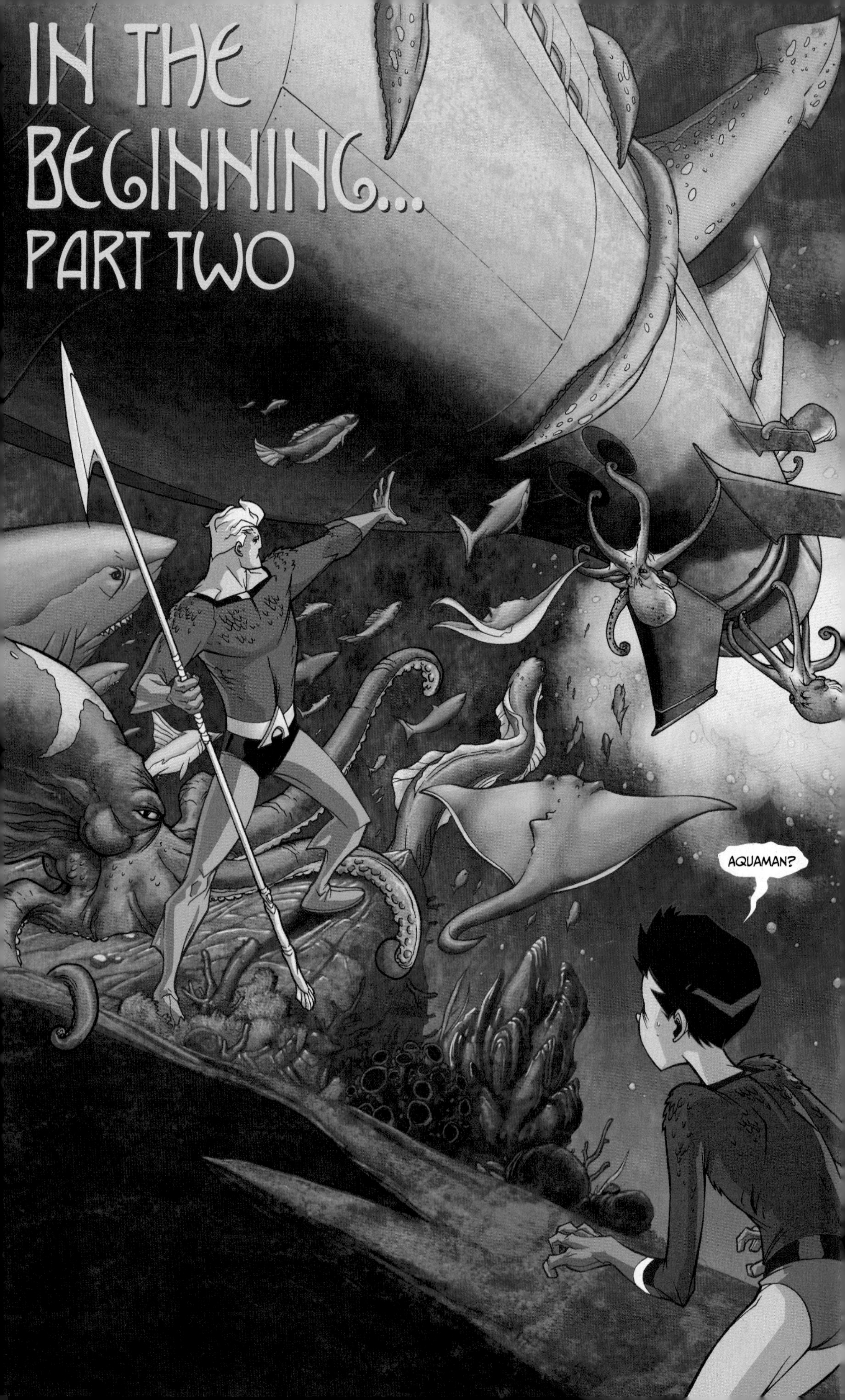
IN THE BEGINNING... PART TWO
AQUAMAN?

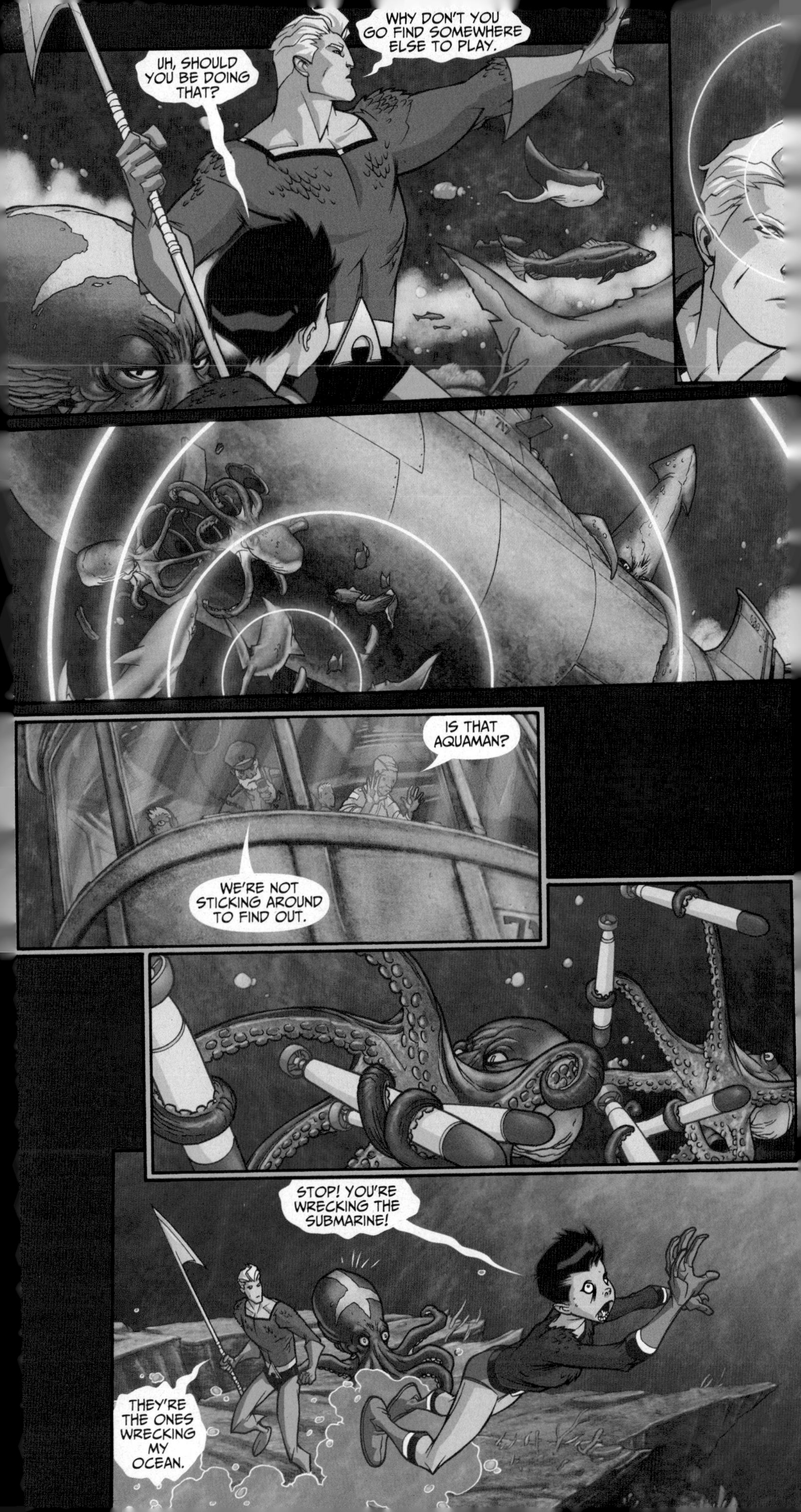
WHY DON'T YOU GO FIND SOMEWHERE ELSE TO PLAY.
UH, SHOULD YOU BE DOING THAT?
IS THAT AQUAMAN?
WE'RE NOT STICKING AROUND TO FIND OUT.
STOP! YOU'RE WRECKING THE SUBMARINE!
THEY'RE THE ONES WRECKING MY OCEAN.

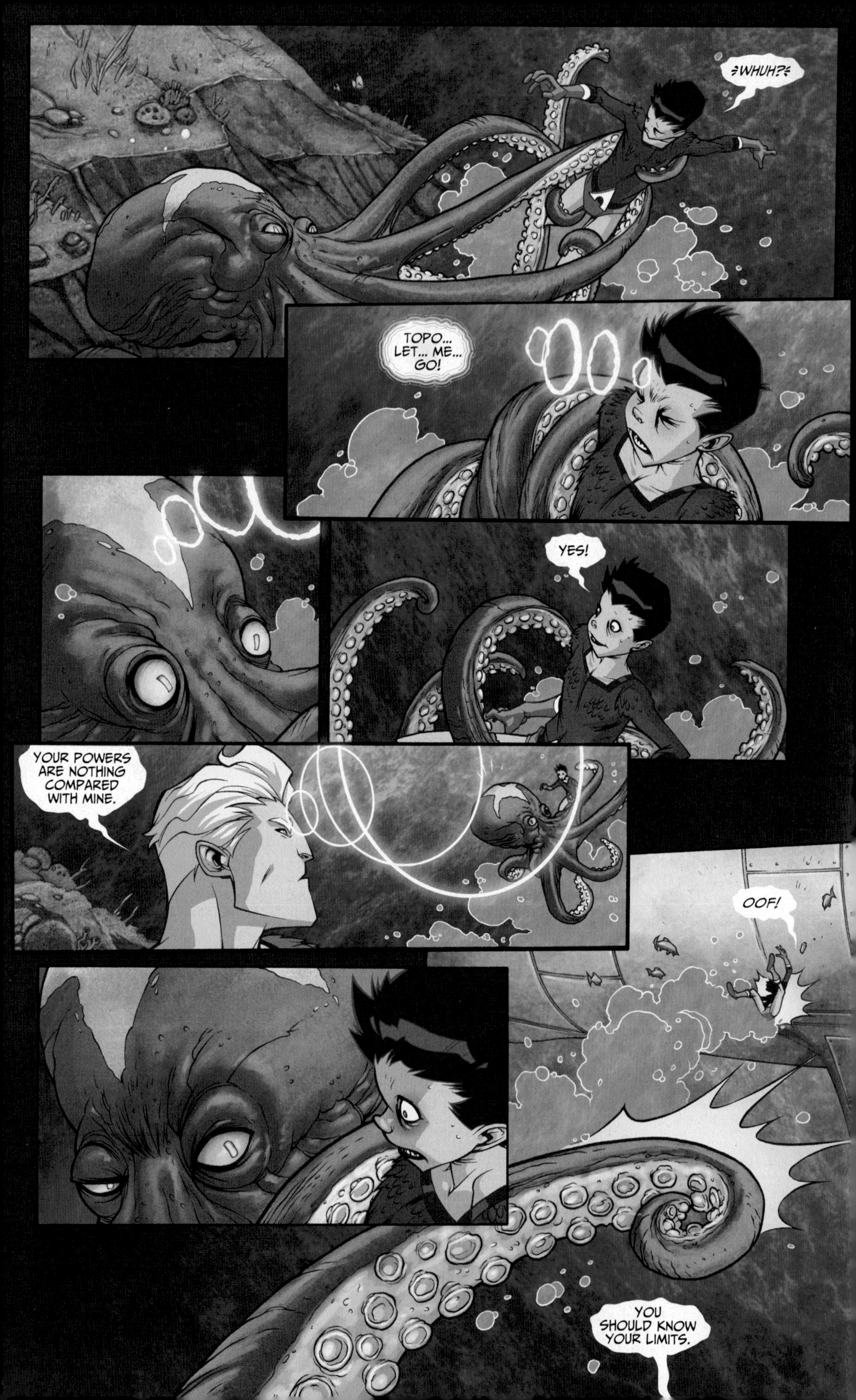
WHUH?
TOPO... LET... ME... GO!
YES!
YOUR POWERS ARE NOTHING COMPARED WITH MINE.
OOF!
YOU SHOULD KNOW YOUR LIMITS.

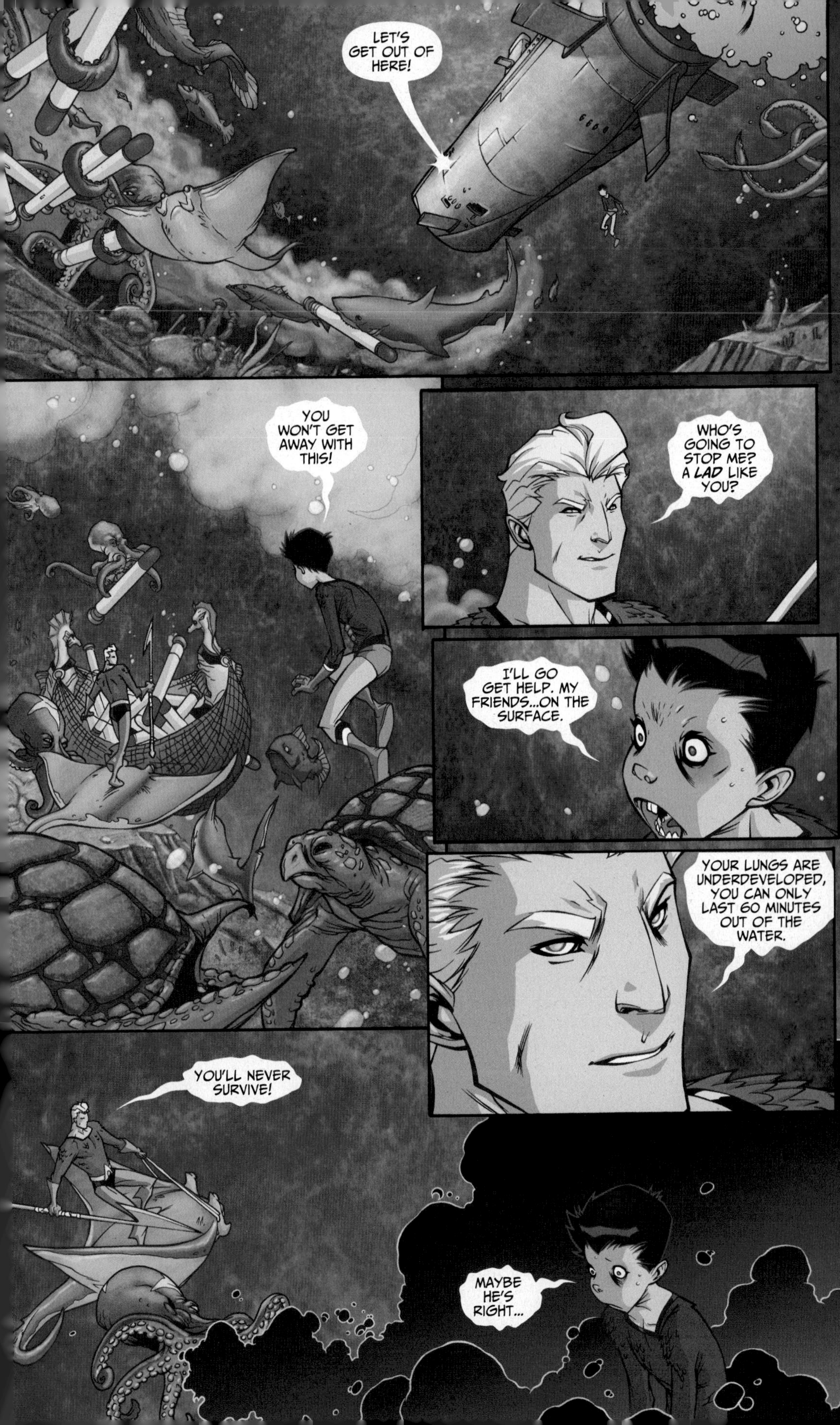
LET'S GET OUT OF HERE!
YOU WON'T GET AWAY WITH THIS!
WHO'S GOING TO STOP ME? A LAD LIKE YOU?
I'LL GO GET HELP. MY FRIENDS...ON THE SURFACE.
YOUR LUNGS ARE UNDERDEVELOPED, YOU CAN ONLY LAST 60 MINUTES OUT OF THE WATER.
YOU'LL NEVER SURVIVE!
MAYBE HE'S RIGHT...

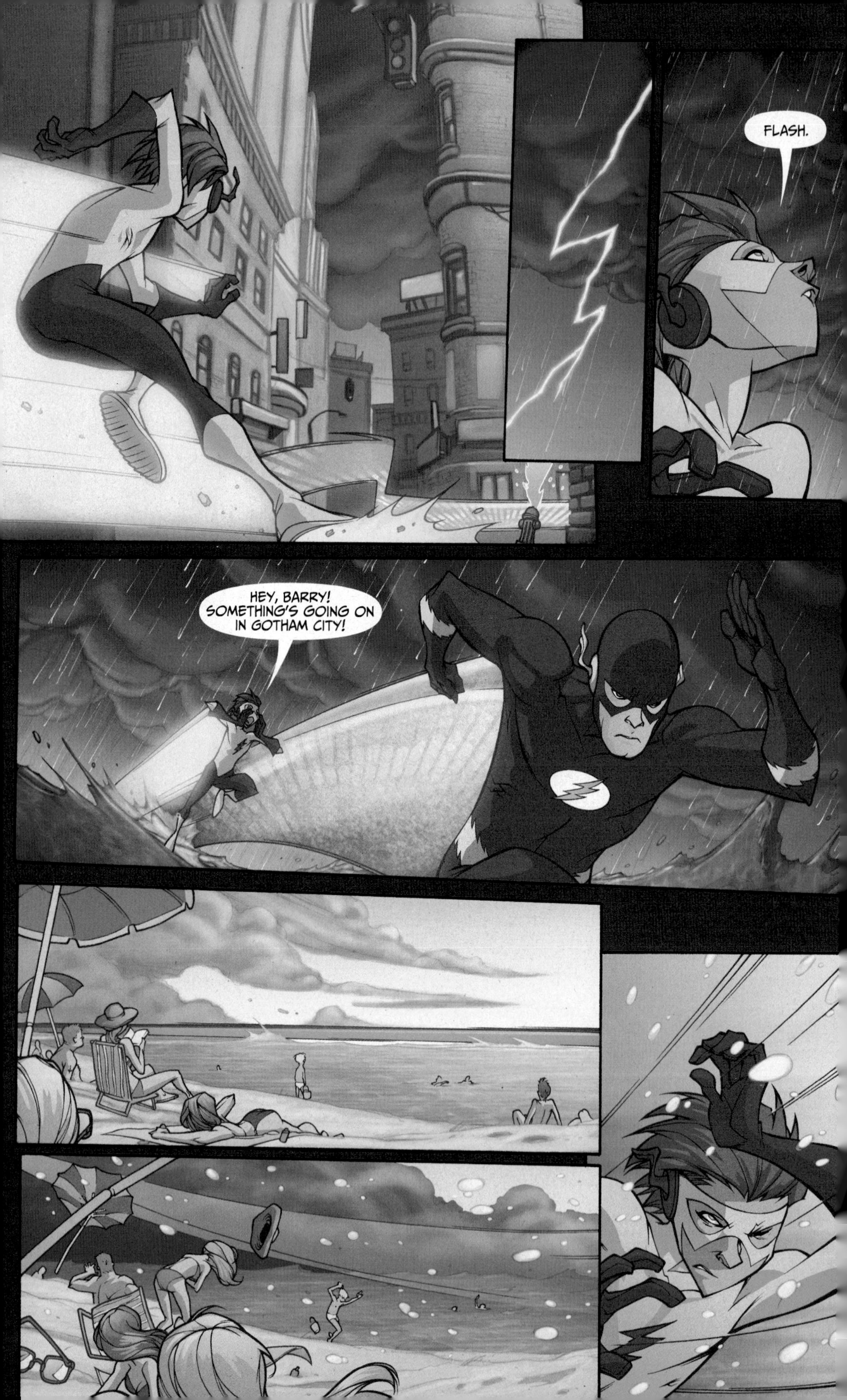
FLASH.
HEY, BARRY! SOMETHING'S GOING ON IN GOTHAM CITY!

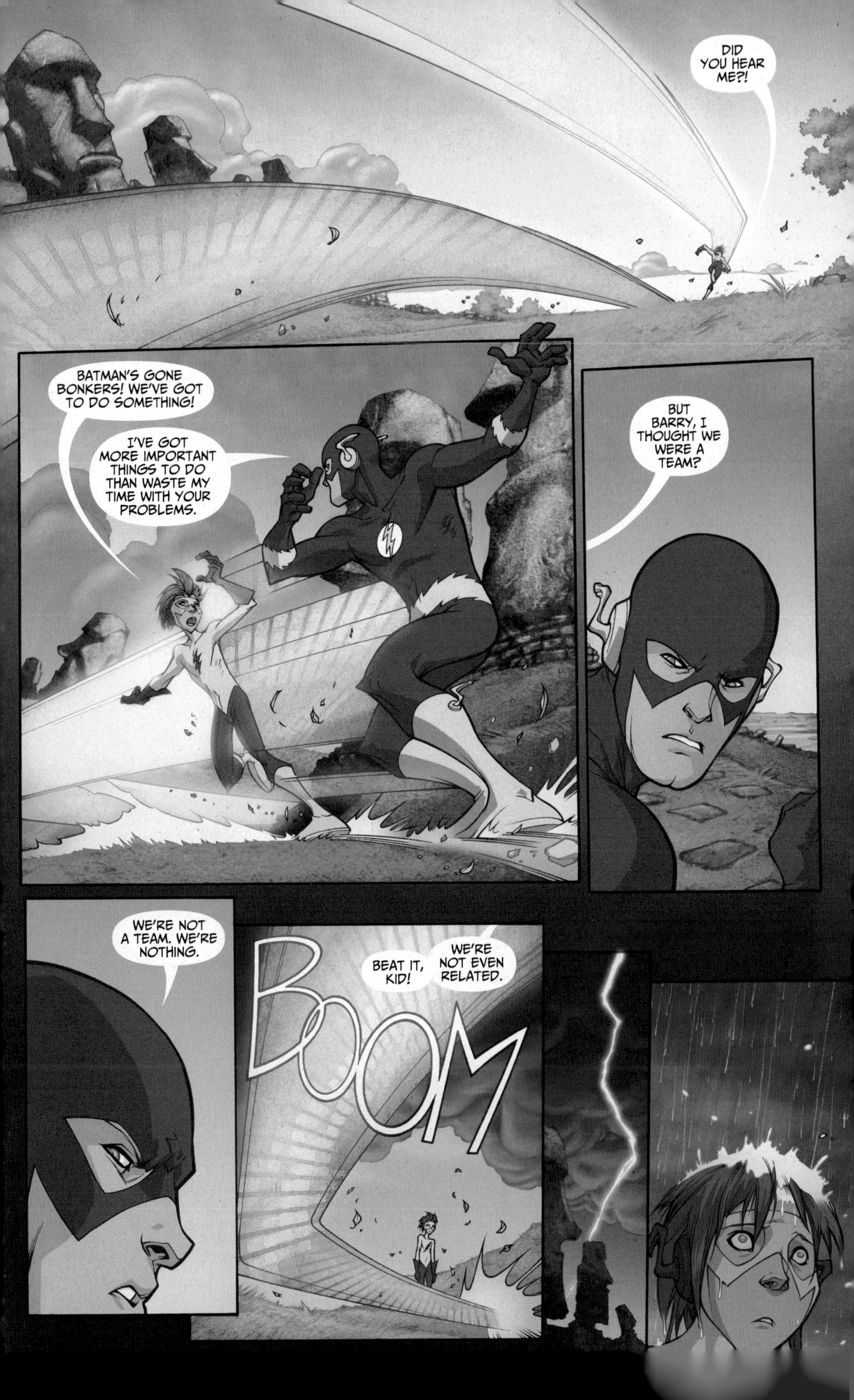
DID YOU HEAR ME?!
BATMAN'S GONE BONKERS! WE'VE GOT TO DO SOMETHING!
I'VE GOT MORE IMPORTANT THINGS TO DO THAN WASTE MY TIME WITH YOUR PROBLEMS.
BUT BARRY, I THOUGHT WE WERE A TEAM?
WE'RE NOT A TEAM. WE'RE NOTHING.
WE'RE NOT EVEN RELATED.
BEAT IT, KID!
BOOM

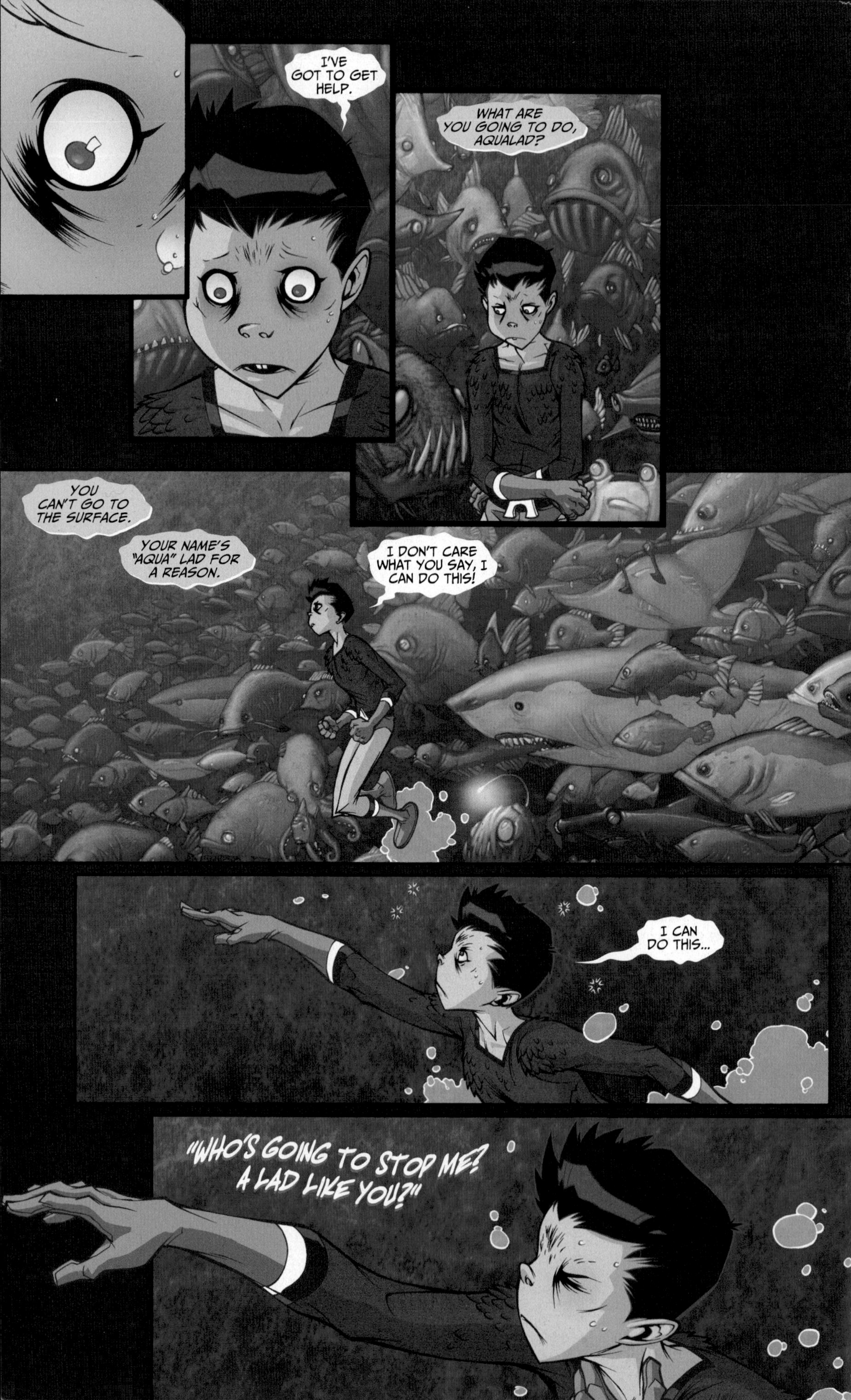
I'VE GOT TO GET HELP.
WHAT ARE YOU GOING TO DO, AQUALAD?
YOU CAN'T GO TO THE SURFACE.
YOUR NAME'S "AQUA" LAD FOR A REASON.
I DON'T CARE WHAT YOU SAY, I CAN DO THIS!
I CAN DO THIS...
"WHO'S GOING TO STOP ME? A LAD LIKE YOU?"

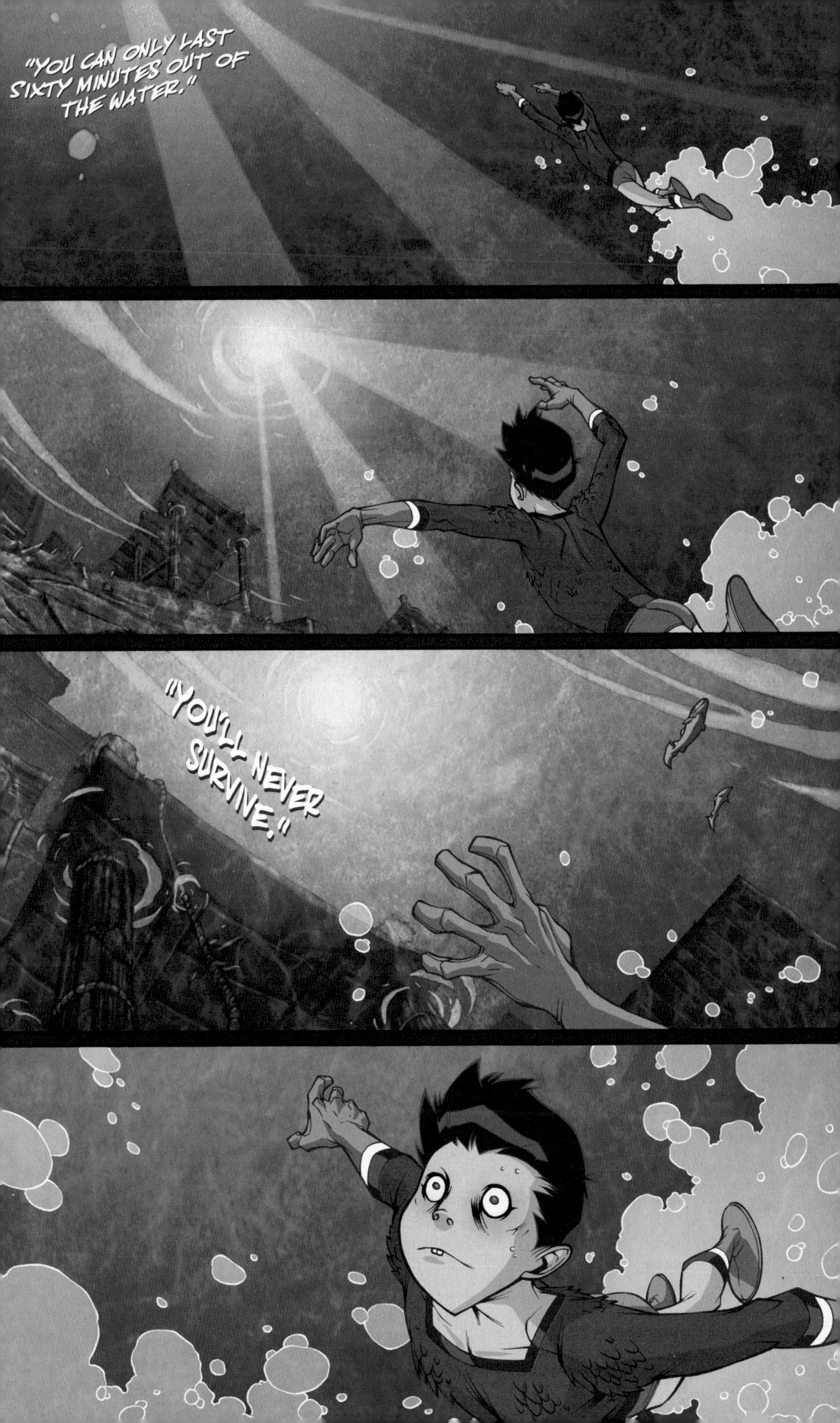
"YOU CAN ONLY LAST SIXTY MINUTES OUT OF THE WATER."
"YOU'LL NEVER SURVIVE."

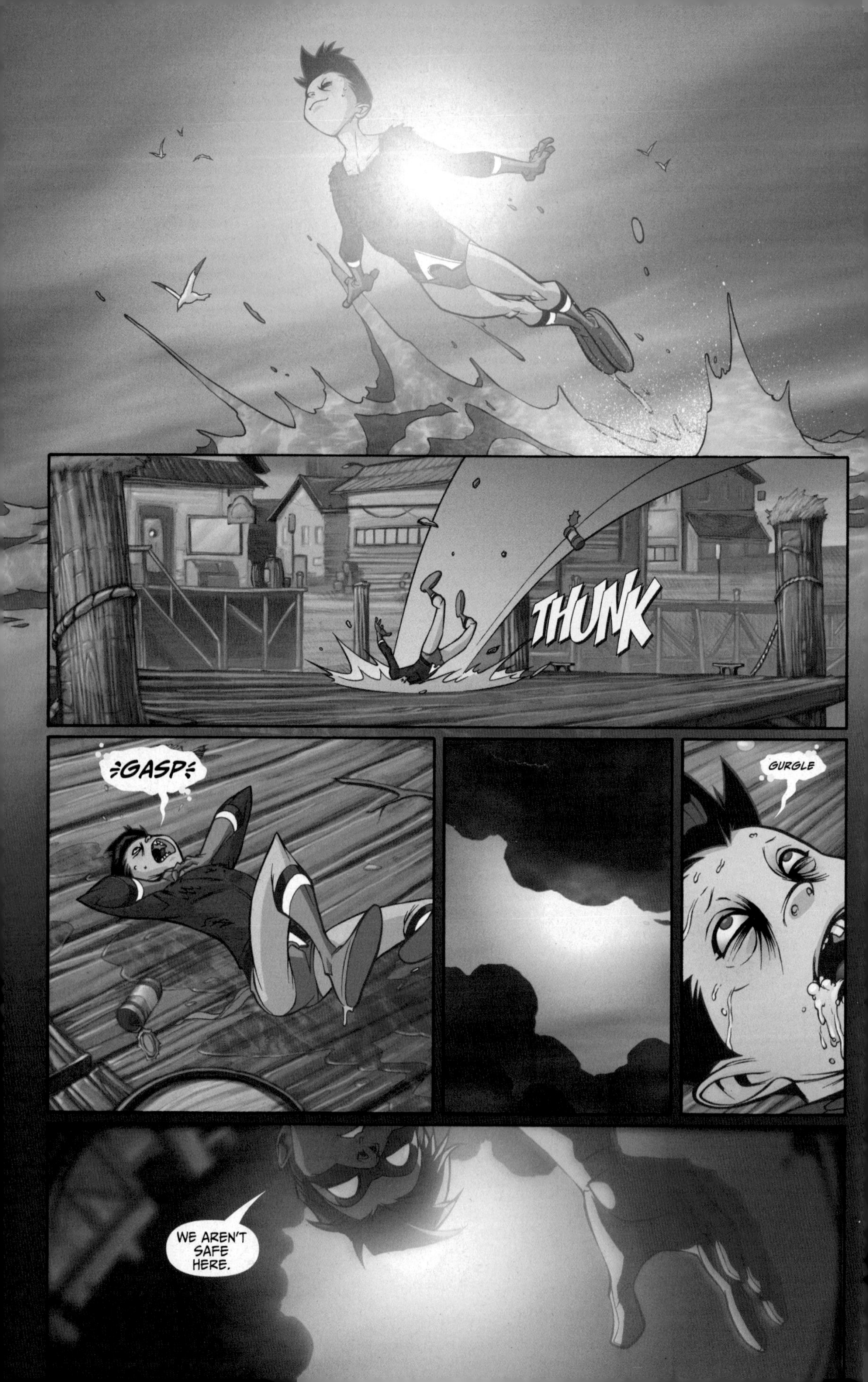
THUNK
GASP
GURGLE
WE AREN'T SAFE HERE.

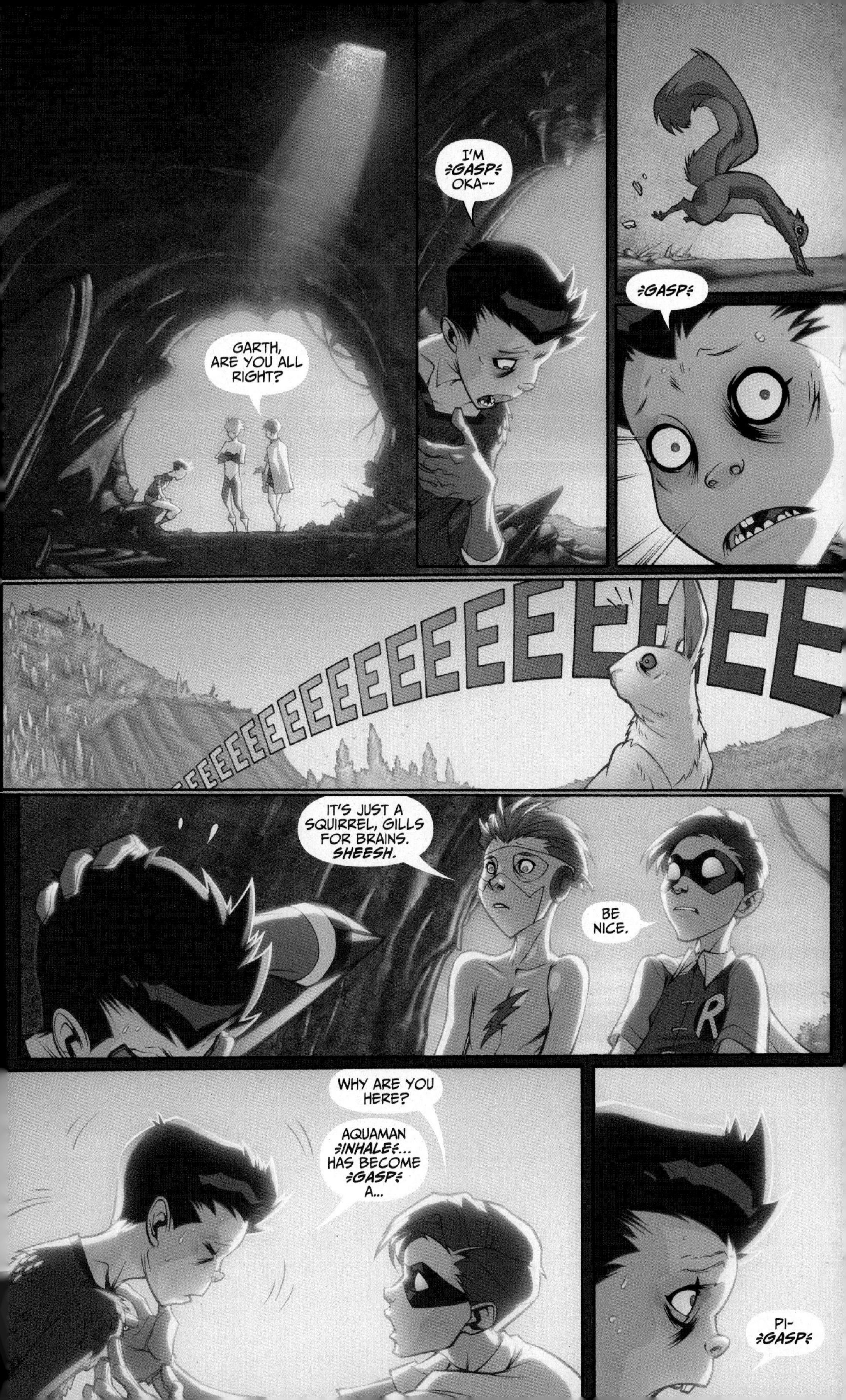
GARTH, ARE YOU ALL RIGHT?
I'M *GASP* OKA--
GASP
EEEEEEEEEEEEEEEEEEEEEEEEEEEE
IT'S JUST A SQUIRREL, GILLS FOR BRAINS. SHEESH.
BE NICE.
WHY ARE YOU HERE?
AQUAMAN *INHALE*... HAS BECOME *GASP* A...
PI- *GASP*

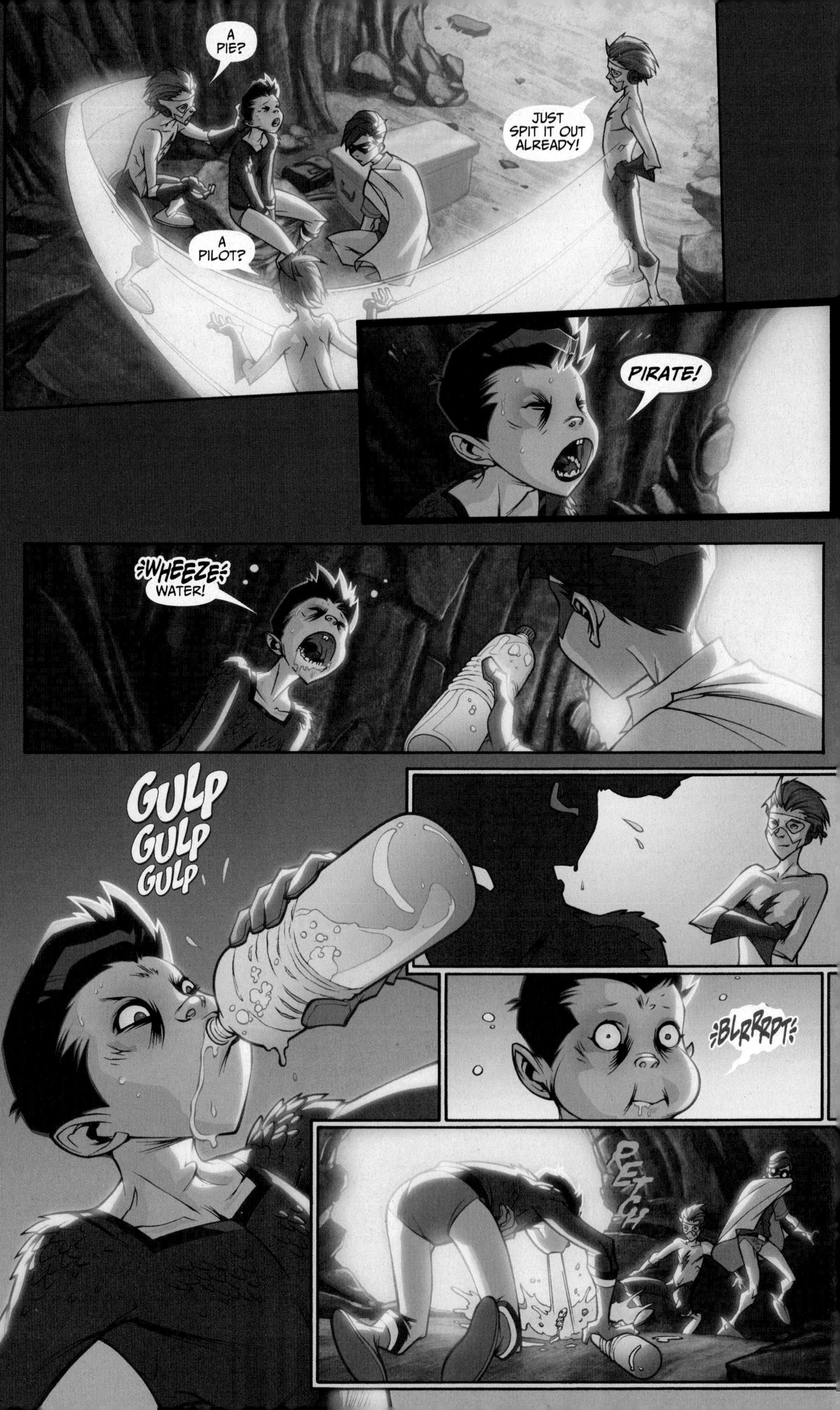
A PIE?
A PILOT?
JUST SPIT IT OUT ALREADY!
PIRATE!
WHEEZE
WATER!
GULP GULP GULP
BLRRRPT
RETCH

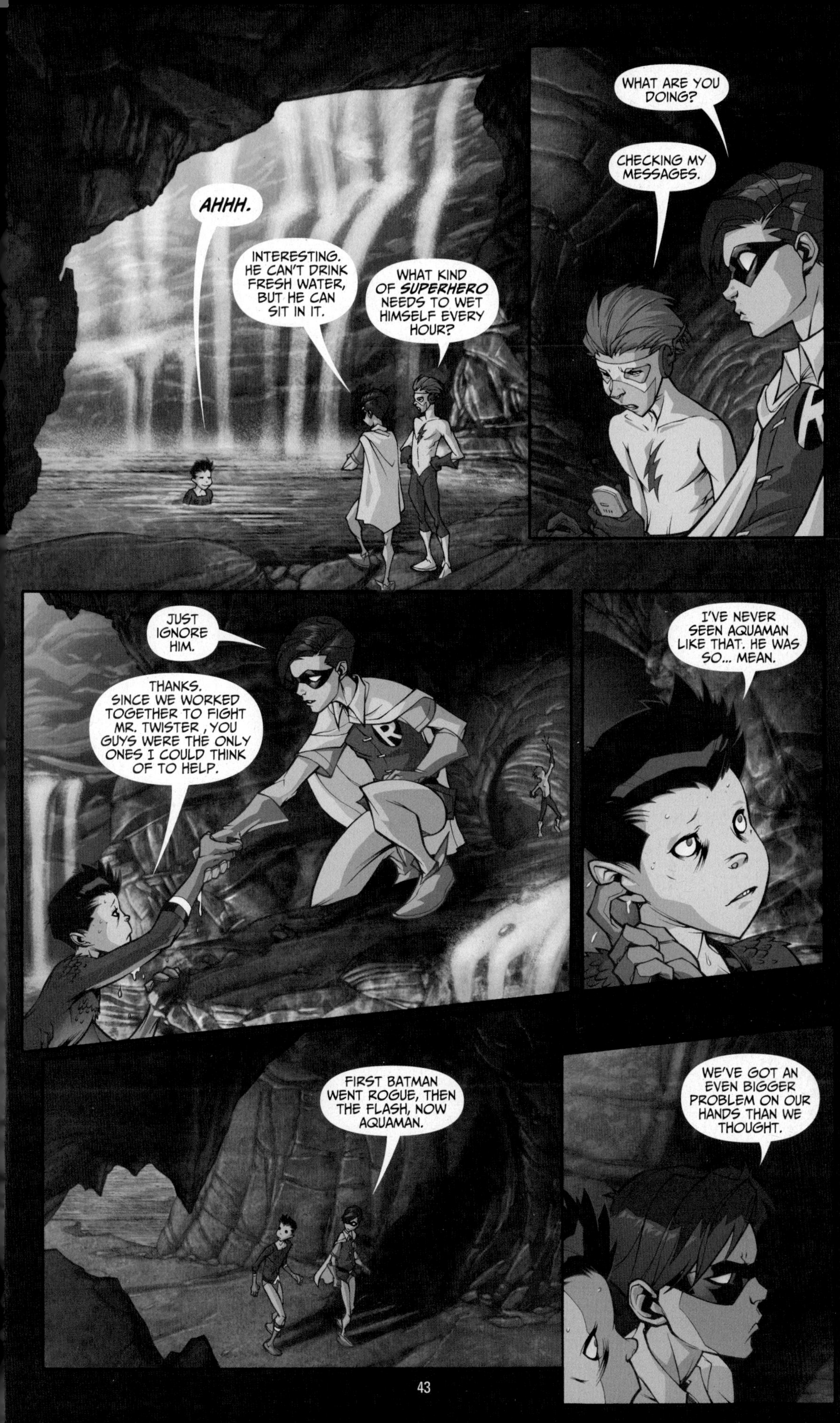
AHHH.
INTERESTING. HE CAN'T DRINK FRESH WATER, BUT HE CAN SIT IN IT.
WHAT KIND OF SUPERHERO NEEDS TO WET HIMSELF EVERY HOUR?
WHAT ARE YOU DOING?
CHECKING MY MESSAGES.
JUST IGNORE HIM.
THANKS. SINCE WE WORKED TOGETHER TO FIGHT MR. TWISTER, YOU GUYS WERE THE ONLY ONES I COULD THINK OF TO HELP.
I'VE NEVER SEEN AQUAMAN LIKE THAT. HE WAS SO... MEAN.
FIRST BATMAN WENT ROGUE, THEN THE FLASH, NOW AQUAMAN.
WE'VE GOT AN EVEN BIGGER PROBLEM ON OUR HANDS THAN WE THOUGHT.

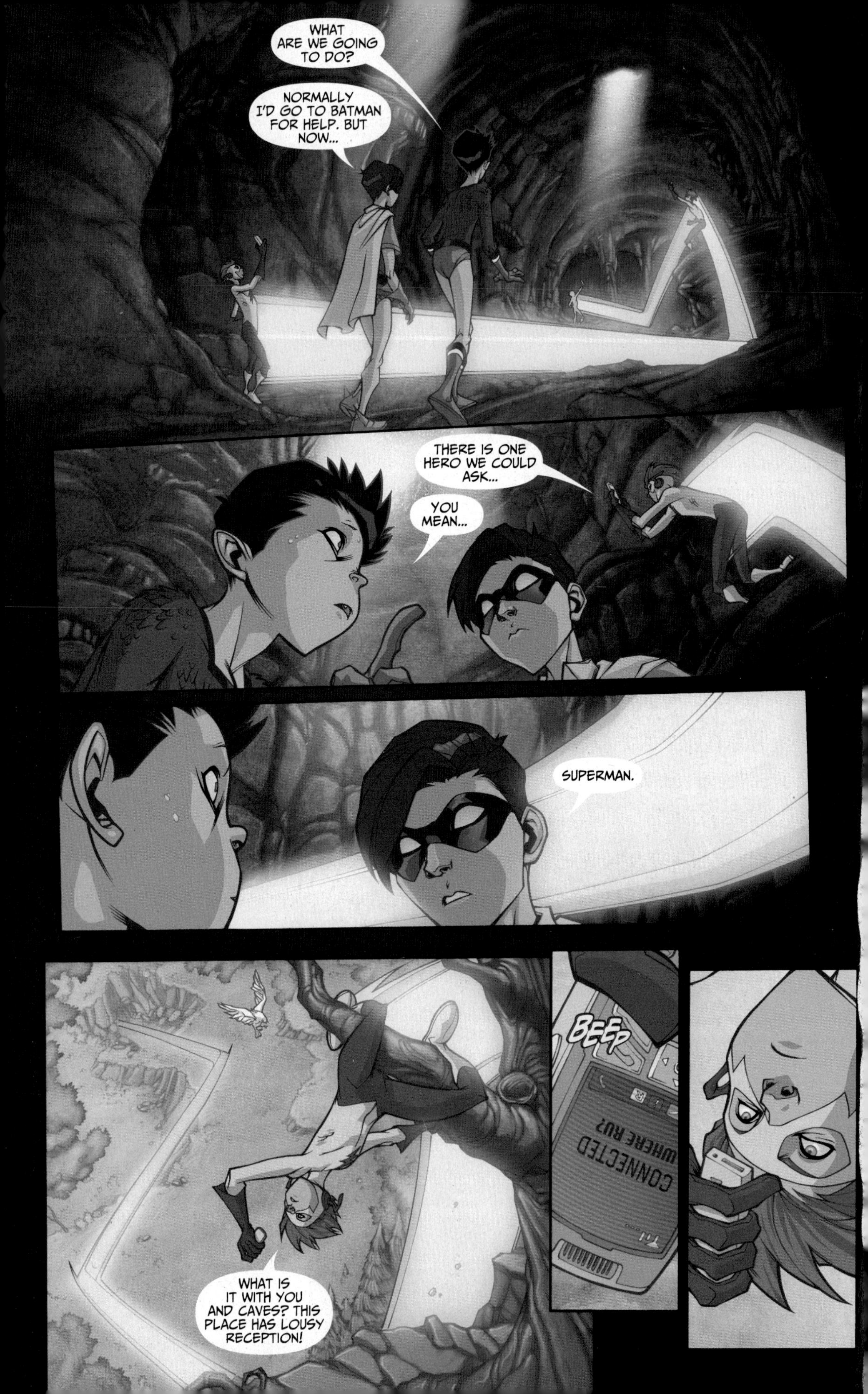
WHAT ARE WE GOING TO DO?
NORMALLY I'D GO TO BATMAN FOR HELP. BUT NOW...
THERE IS ONE HERO WE COULD ASK...
YOU MEAN...
SUPERMAN.
WHAT IS IT WITH YOU AND CAVES? THIS PLACE HAS LOUSY RECEPTION!
BEEP
CONNECTED
WHERE RU?

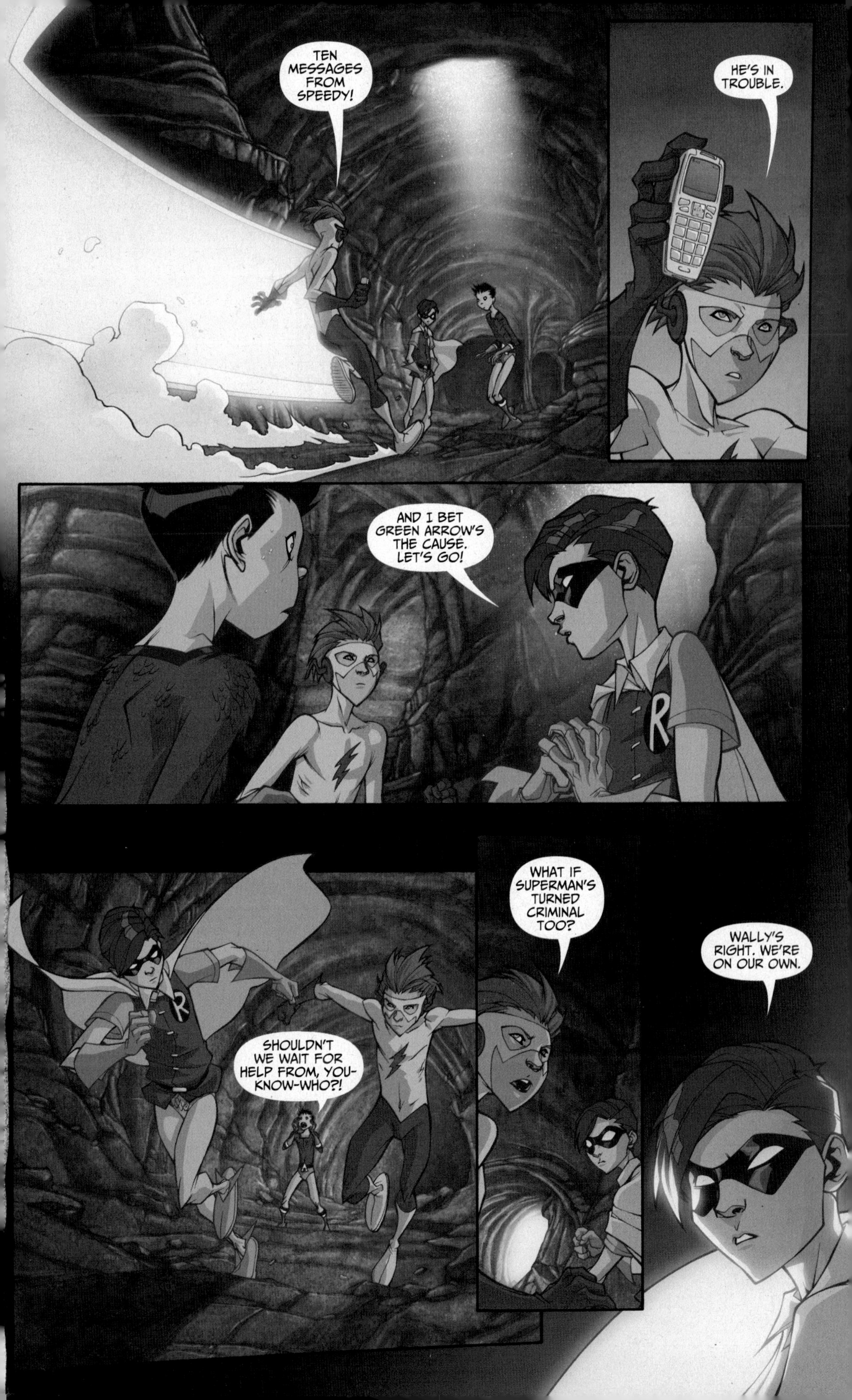
TEN MESSAGES FROM SPEEDY!
HE'S IN TROUBLE.
AND I BET GREEN ARROW'S THE CAUSE. LET'S GO!
SHOULDN'T WE WAIT FOR HELP FROM, YOU-KNOW-WHO?!
WHAT IF SUPERMAN'S TURNED CRIMINAL TOO?
WALLY'S RIGHT. WE'RE ON OUR OWN.

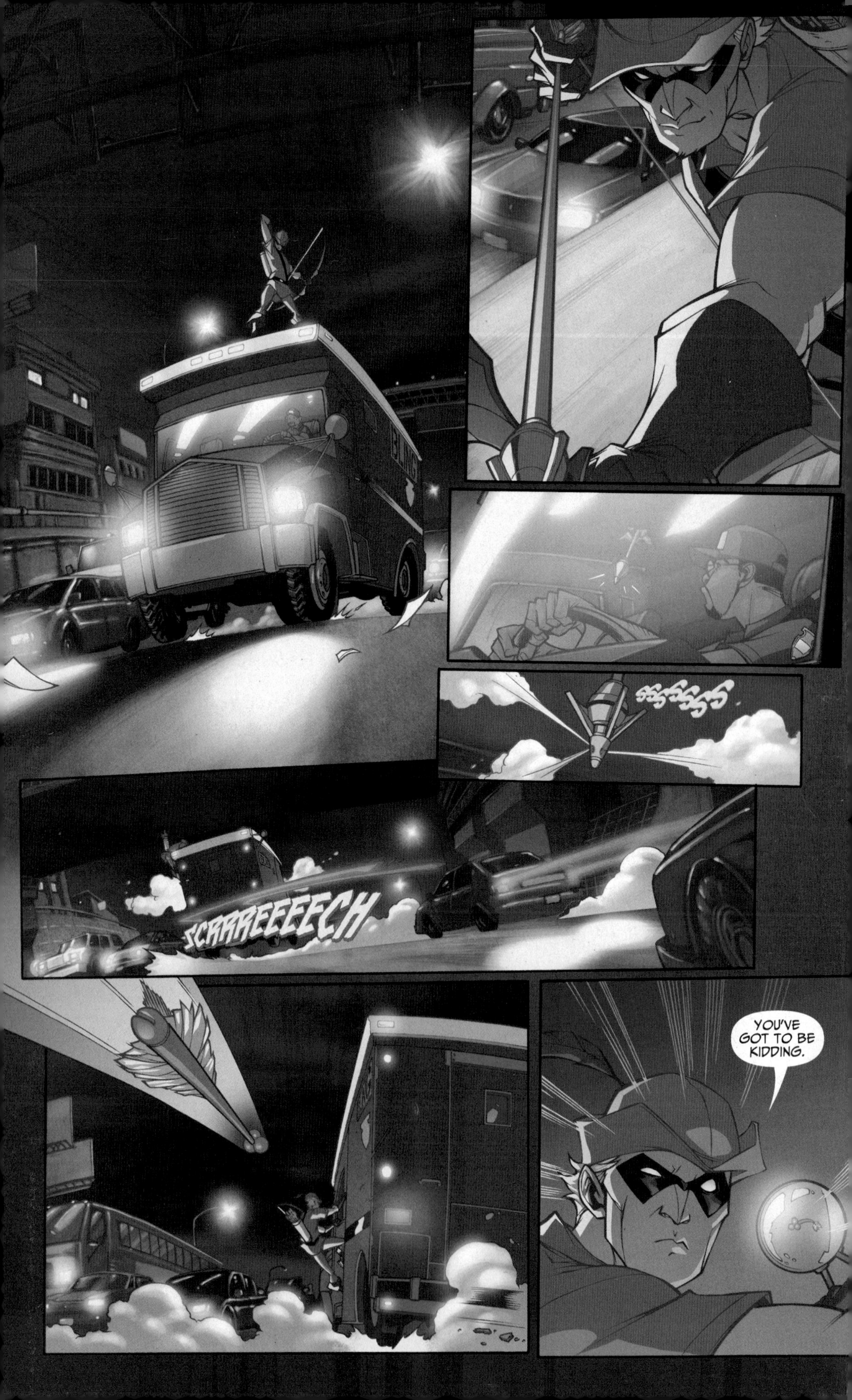
SSSSSSS
SCRRREEEEECH
YOU'VE GOT TO BE KIDDING.

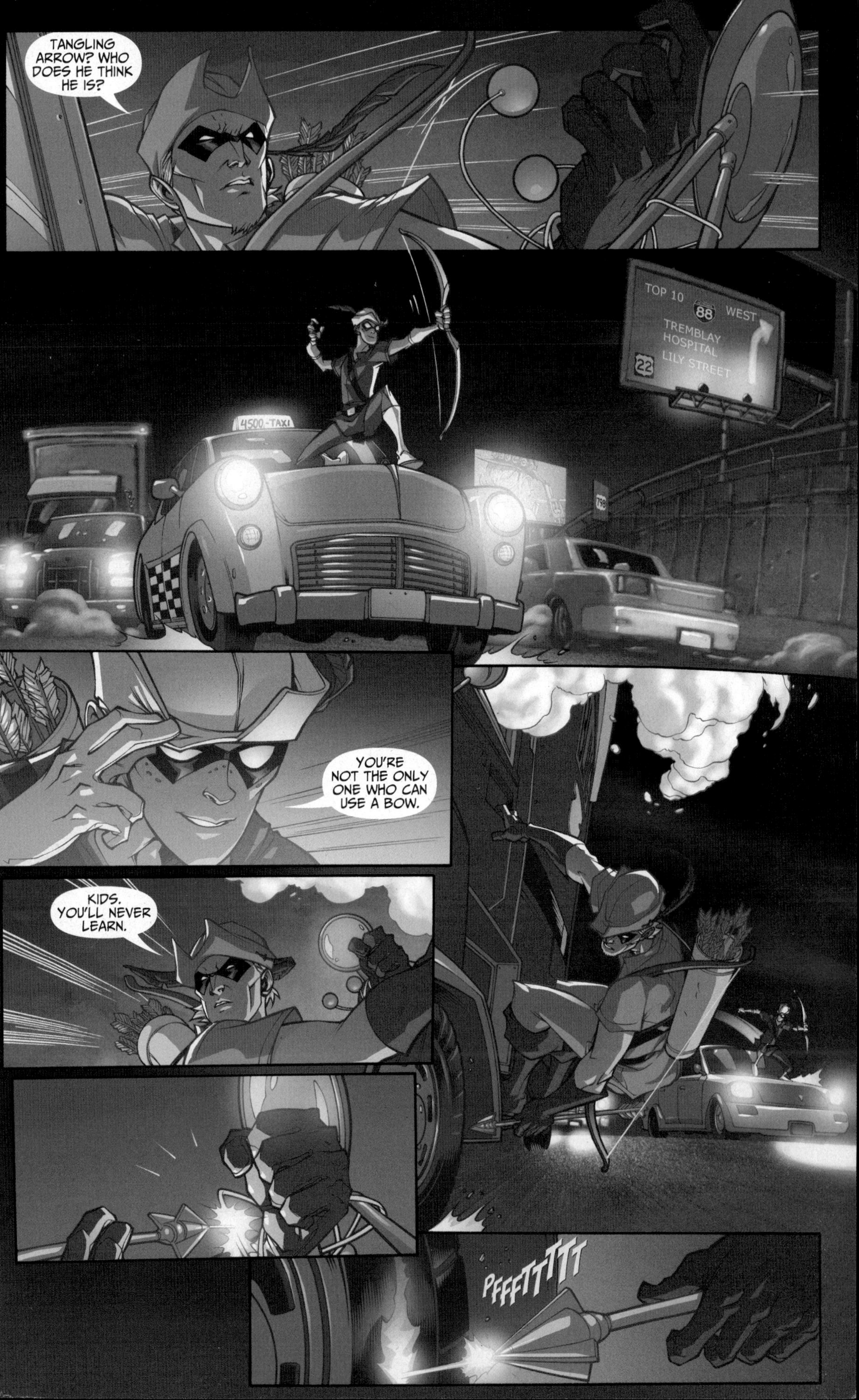
TANGLING ARROW? WHO DOES HE THINK HE IS?
TOP 10
88
WEST
TREMBLAY HOSPITAL
22
LILY STREET
4500-TAXI
798
YOU'RE NOT THE ONLY ONE WHO CAN USE A BOW.
KIDS. YOU'LL NEVER LEARN.
PFFFTTTTT

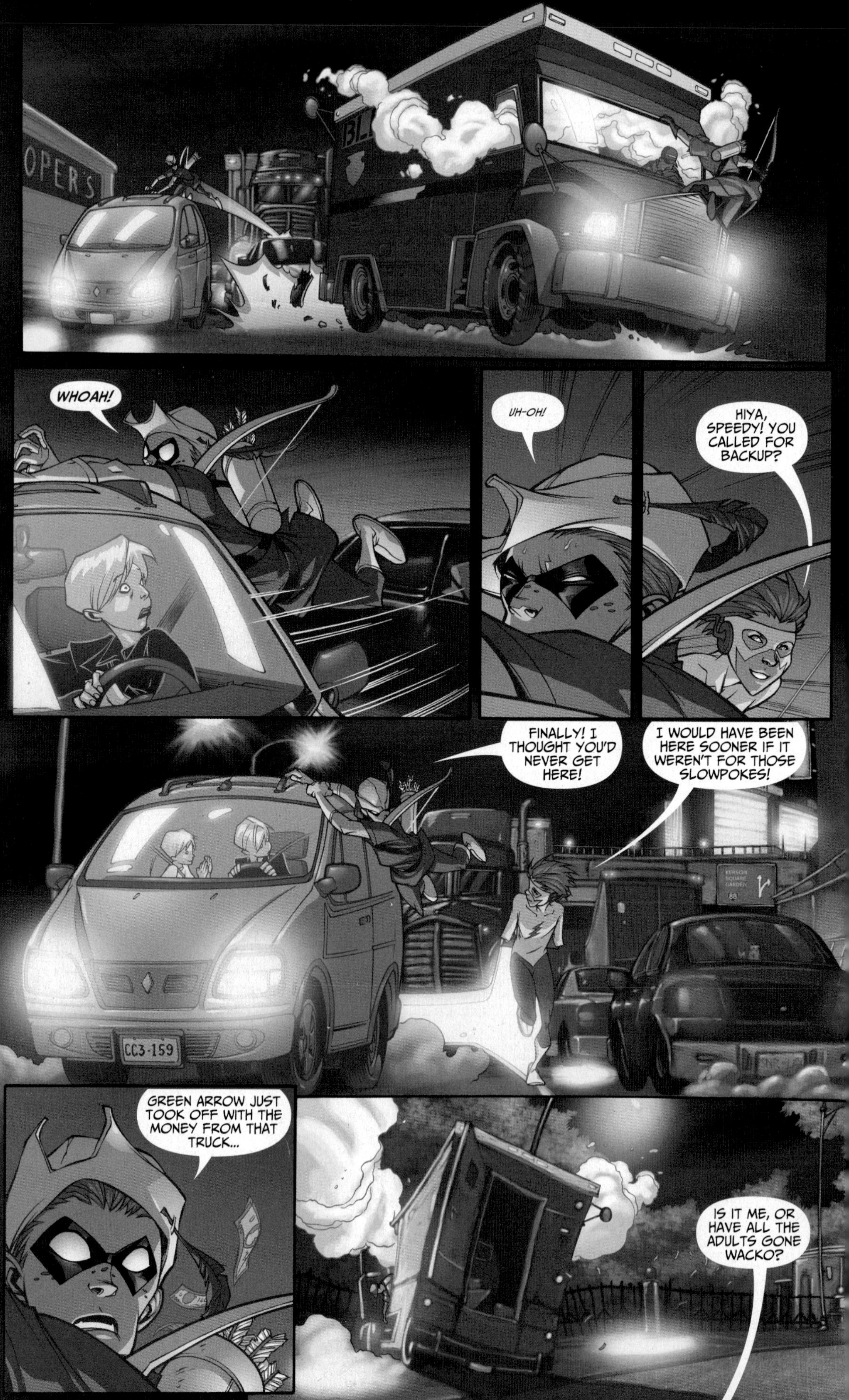
WHOAH!
UH-OH!
HIYA, SPEEDY! YOU CALLED FOR BACKUP?
FINALLY! I THOUGHT YOU'D NEVER GET HERE!
I WOULD HAVE BEEN HERE SOONER IF IT WEREN'T FOR THOSE SLOWPOKES!
GREEN ARROW JUST TOOK OFF WITH THE MONEY FROM THAT TRUCK...
IS IT ME, OR HAVE ALL THE ADULTS GONE WACKO?

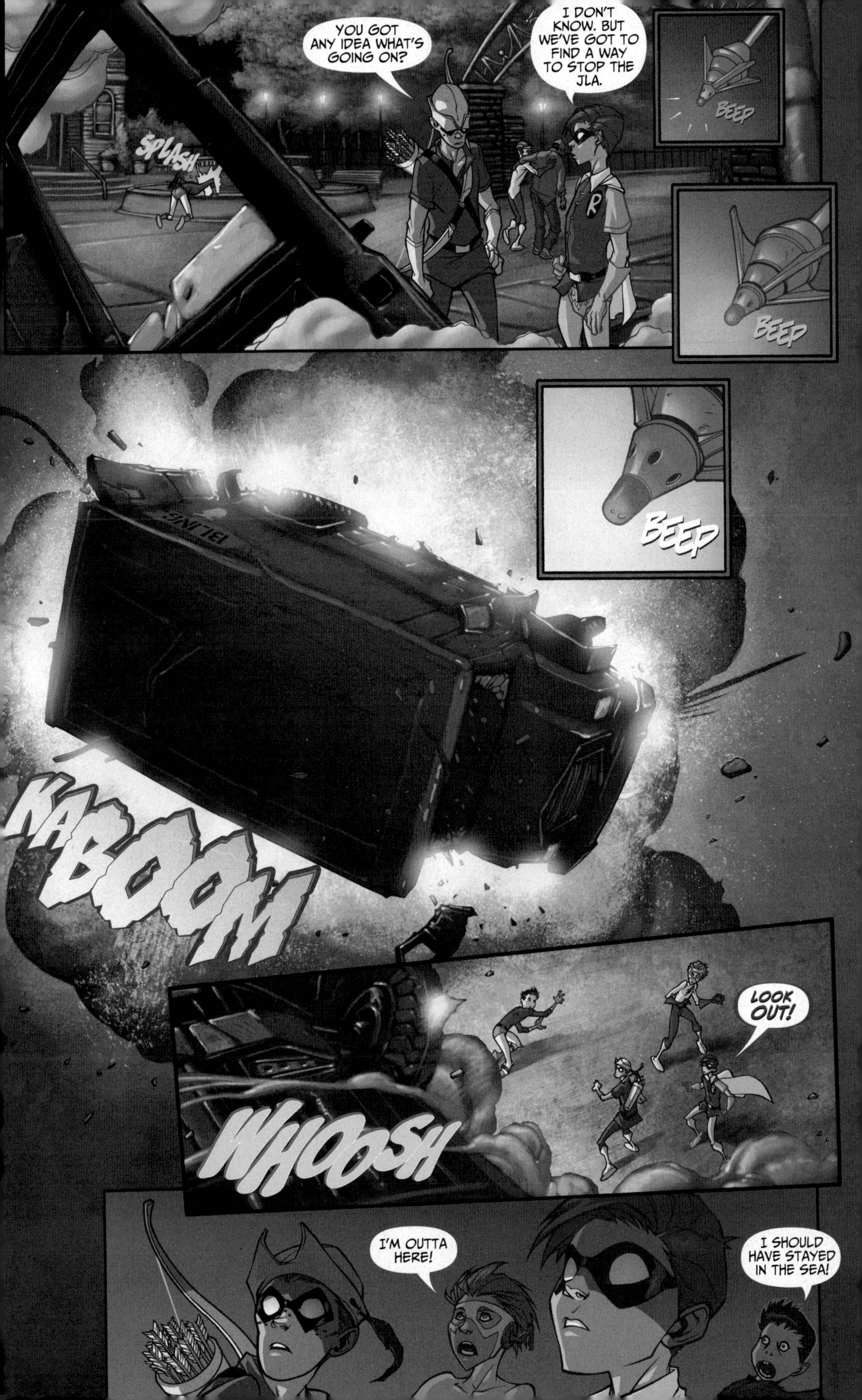
SPLASH
YOU GOT ANY IDEA WHAT'S GOING ON?
I DON'T KNOW. BUT WE'VE GOT TO FIND A WAY TO STOP THE JLA.
BEEP
BEEP
BEEP
KABOOM
WHOOSH
LOOK OUT!
I'M OUTTA HERE!
I SHOULD HAVE STAYED IN THE SEA!

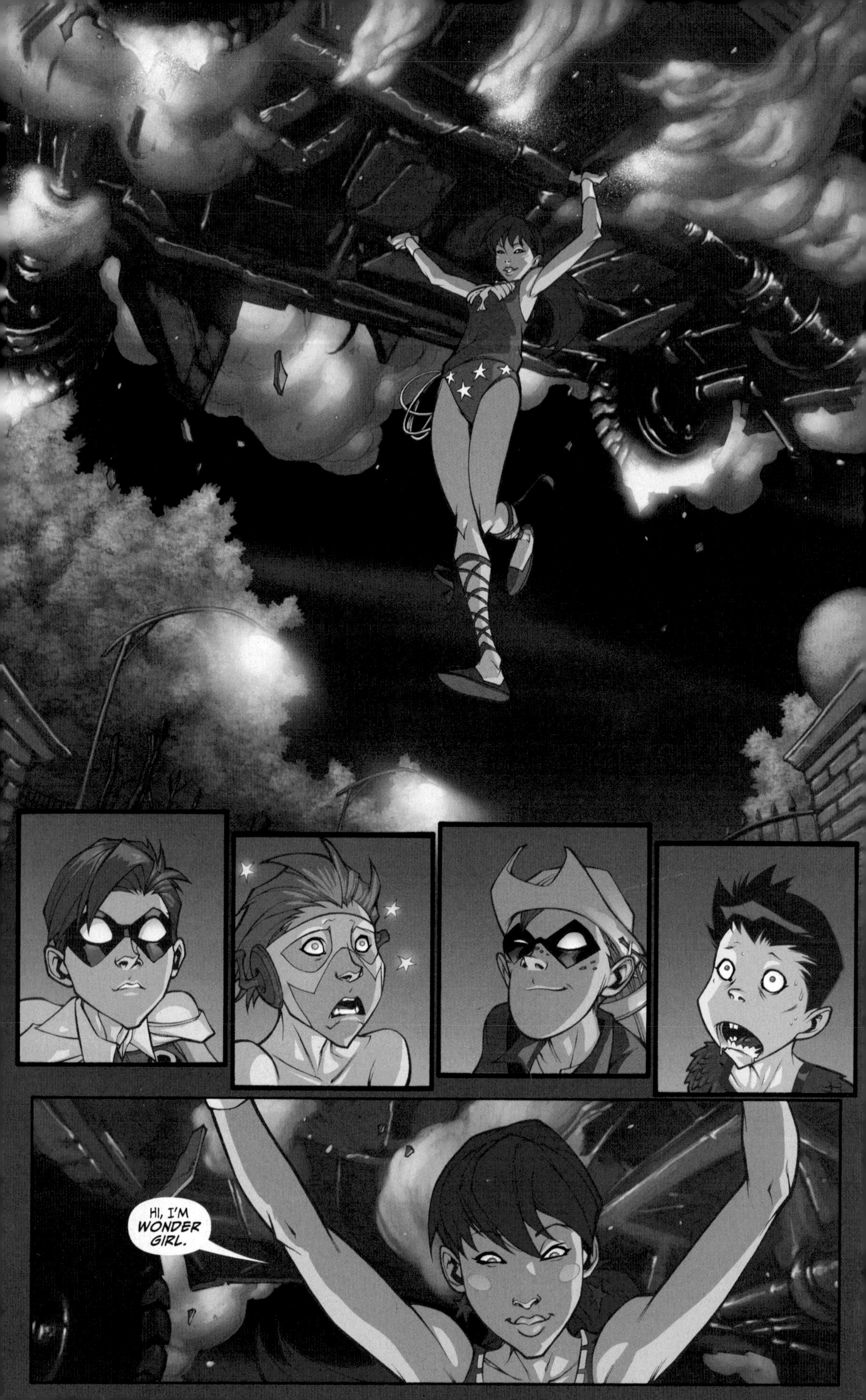
HI, I'M WONDER GIRL.

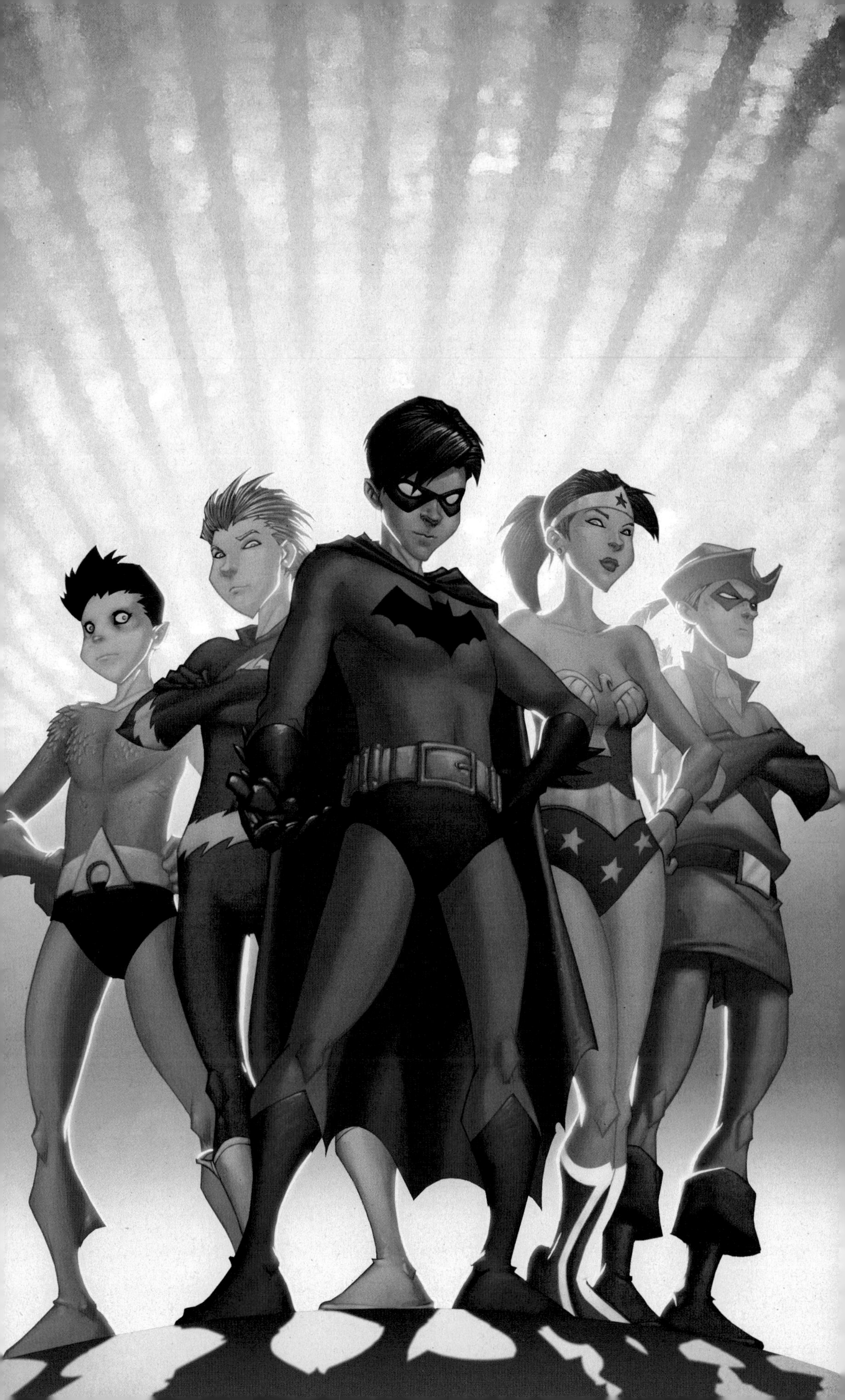

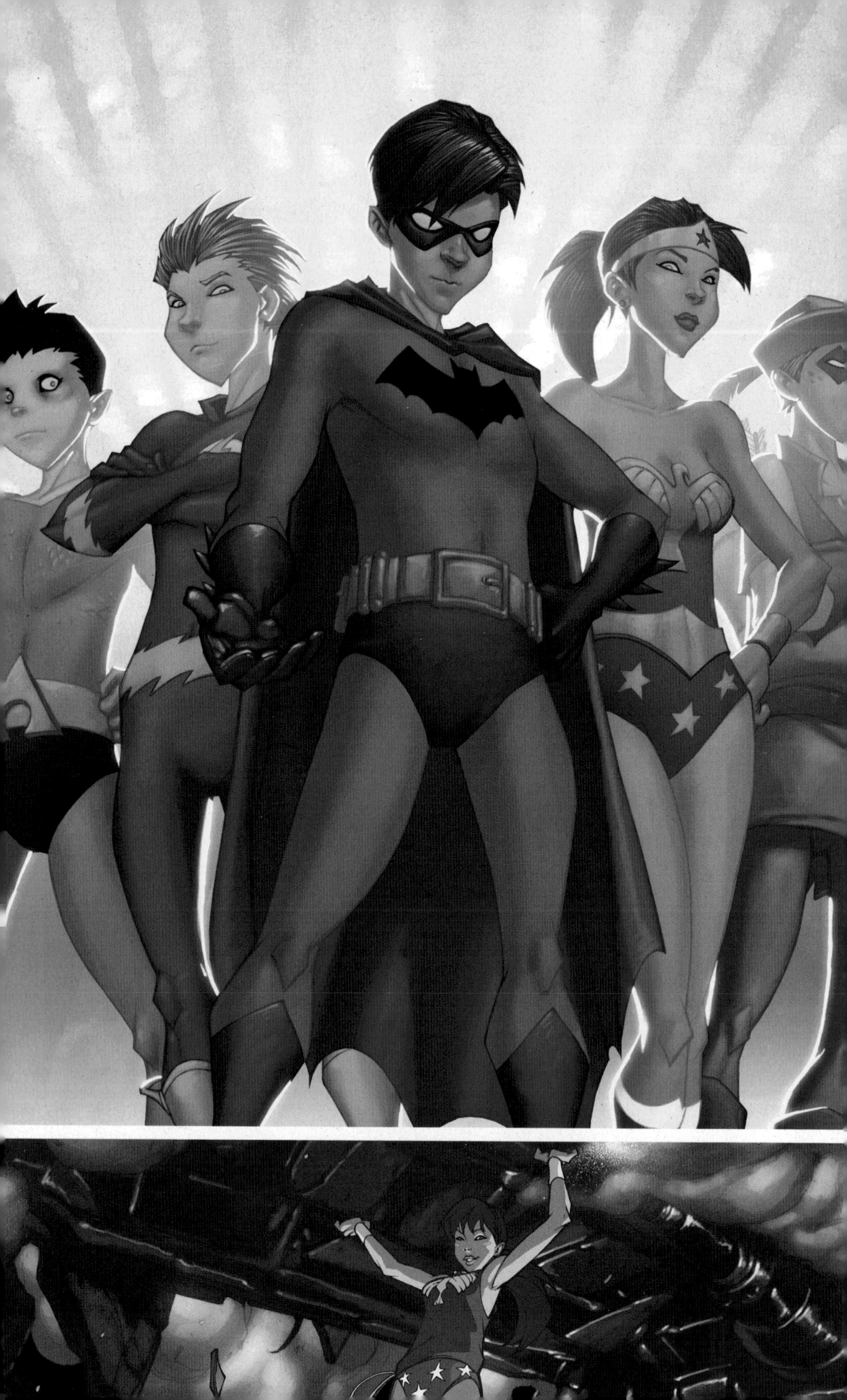

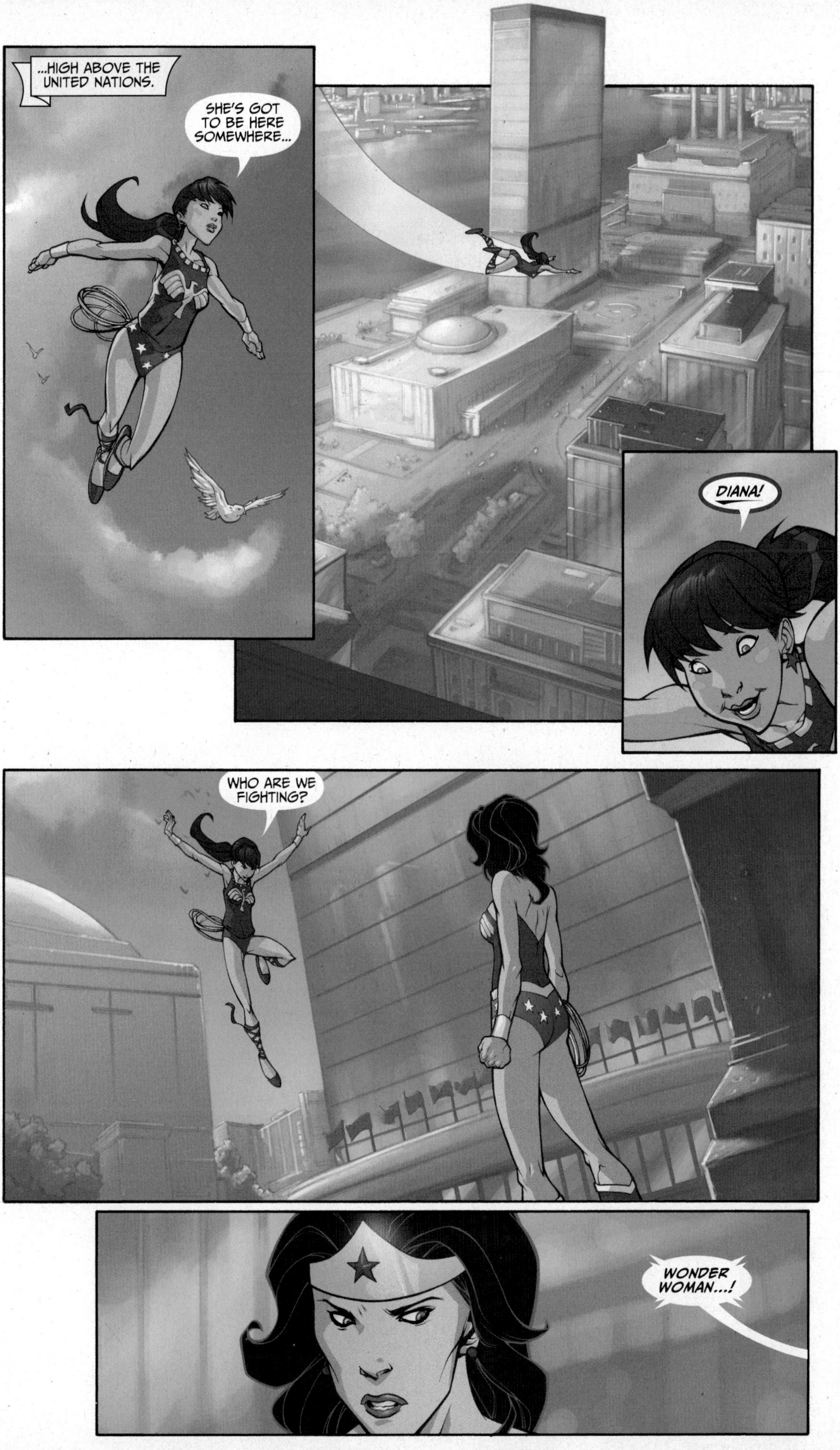
...HIGH ABOVE THE UNITED NATIONS.
SHE'S GOT TO BE HERE SOMEWHERE...
DIANA!
WHO ARE WE FIGHTING?
WONDER WOMAN...!

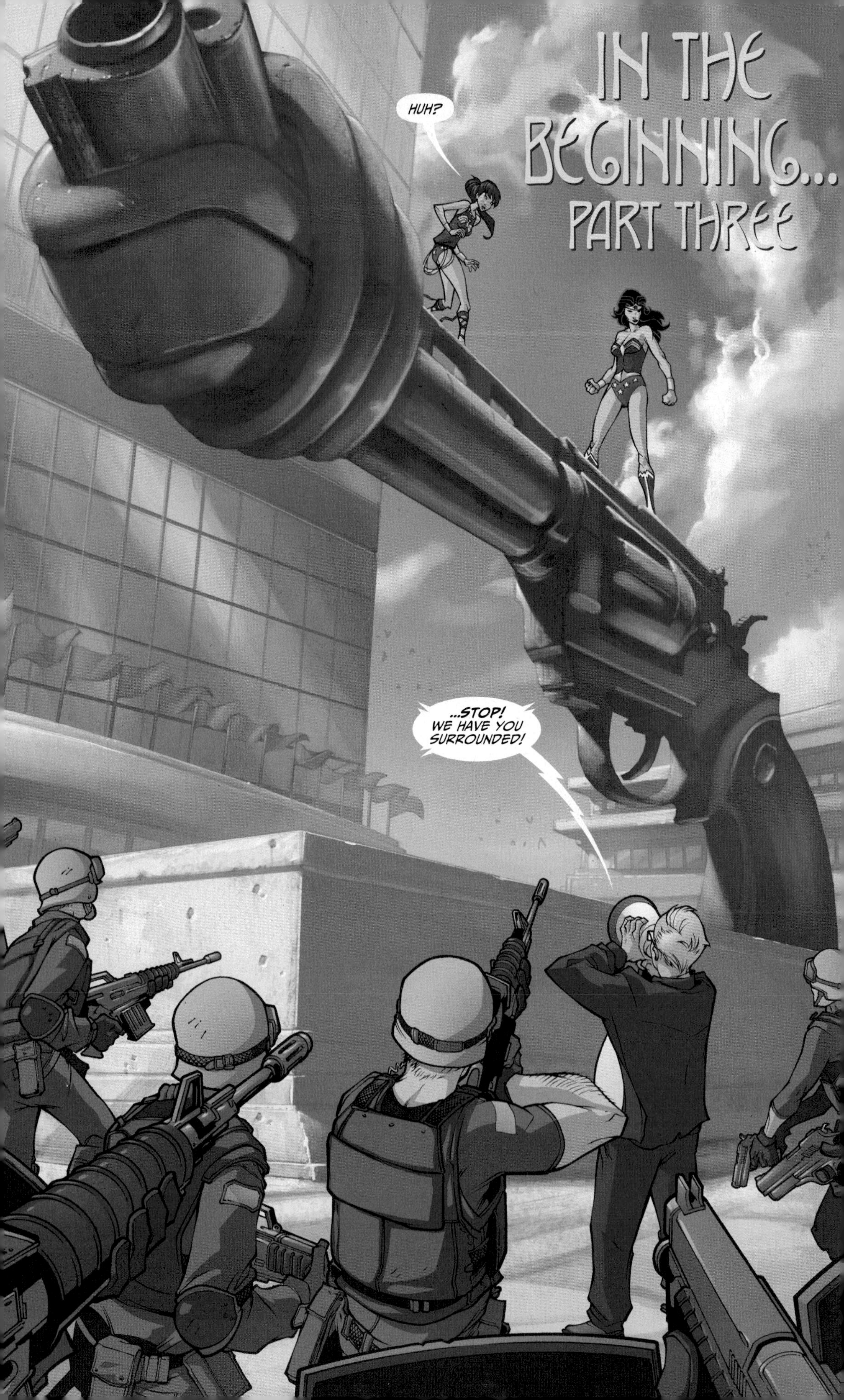
IN THE BEGINNING... PART THREE
HUH?
...STOP! WE HAVE YOU SURROUNDED!

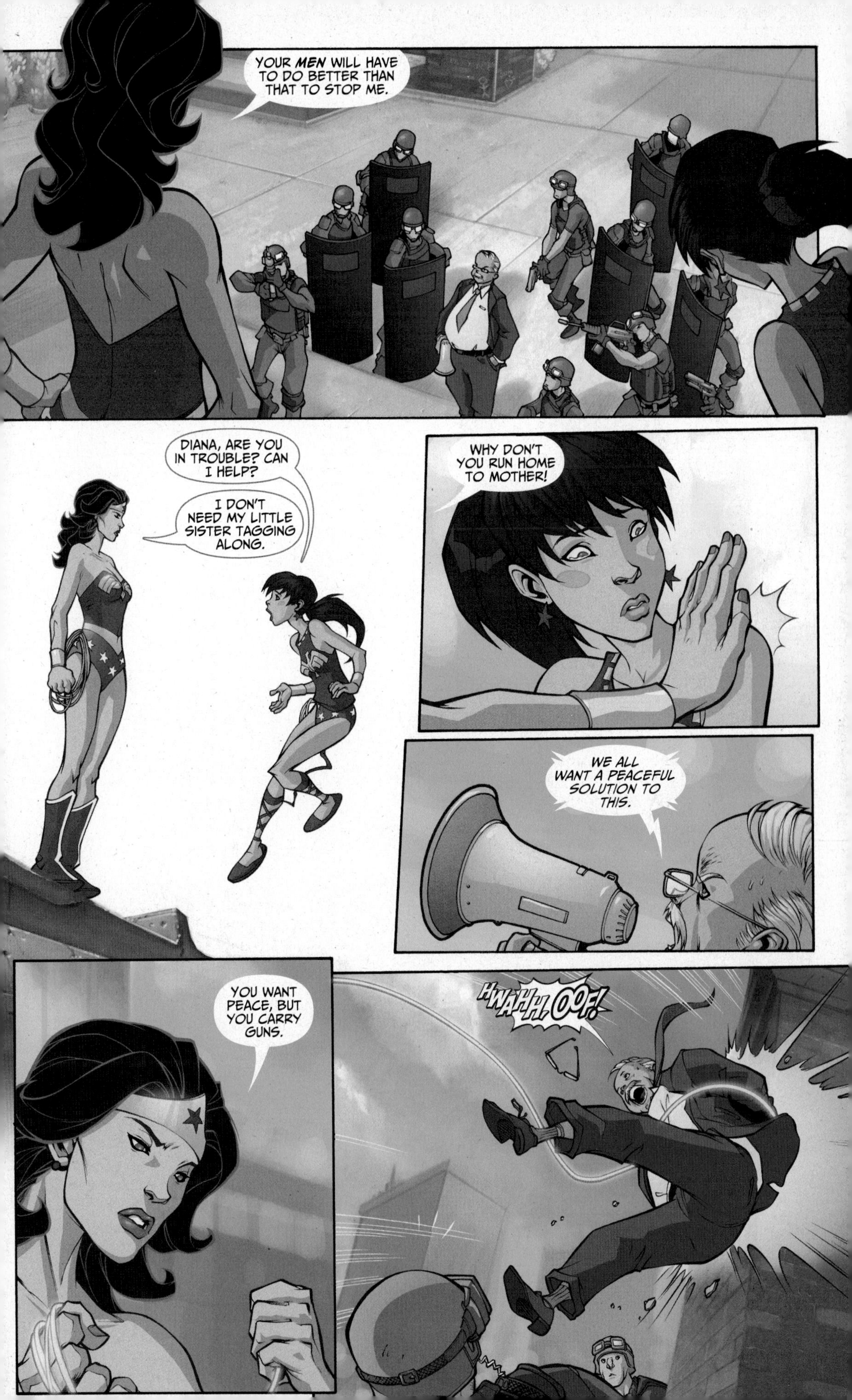
YOUR MEN WILL HAVE TO DO BETTER THAN THAT TO STOP ME.
DIANA, ARE YOU IN TROUBLE? CAN I HELP?
I DON'T NEED MY LITTLE SISTER TAGGING ALONG.
WHY DON'T YOU RUN HOME TO MOTHER!
WE ALL WANT A PEACEFUL SOLUTION TO THIS.
YOU WANT PEACE, BUT YOU CARRY GUNS.
HWAHH, OOF!

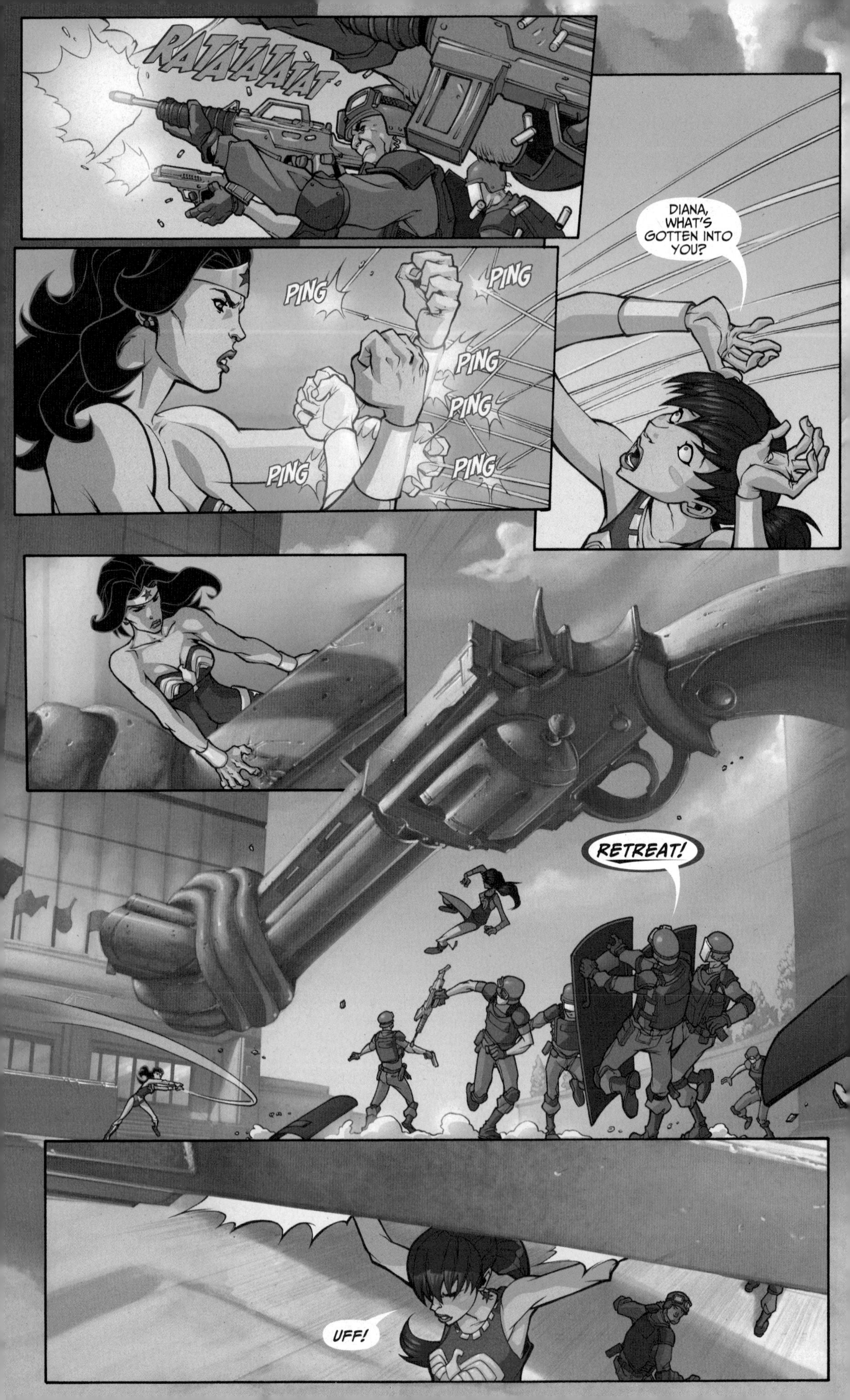
RATATATATAT
PING
PING
PING
PING
PING
PING
DIANA, WHAT'S GOTTEN INTO YOU?
RETREAT!
UFF!

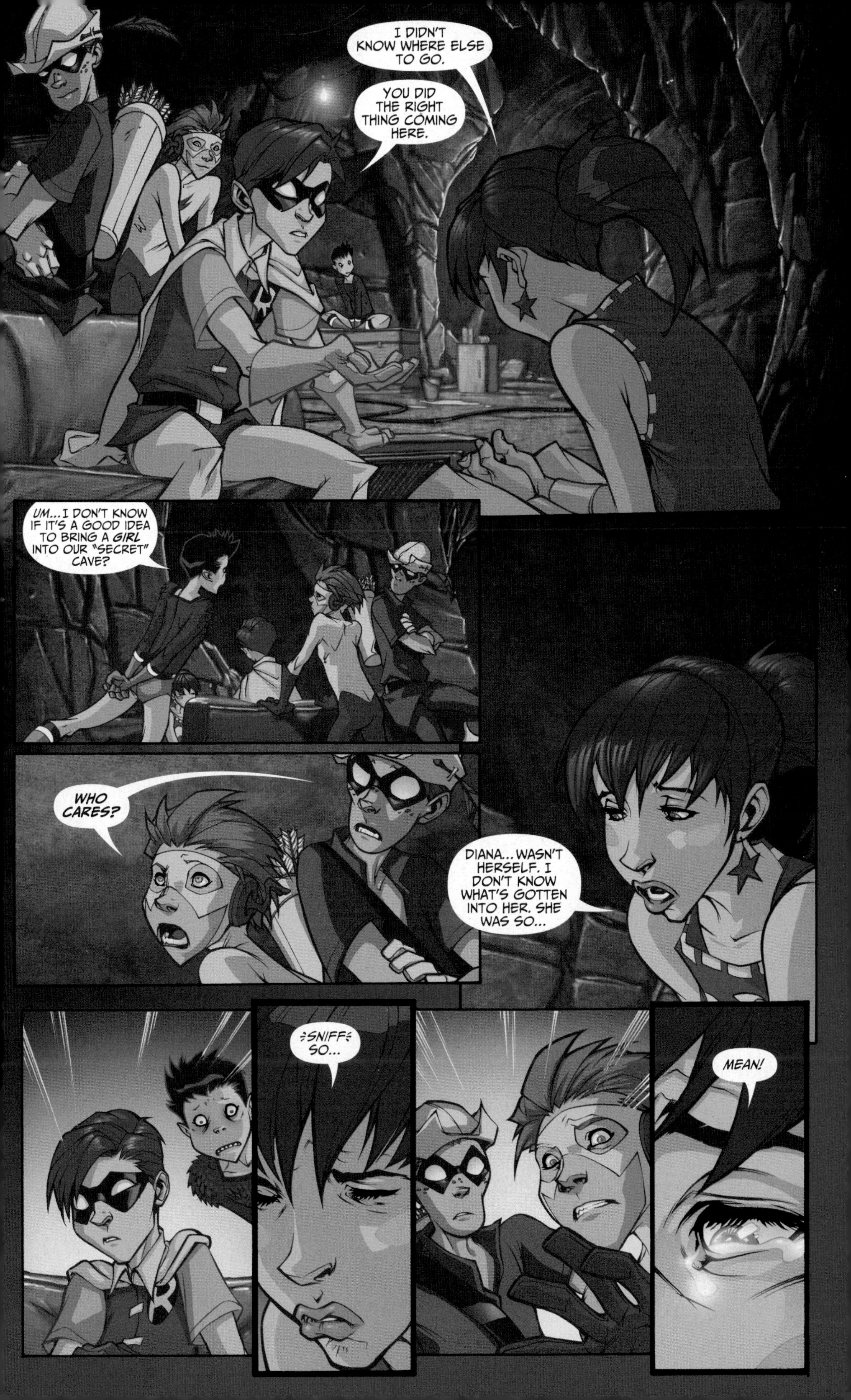
I DIDN'T KNOW WHERE ELSE TO GO.
YOU DID THE RIGHT THING COMING HERE.
UM...I DON'T KNOW IF IT'S A GOOD IDEA TO BRING A *GIRL* INTO OUR "SECRET" CAVE?
WHO CARES?
DIANA...WASN'T HERSELF. I DON'T KNOW WHAT'S GOTTEN INTO HER. SHE WAS SO...
SNIFF SO...
MEAN!

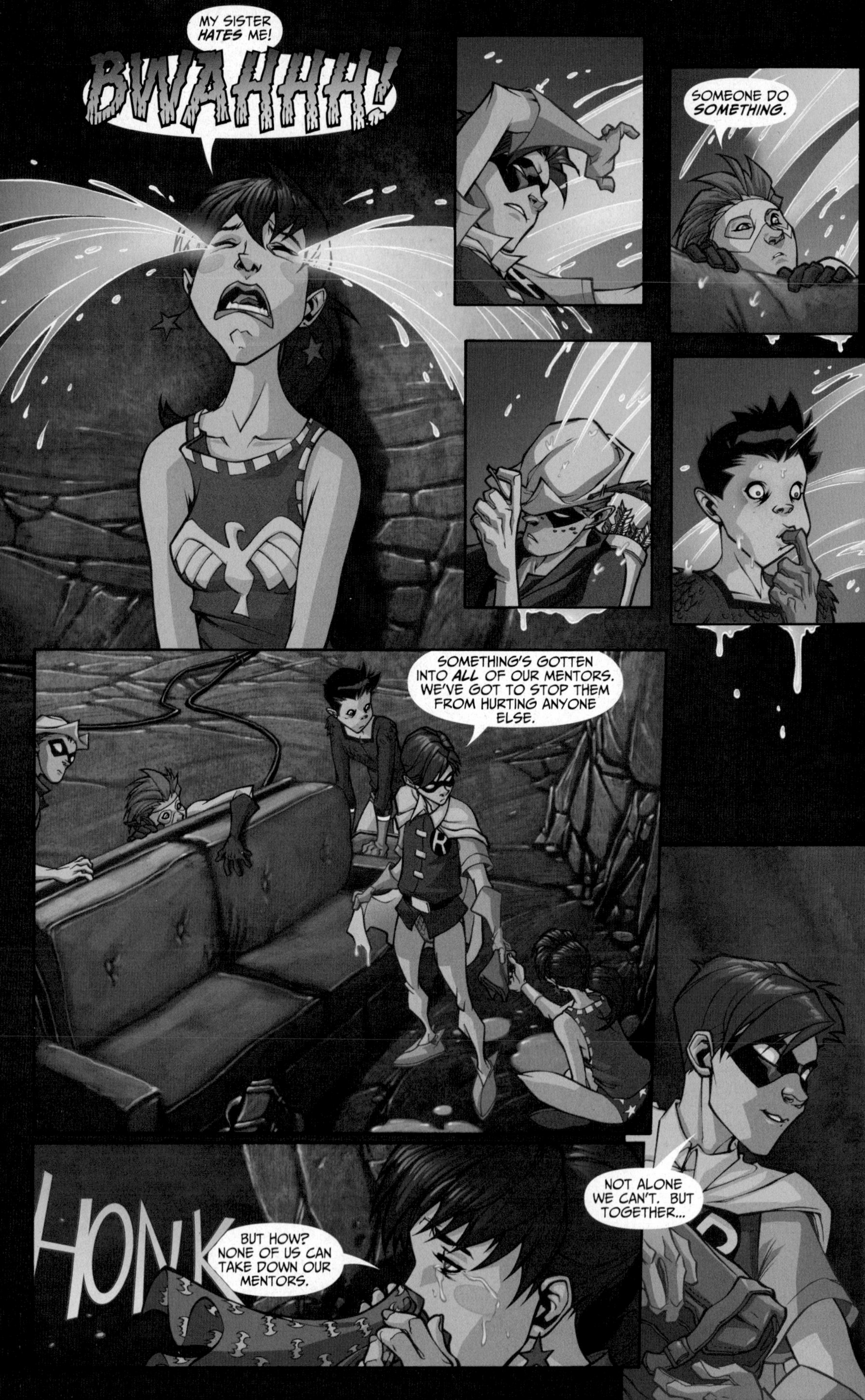
MY SISTER HATES ME!
BWAHHH!
SOMEONE DO SOMETHING.
SOMETHING'S GOTTEN INTO ALL OF OUR MENTORS. WE'VE GOT TO STOP THEM FROM HURTING ANYONE ELSE.
HONK
BUT HOW? NONE OF US CAN TAKE DOWN OUR MENTORS.
NOT ALONE WE CAN'T. BUT TOGETHER...

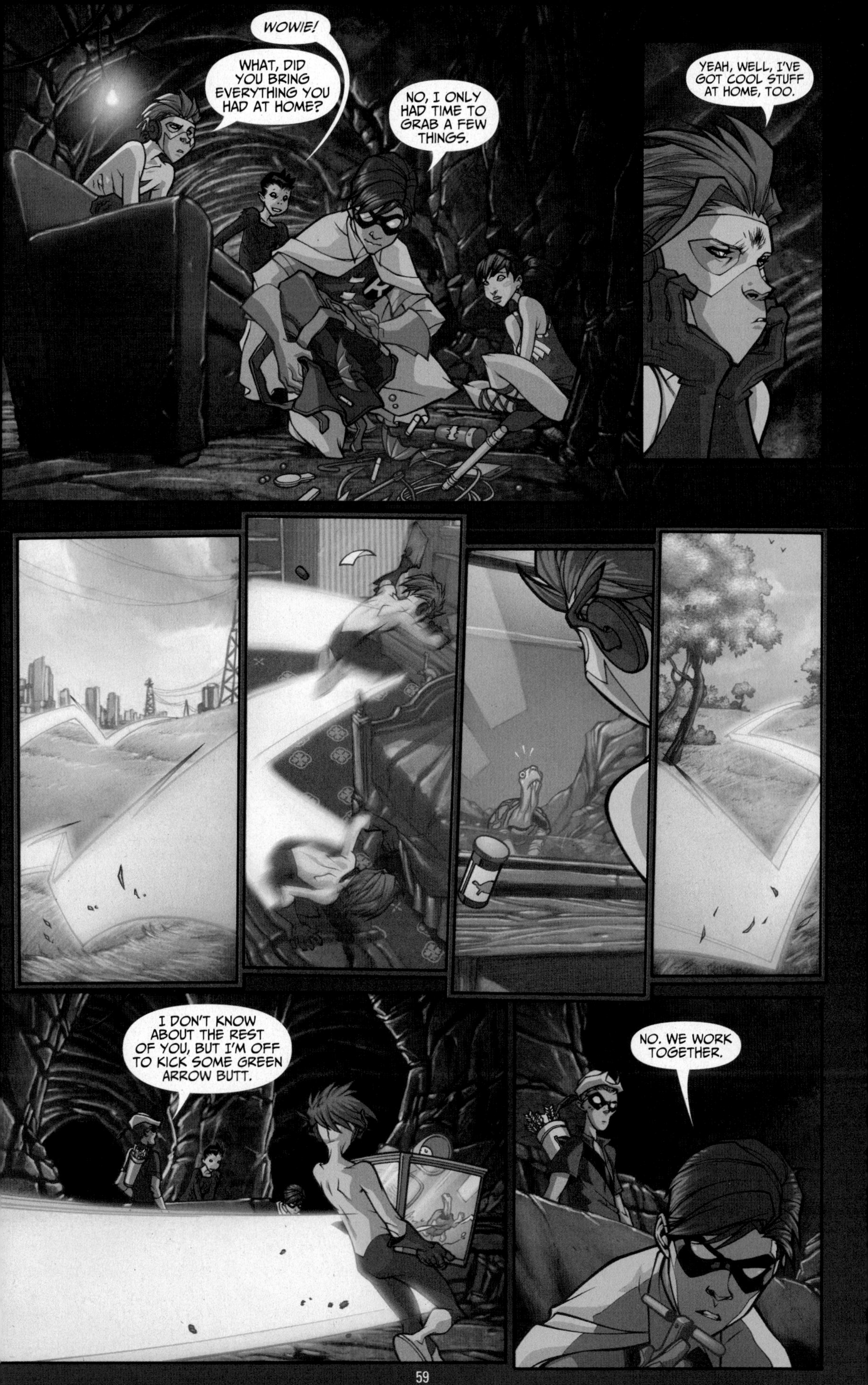
WOWIE!
WHAT, DID YOU BRING EVERYTHING YOU HAD AT HOME?
NO, I ONLY HAD TIME TO GRAB A FEW THINGS.
YEAH, WELL, I'VE GOT COOL STUFF AT HOME, TOO.
I DON'T KNOW ABOUT THE REST OF YOU, BUT I'M OFF TO KICK SOME GREEN ARROW BUTT.
NO. WE WORK TOGETHER.

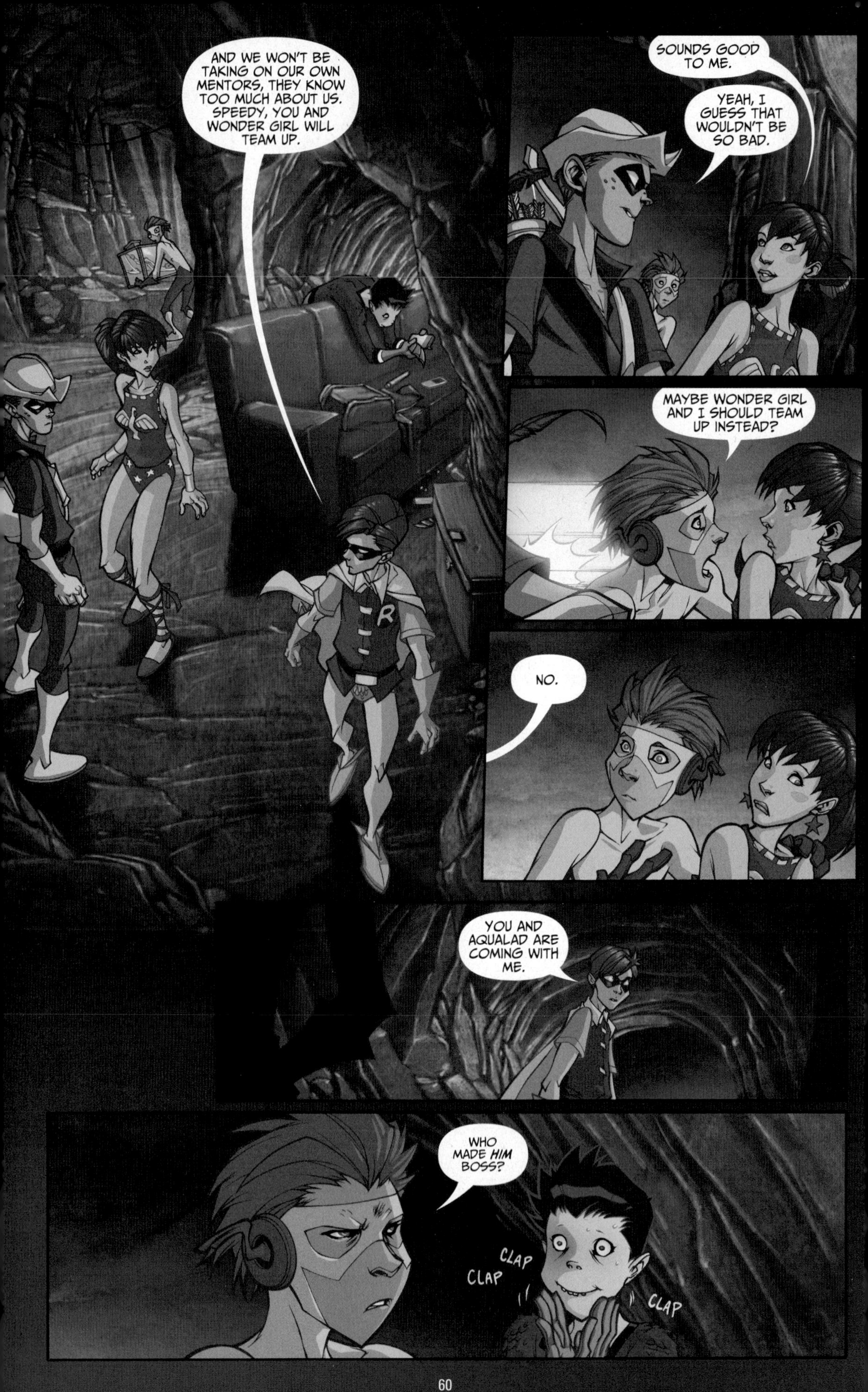
AND WE WON'T BE TAKING ON OUR OWN MENTORS, THEY KNOW TOO MUCH ABOUT US. SPEEDY, YOU AND WONDER GIRL WILL TEAM UP.
SOUNDS GOOD TO ME.
YEAH, I GUESS THAT WOULDN'T BE SO BAD.
MAYBE WONDER GIRL AND I SHOULD TEAM UP INSTEAD?
NO.
YOU AND AQUALAD ARE COMING WITH ME.
WHO MADE *HIM* BOSS?
CLAP
CLAP
CLAP

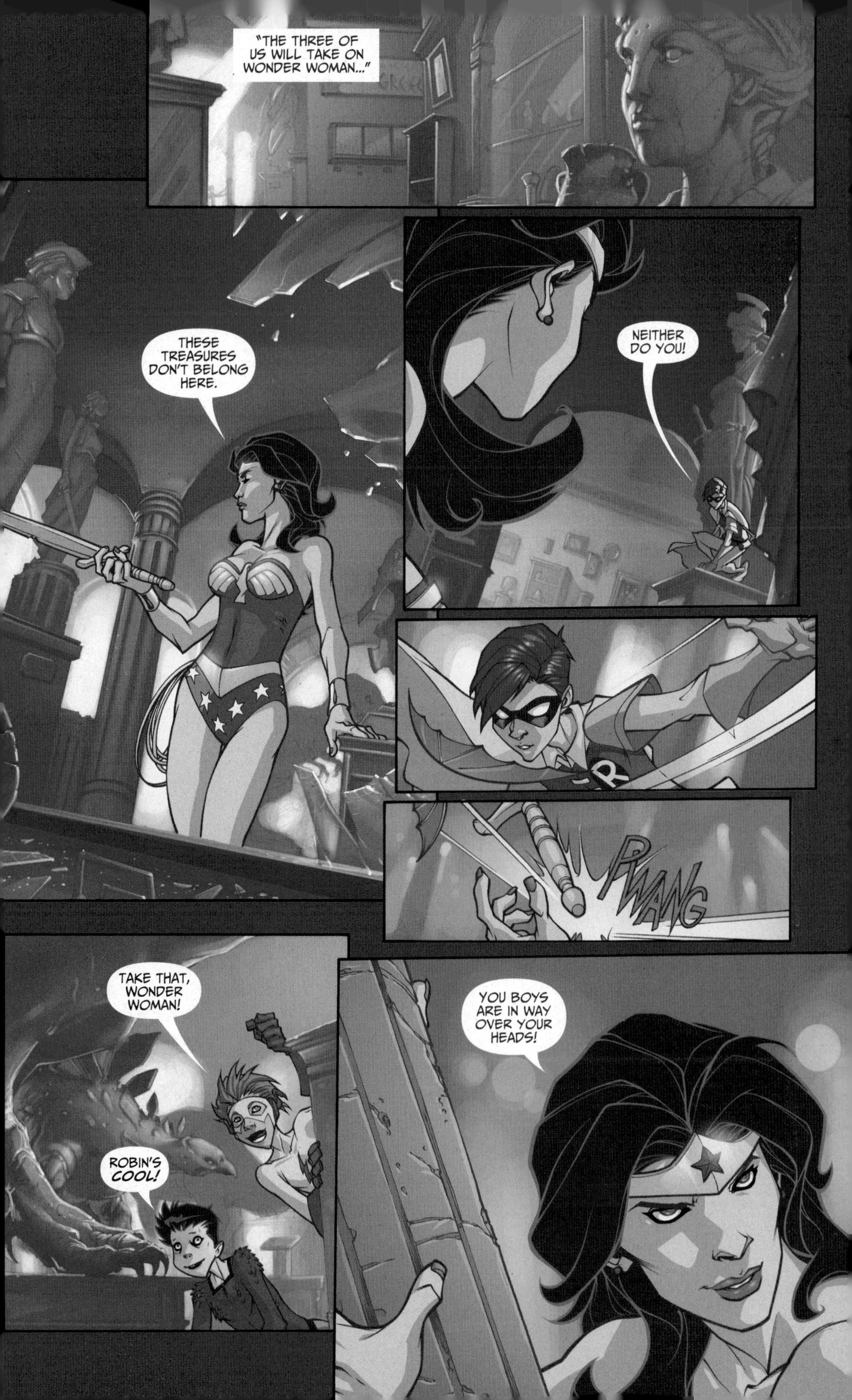
"THE THREE OF US WILL TAKE ON WONDER WOMAN..."
THESE TREASURES DON'T BELONG HERE.
NEITHER DO YOU!
PWANG
TAKE THAT, WONDER WOMAN!
ROBIN'S COOL!
YOU BOYS ARE IN WAY OVER YOUR HEADS!

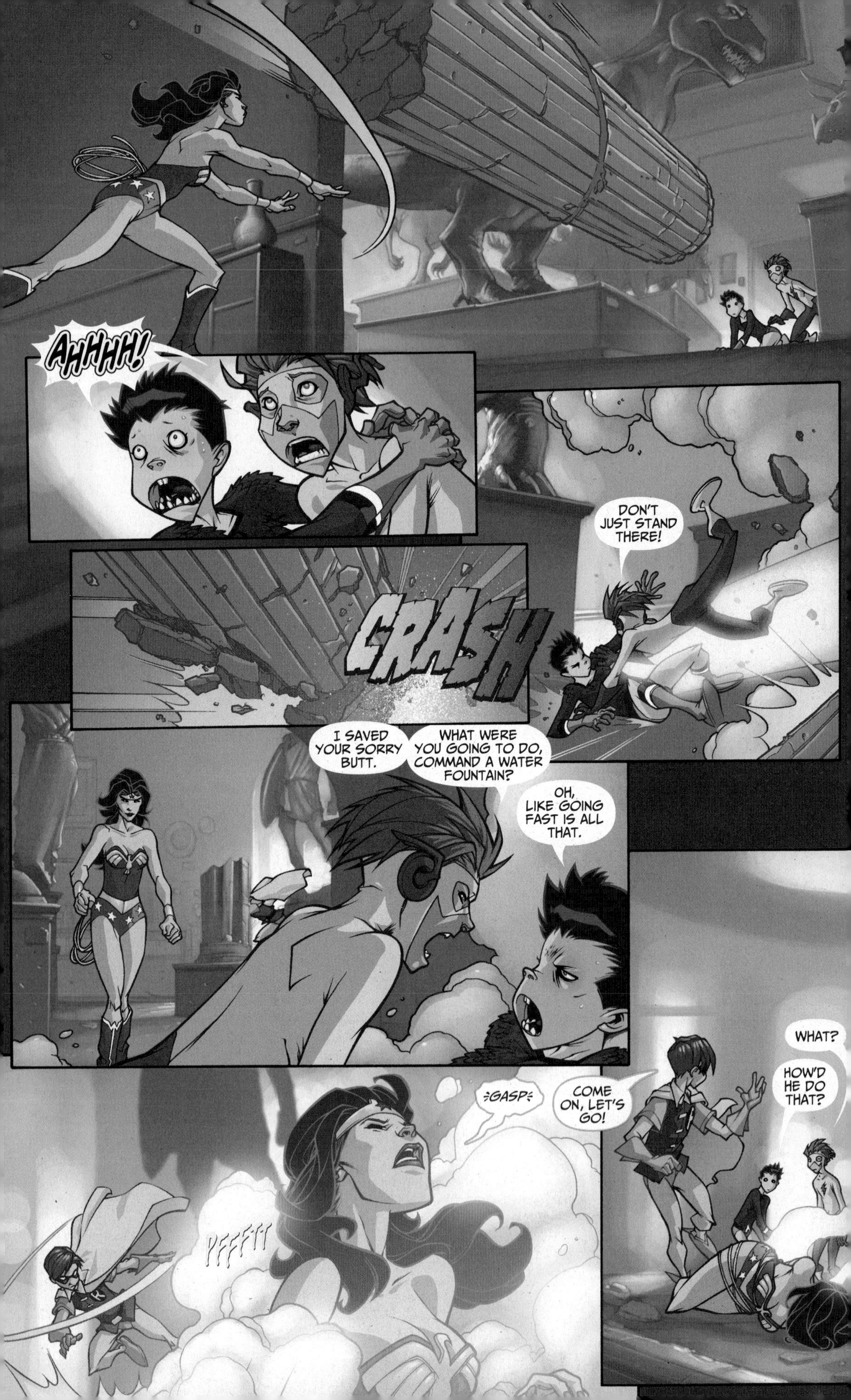
AHHHH!
DON'T JUST STAND THERE!
CRASH
I SAVED YOUR SORRY BUTT.
WHAT WERE YOU GOING TO DO, COMMAND A WATER FOUNTAIN?
OH, LIKE GOING FAST IS ALL THAT.
PFFFTT
GASP
COME ON, LET'S GO!
WHAT?
HOW'D HE DO THAT?

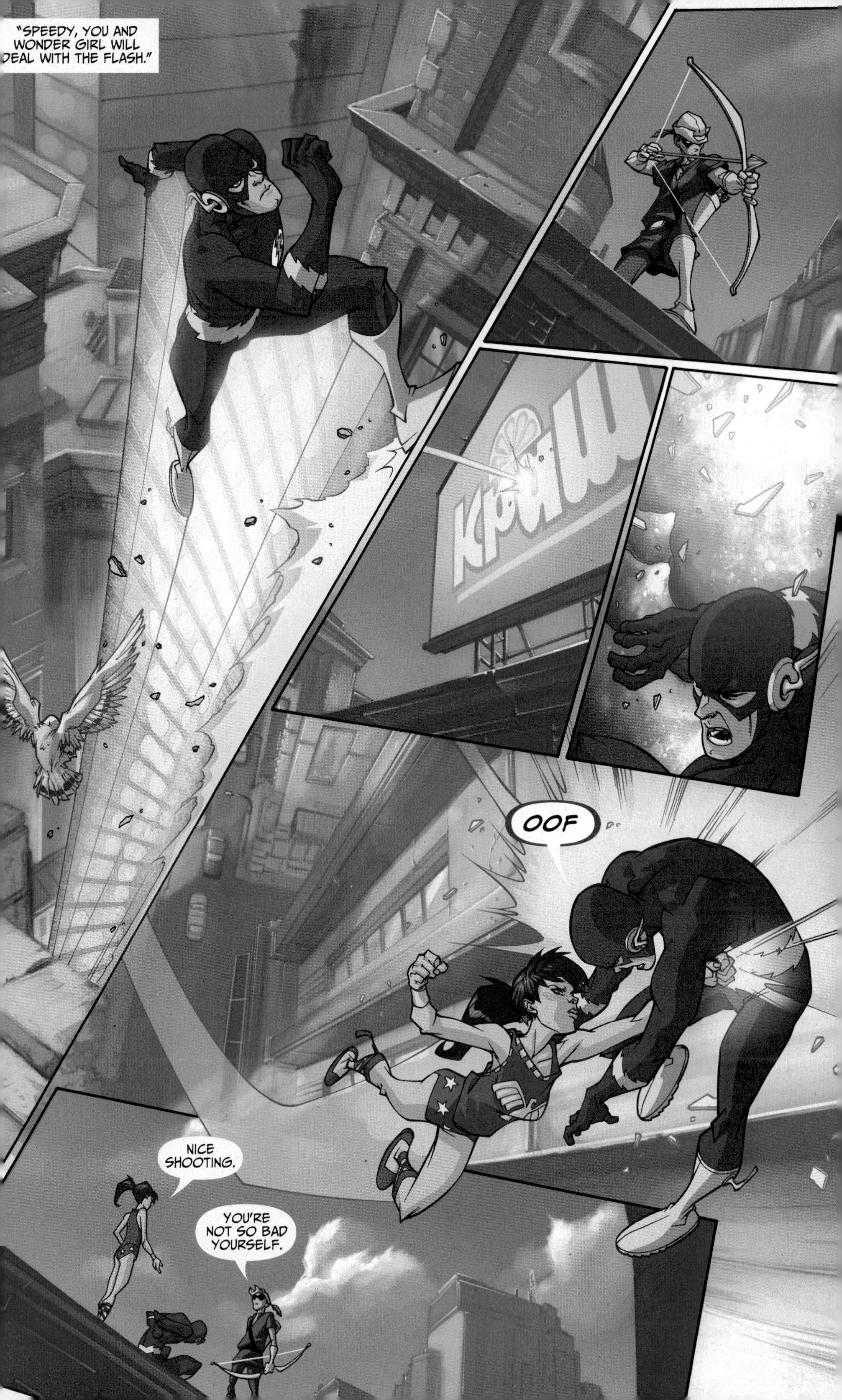
"SPEEDY, YOU AND WONDER GIRL WILL DEAL WITH THE FLASH."
OOF
NICE SHOOTING.
YOU'RE NOT SO BAD YOURSELF.

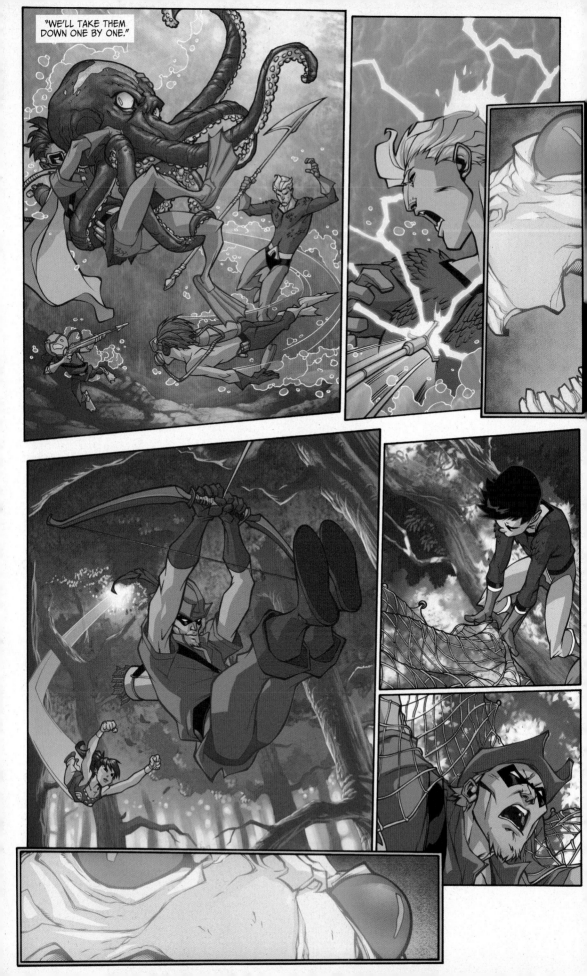

"WE'LL TAKE THEM DOWN ONE BY ONE."

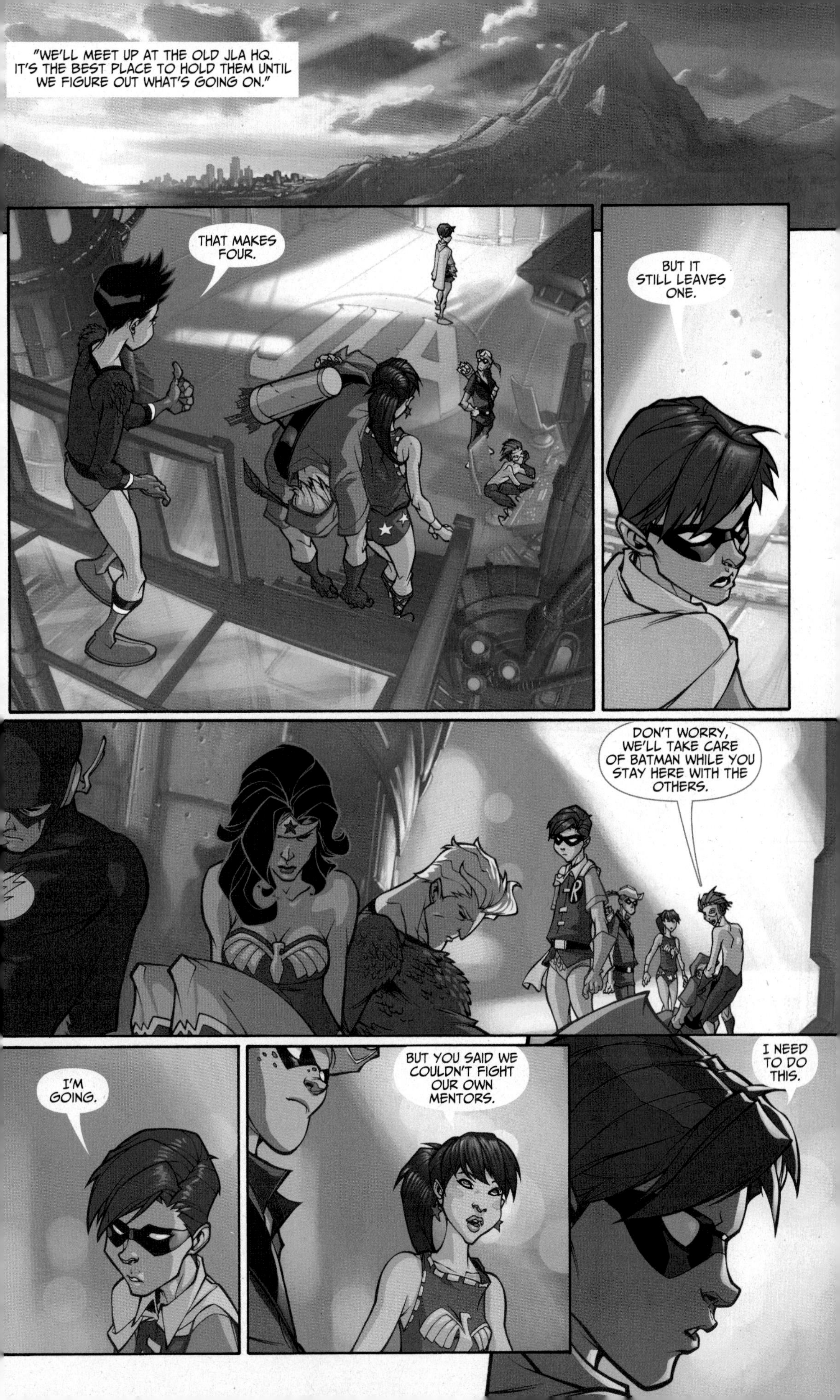
"WE'LL MEET UP AT THE OLD JLA HQ. IT'S THE BEST PLACE TO HOLD THEM UNTIL WE FIGURE OUT WHAT'S GOING ON."
THAT MAKES FOUR.
BUT IT STILL LEAVES ONE.
DON'T WORRY, WE'LL TAKE CARE OF BATMAN WHILE YOU STAY HERE WITH THE OTHERS.
I'M GOING.
BUT YOU SAID WE COULDN'T FIGHT OUR OWN MENTORS.
I NEED TO DO THIS.

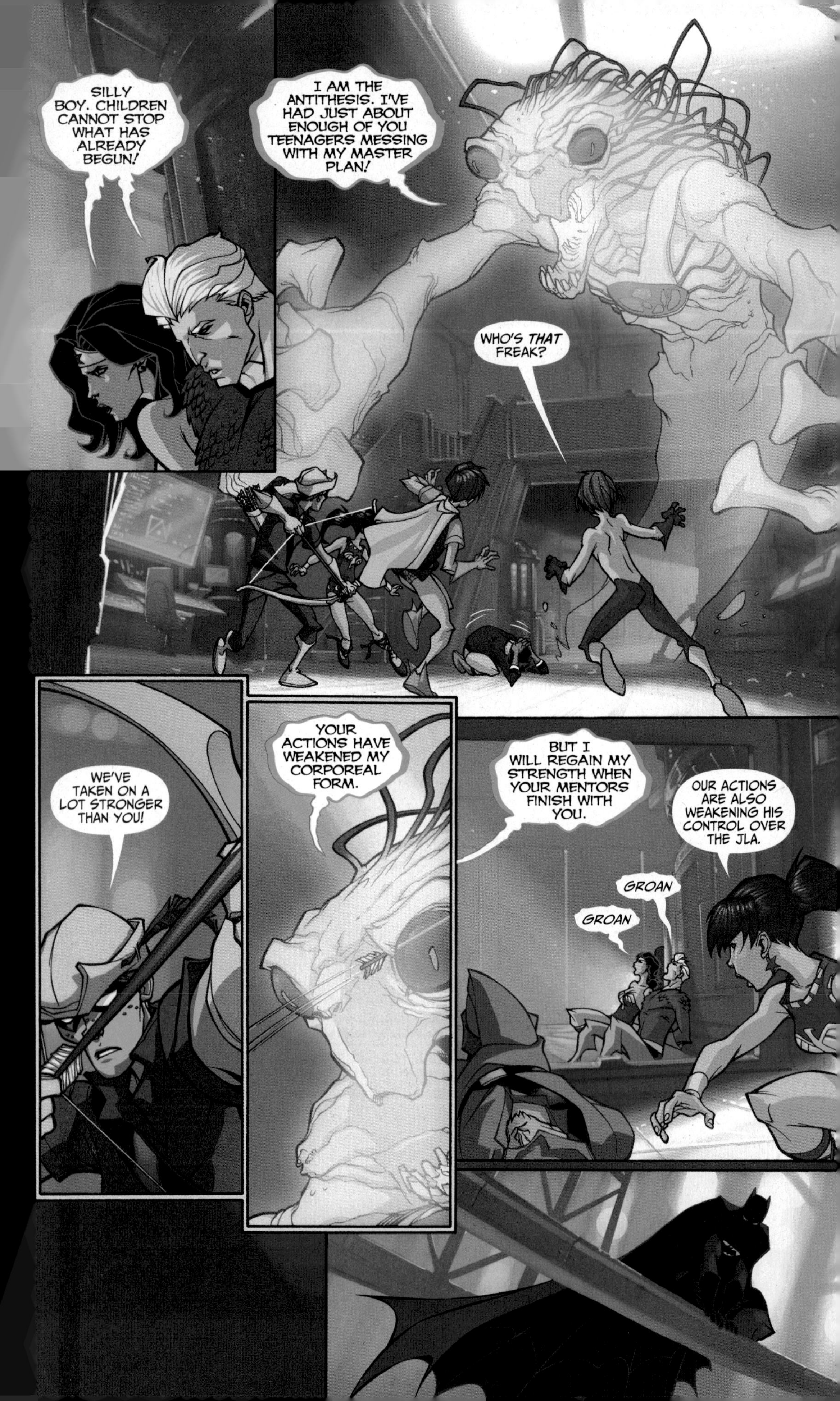
SILLY BOY. CHILDREN CANNOT STOP WHAT HAS ALREADY BEGUN!
I AM THE ANTITHESIS. I'VE HAD JUST ABOUT ENOUGH OF YOU TEENAGERS MESSING WITH MY MASTER PLAN!
WHO'S THAT FREAK?
WE'VE TAKEN ON A LOT STRONGER THAN YOU!
YOUR ACTIONS HAVE WEAKENED MY CORPOREAL FORM.
BUT I WILL REGAIN MY STRENGTH WHEN YOUR MENTORS FINISH WITH YOU.
OUR ACTIONS ARE ALSO WEAKENING HIS CONTROL OVER THE JLA.
GROAN
GROAN

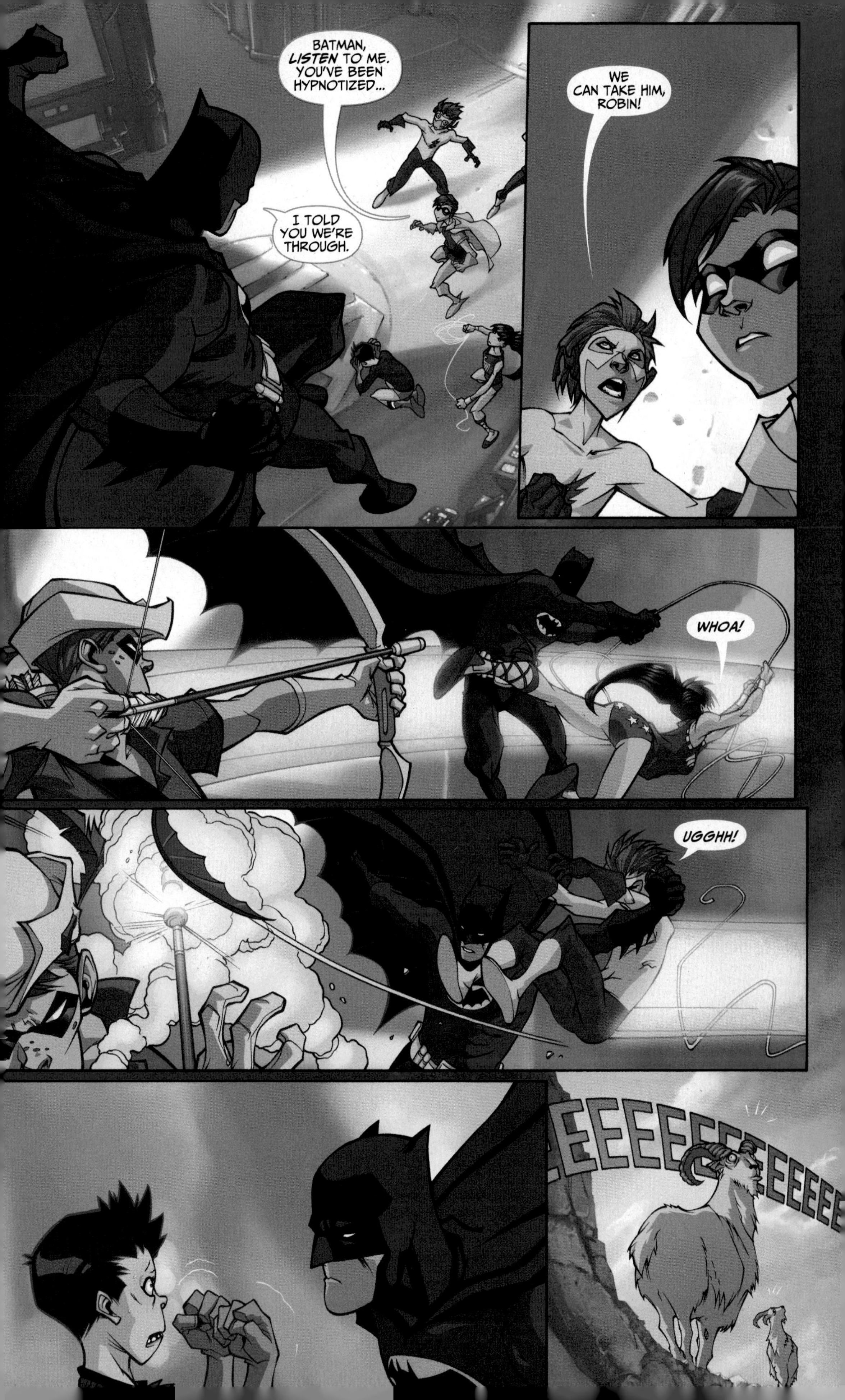
BATMAN, LISTEN TO ME. YOU'VE BEEN HYPNOTIZED...
I TOLD YOU WE'RE THROUGH.
WE CAN TAKE HIM, ROBIN!
WHOA!
UGGHH!
EEEEEEEEEEEEEEEE

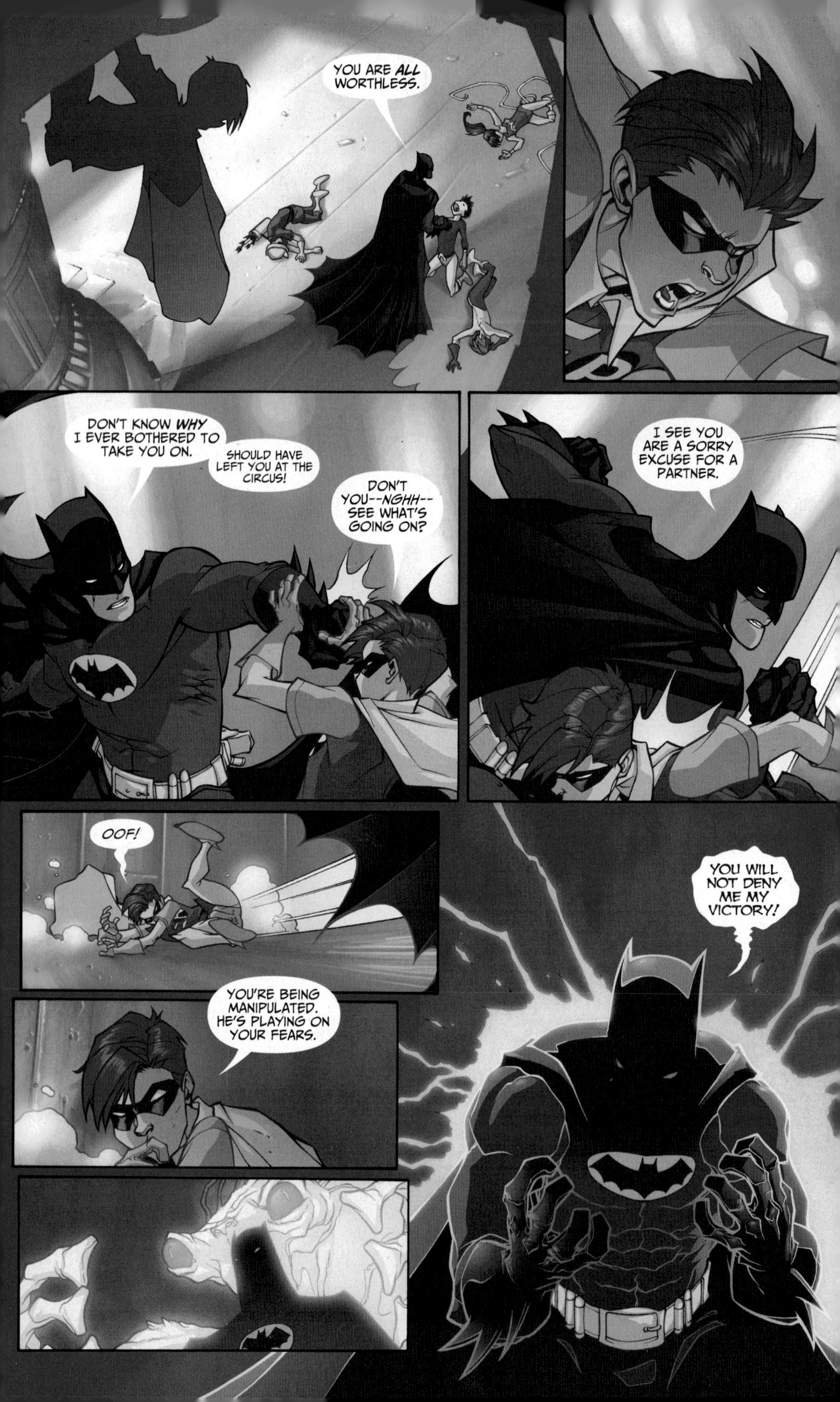
YOU ARE ***ALL*** WORTHLESS.
DON'T KNOW ***WHY*** I EVER BOTHERED TO TAKE YOU ON.
SHOULD HAVE LEFT YOU AT THE CIRCUS!
DON'T YOU--*NGHH*--SEE WHAT'S GOING ON?
I SEE YOU ARE A SORRY EXCUSE FOR A PARTNER.
OOF!
YOU'RE BEING MANIPULATED. HE'S PLAYING ON YOUR FEARS.
YOU WILL NOT DENY ME MY VICTORY!

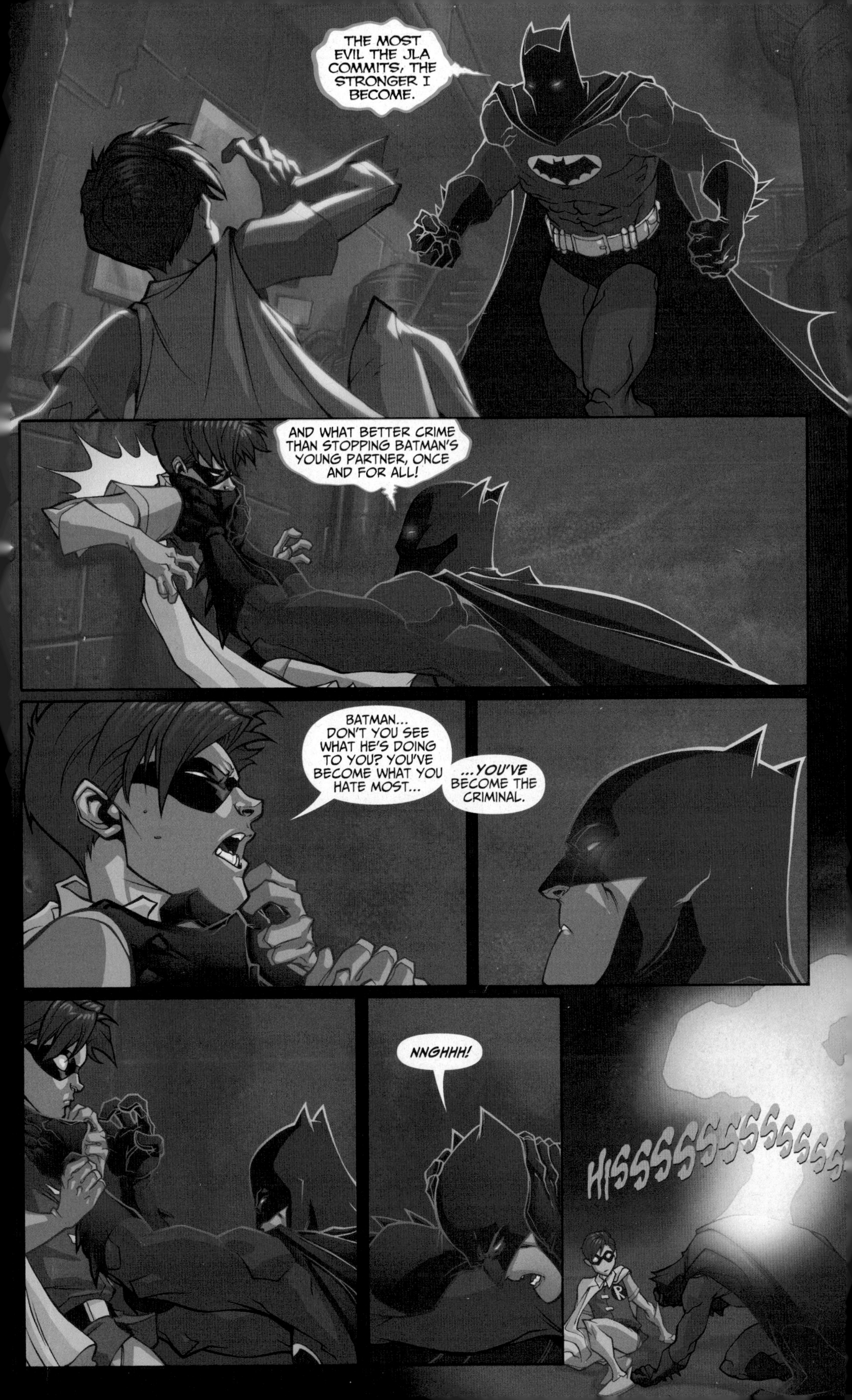
THE MOST EVIL THE JLA COMMITS, THE STRONGER I BECOME.
AND WHAT BETTER CRIME THAN STOPPING BATMAN'S YOUNG PARTNER, ONCE AND FOR ALL!
BATMAN... DON'T YOU SEE WHAT HE'S DOING TO YOU? YOU'VE BECOME WHAT YOU HATE MOST...
...YOU'VE BECOME THE CRIMINAL.
NNGHHH!
HISSSSSSSSSSSSS

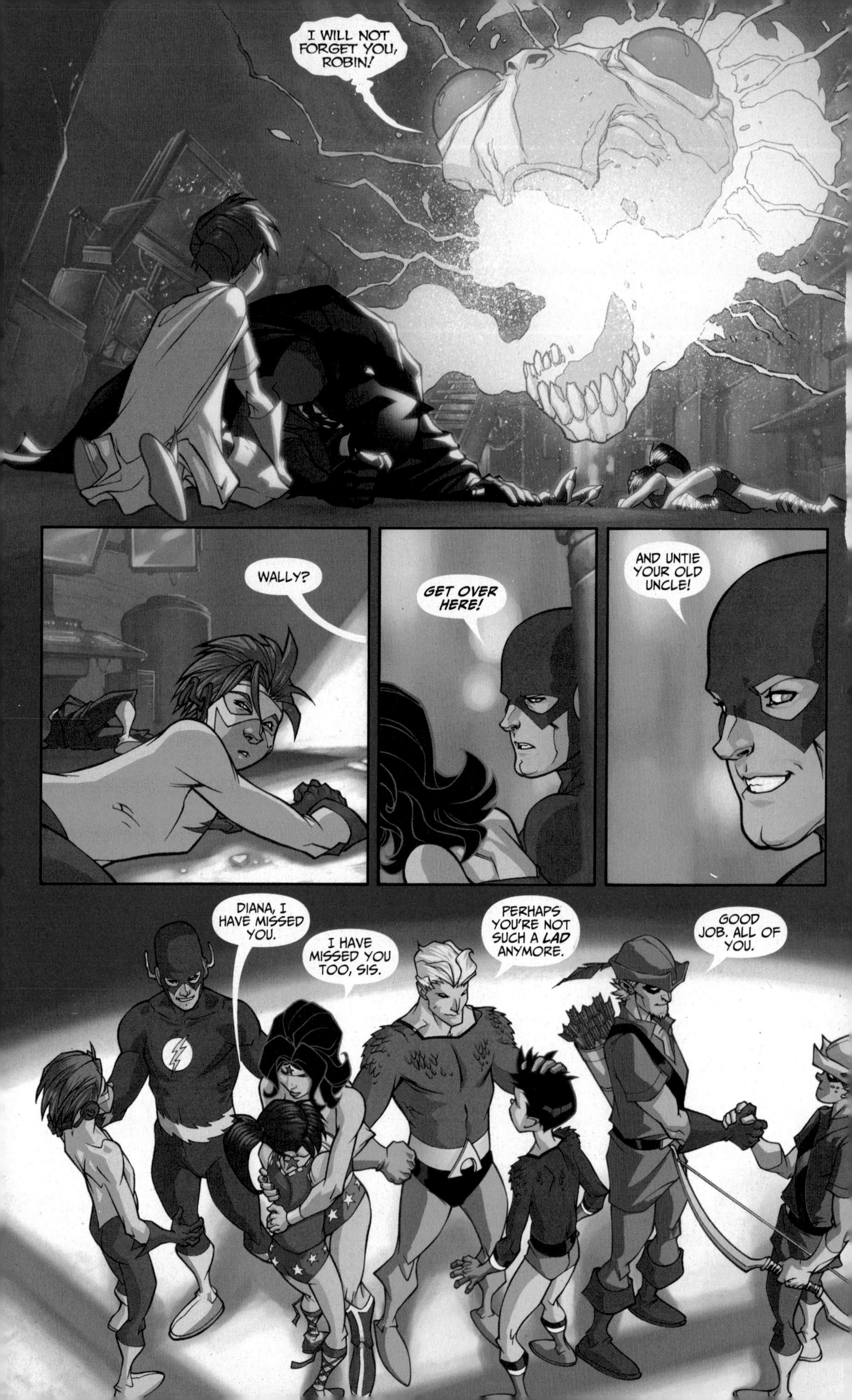
I WILL NOT FORGET YOU, ROBIN!
WALLY?
GET OVER HERE!
AND UNTIE YOUR OLD UNCLE!
DIANA, I HAVE MISSED YOU.
I HAVE MISSED YOU TOO, SIS.
PERHAPS YOU'RE NOT SUCH A *LAD* ANYMORE.
GOOD JOB. ALL OF YOU.

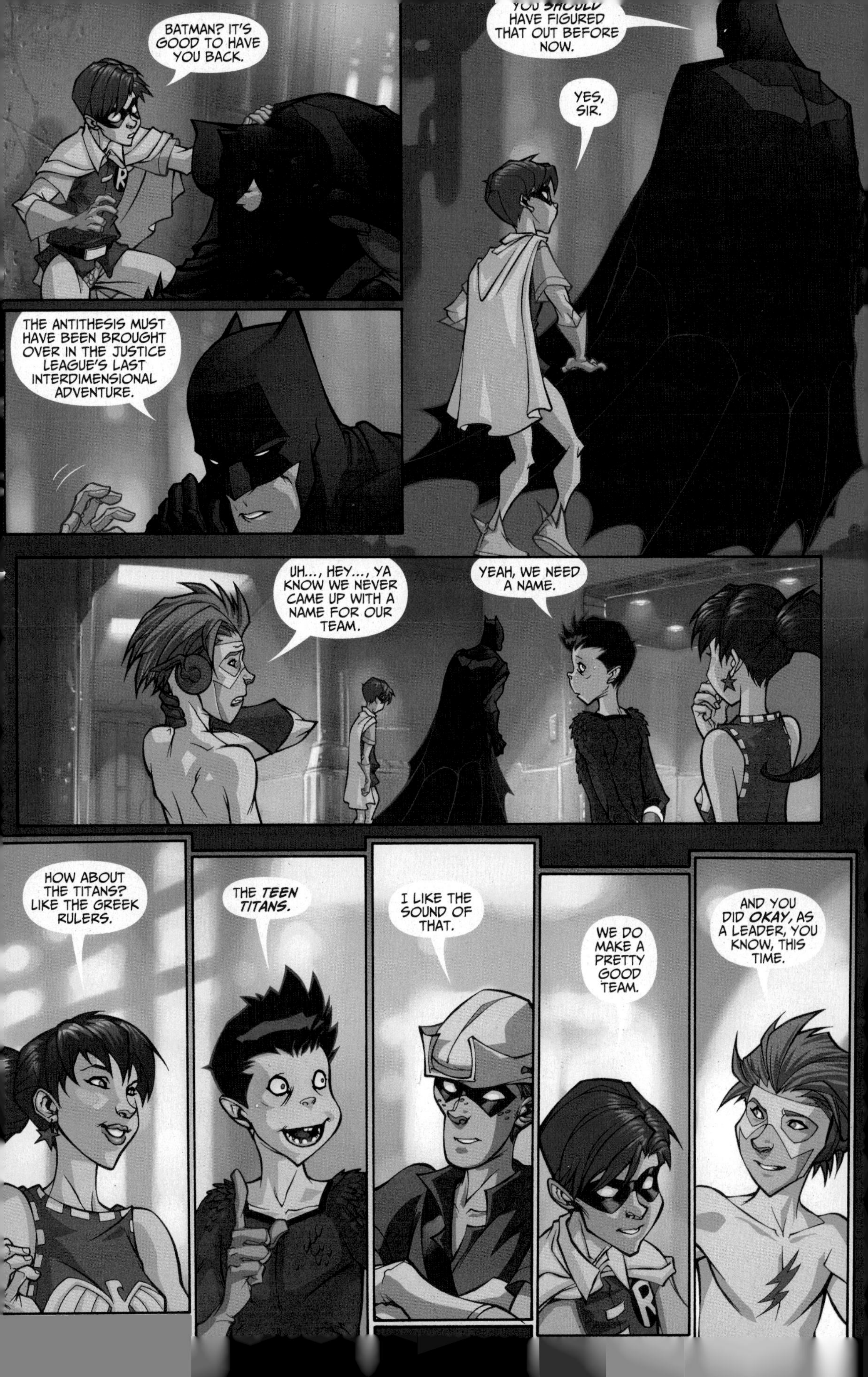
BATMAN? IT'S GOOD TO HAVE YOU BACK.
THE ANTITHESIS MUST HAVE BEEN BROUGHT OVER IN THE JUSTICE LEAGUE'S LAST INTERDIMENSIONAL ADVENTURE.
HAVE FIGURED THAT OUT BEFORE NOW.
YES, SIR.
UH..., HEY..., YA KNOW WE NEVER CAME UP WITH A NAME FOR OUR TEAM.
YEAH, WE NEED A NAME.
HOW ABOUT THE TITANS? LIKE THE GREEK RULERS.
THE *TEEN TITANS.*
I LIKE THE SOUND OF THAT.
WE DO MAKE A PRETTY GOOD TEAM.
AND YOU DID *OKAY,* AS A LEADER, YOU KNOW, THIS TIME.

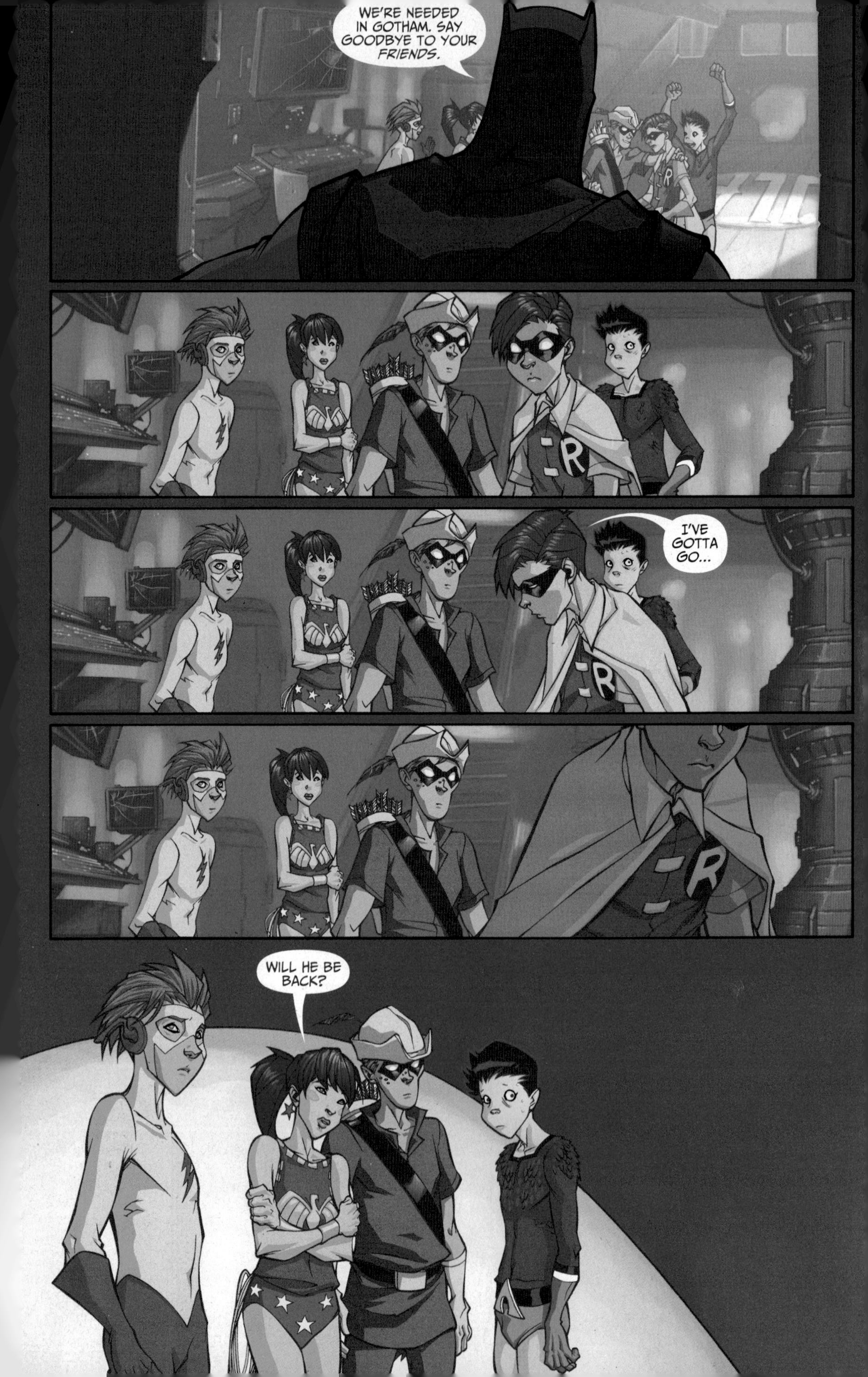
WE'RE NEEDED IN GOTHAM. SAY GOODBYE TO YOUR FRIENDS.
I'VE GOTTA GO...
WILL HE BE BACK?

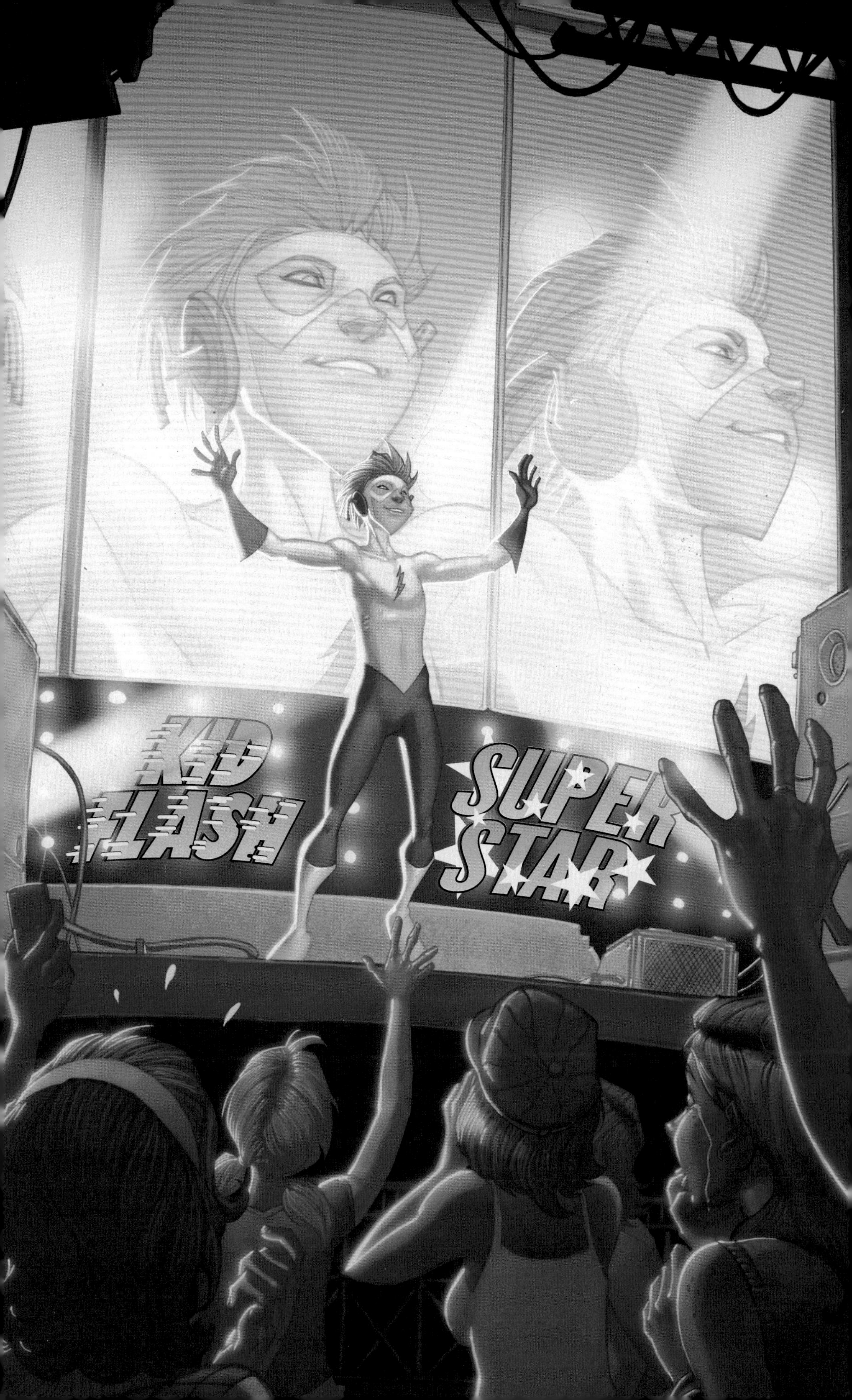
KID FLASH
SUPER STAR

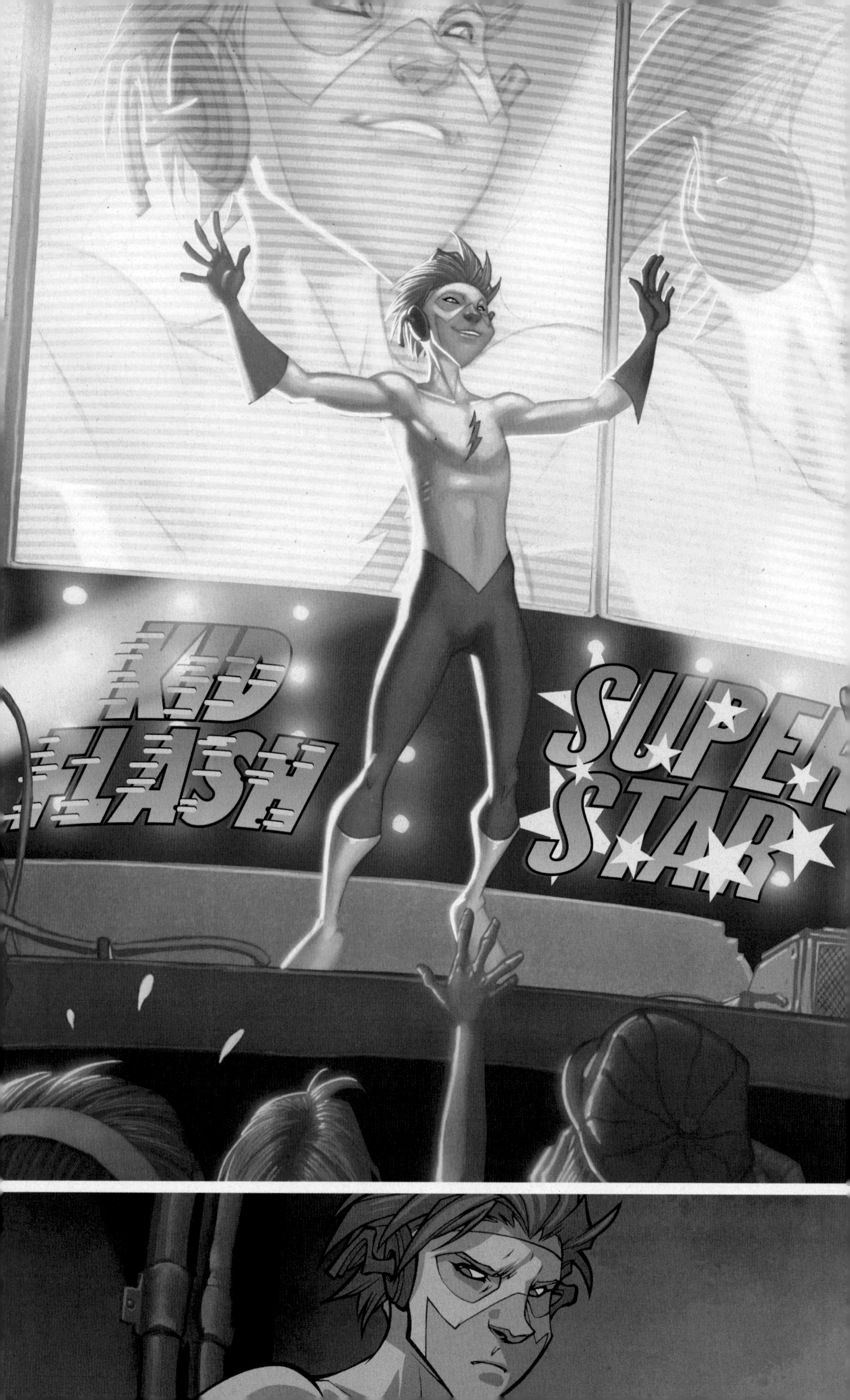
KID FLASH
SUPERSTAR

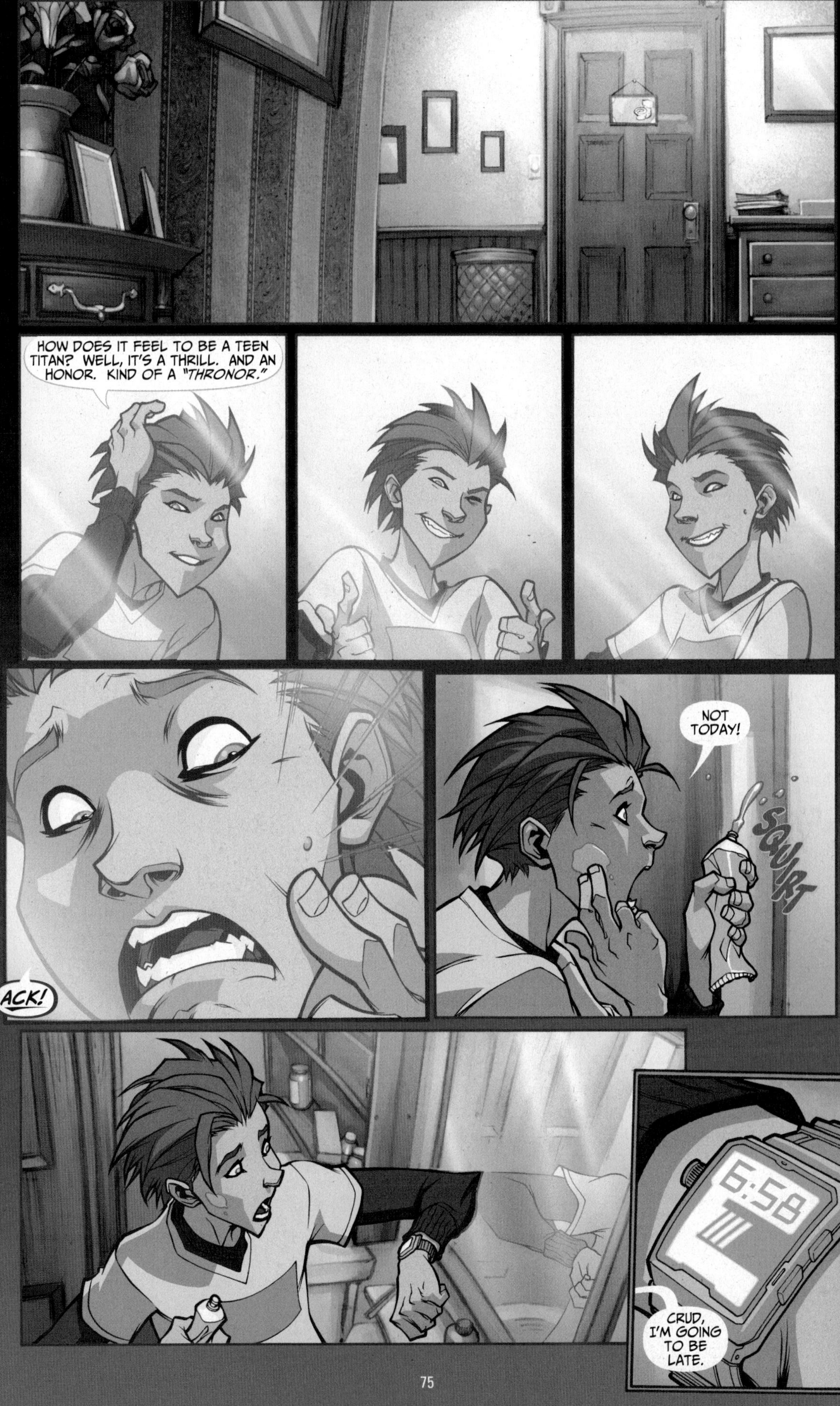
HOW DOES IT FEEL TO BE A TEEN TITAN? WELL, IT'S A THRILL. AND AN HONOR. KIND OF A "THRONOR."
ACK!
NOT TODAY!
SQUIRT
6:58
CRUD, I'M GOING TO BE LATE.

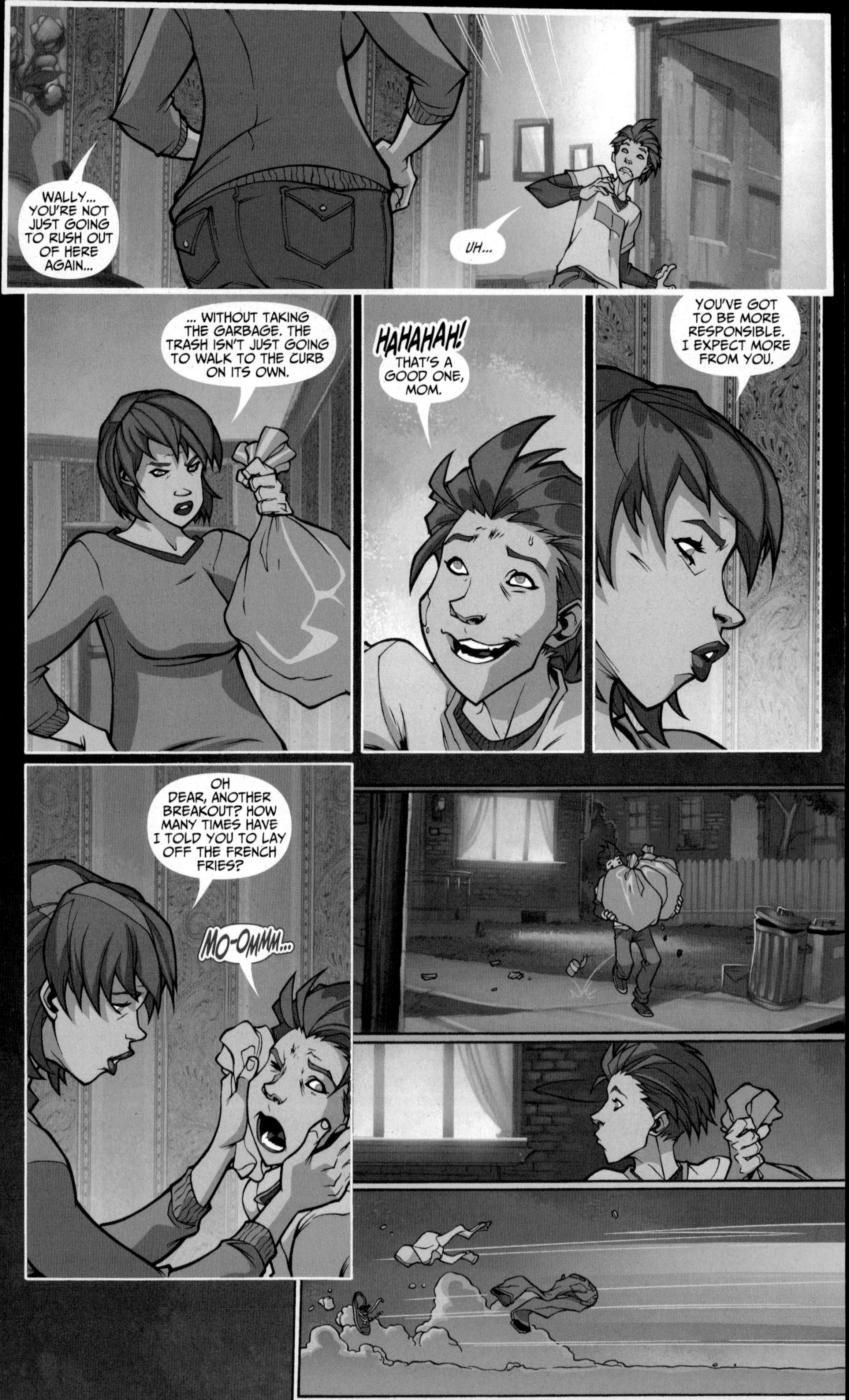
WALLY... YOU'RE NOT JUST GOING TO RUSH OUT OF HERE AGAIN...
UH...
... WITHOUT TAKING THE GARBAGE. THE TRASH ISN'T JUST GOING TO WALK TO THE CURB ON ITS OWN.
HAHAHAH!
THAT'S A GOOD ONE, MOM.
YOU'VE GOT TO BE MORE RESPONSIBLE. I EXPECT MORE FROM YOU.
OH DEAR, ANOTHER BREAKOUT? HOW MANY TIMES HAVE I TOLD YOU TO LAY OFF THE FRENCH FRIES?
MO-OMMM...

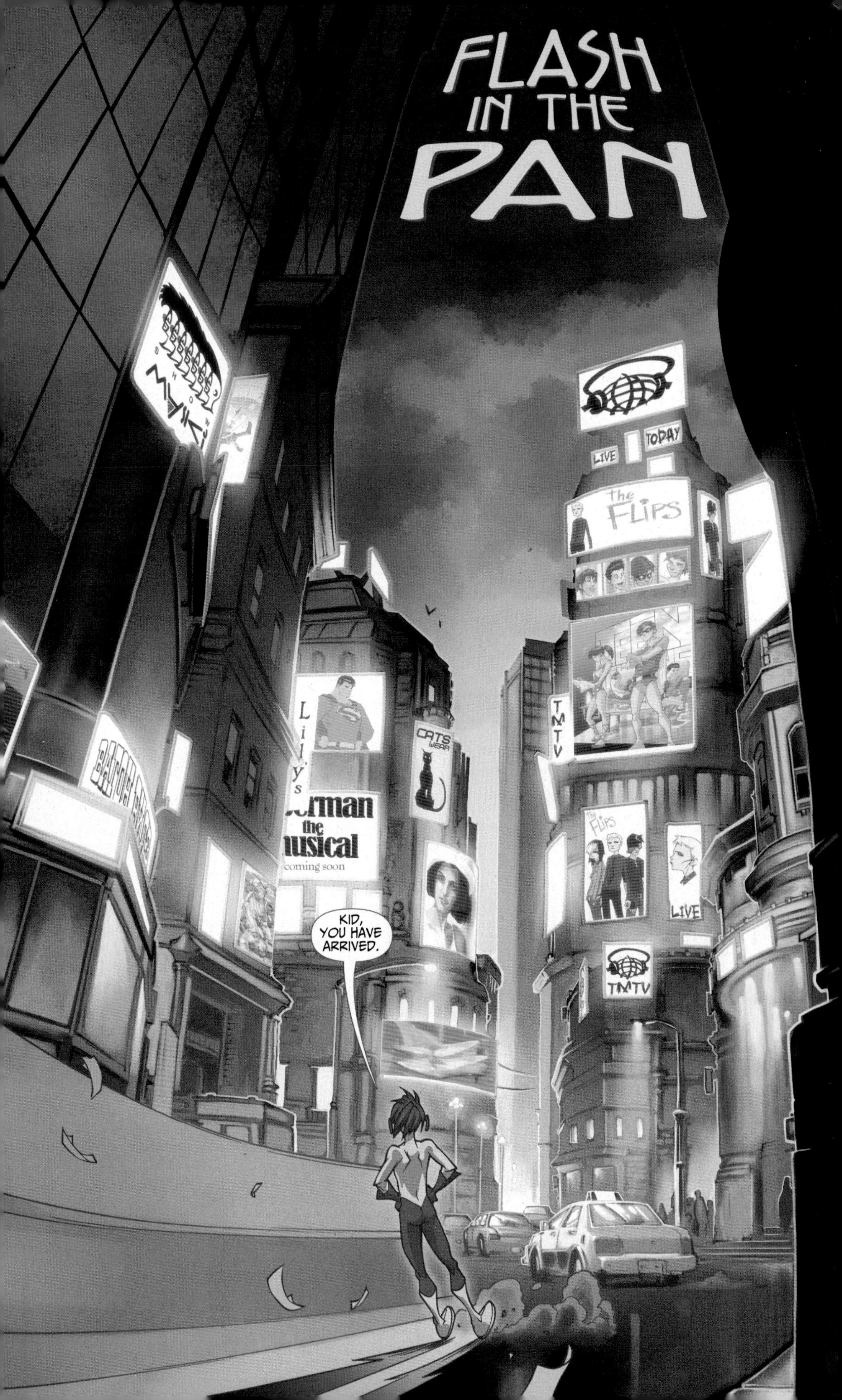
FLASH IN THE PAN
LIVE
TODAY
the FLIPS
TMTV
CATS WEAR
coming soon
the FLIPS
LIVE
TMTV
KID, YOU HAVE ARRIVED.

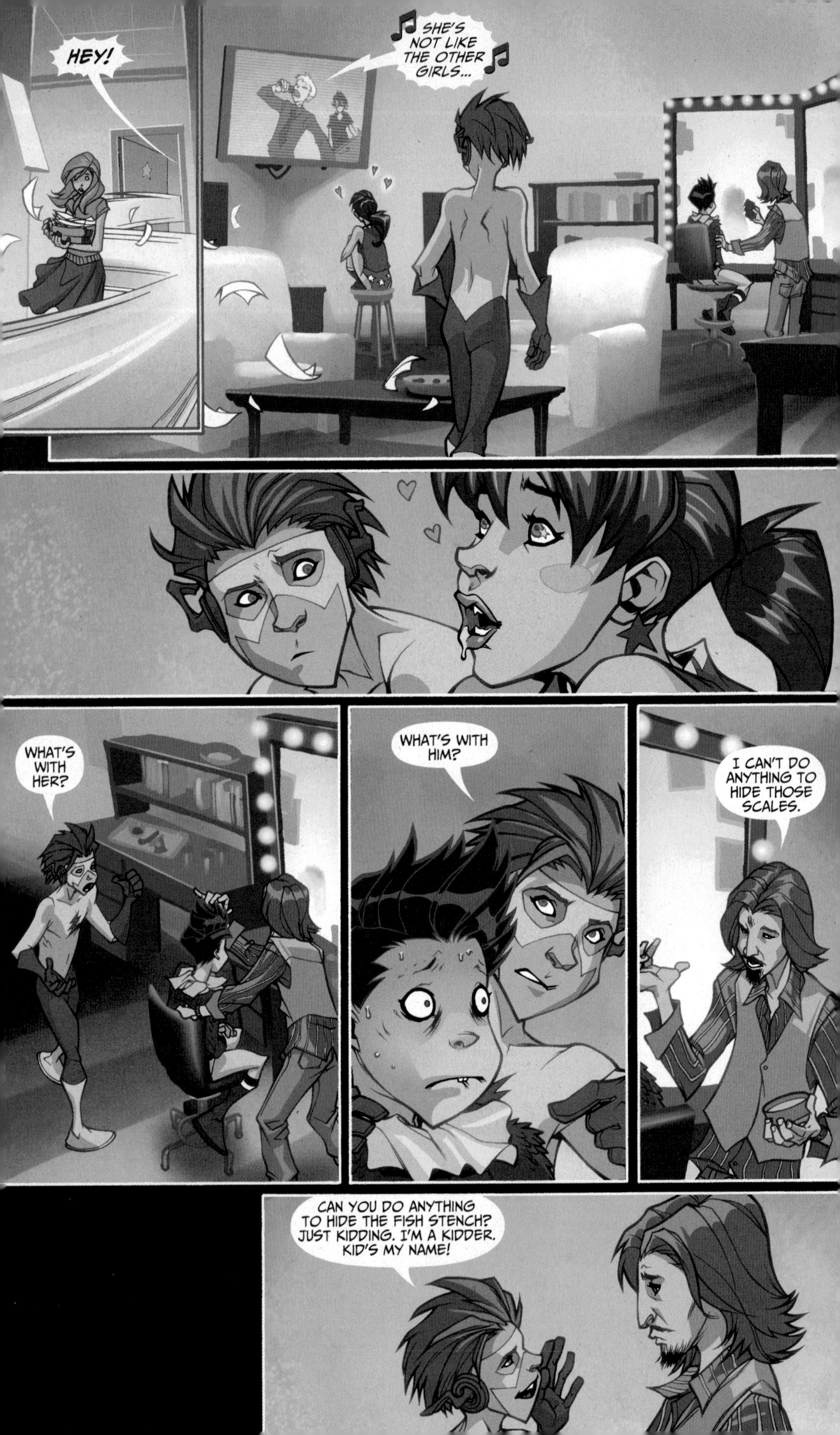
HEY!
SHE'S NOT LIKE THE OTHER GIRLS...
WHAT'S WITH HER?
WHAT'S WITH HIM?
I CAN'T DO ANYTHING TO HIDE THOSE SCALES.
CAN YOU DO ANYTHING TO HIDE THE FISH STENCH? JUST KIDDING. I'M A KIDDER. KID'S MY NAME!

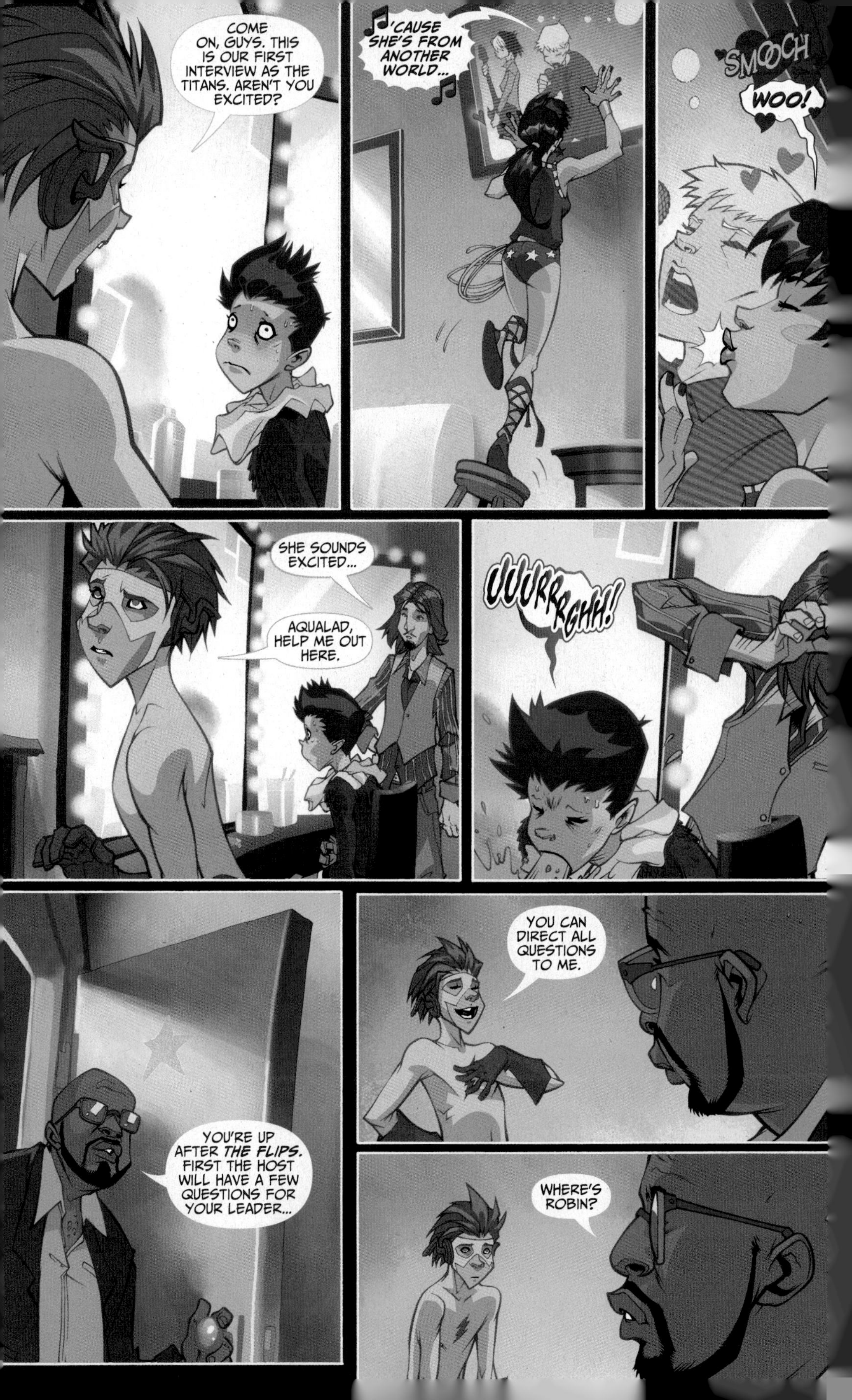
COME ON, GUYS. THIS IS OUR FIRST INTERVIEW AS THE TITANS. AREN'T YOU EXCITED?
'CAUSE SHE'S FROM ANOTHER WORLD...
SMOOCH
WOO!
SHE SOUNDS EXCITED...
AQUALAD, HELP ME OUT HERE.
UUURRRGHH!
YOU'RE UP AFTER THE FLIPS. FIRST THE HOST WILL HAVE A FEW QUESTIONS FOR YOUR LEADER...
YOU CAN DIRECT ALL QUESTIONS TO ME.
WHERE'S ROBIN?

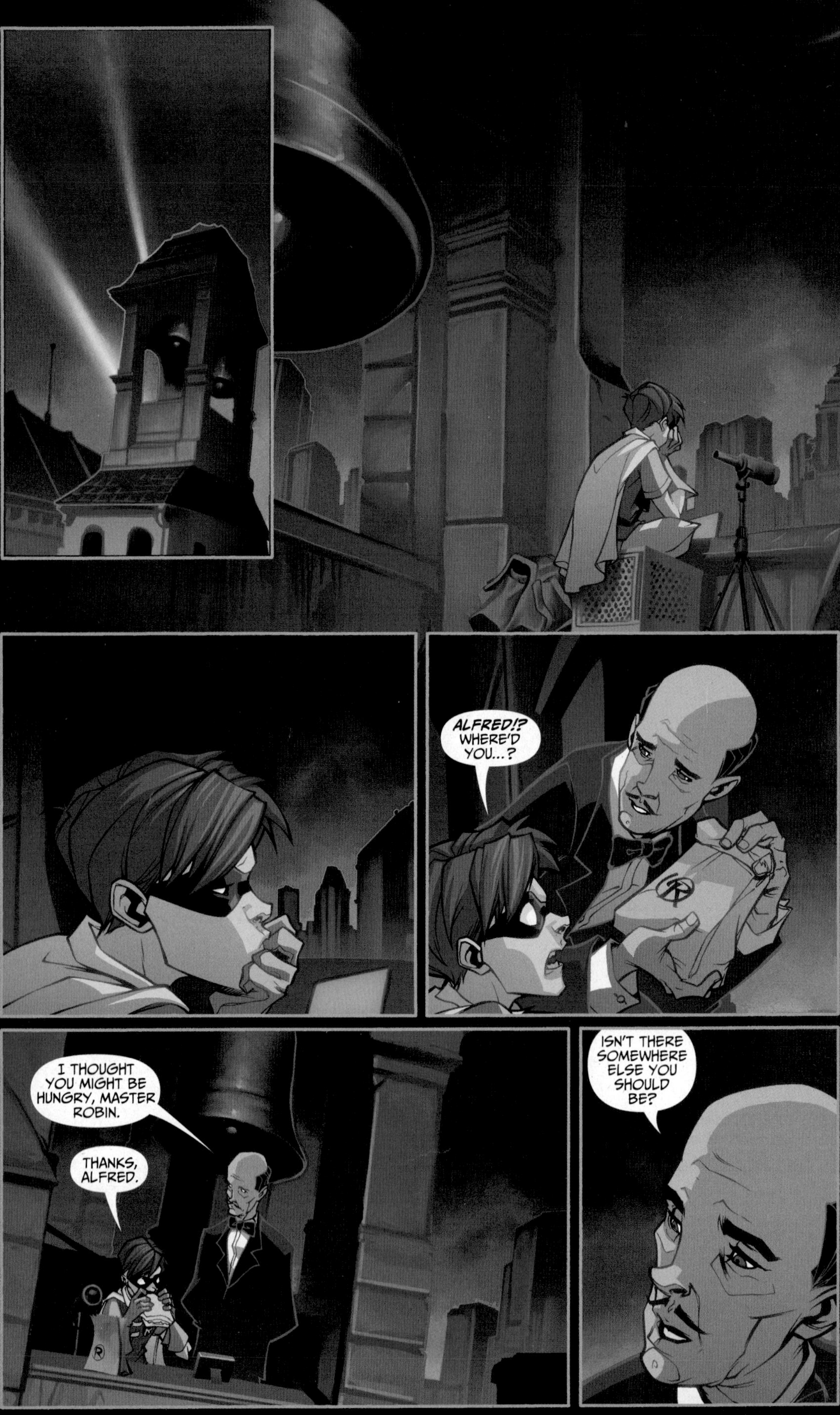
ALFRED!? WHERE'D YOU...?
I THOUGHT YOU MIGHT BE HUNGRY, MASTER ROBIN.
THANKS, ALFRED.
ISN'T THERE SOMEWHERE ELSE YOU SHOULD BE?

BATMAN TOLD ME TO STAY HERE.

INDEED.

THEN I AM CERTAIN YOU KNOW WHERE YOU BELONG.

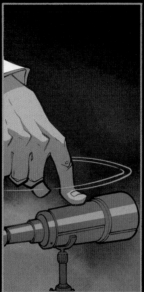

the FLIPS

LIVE   TODAY

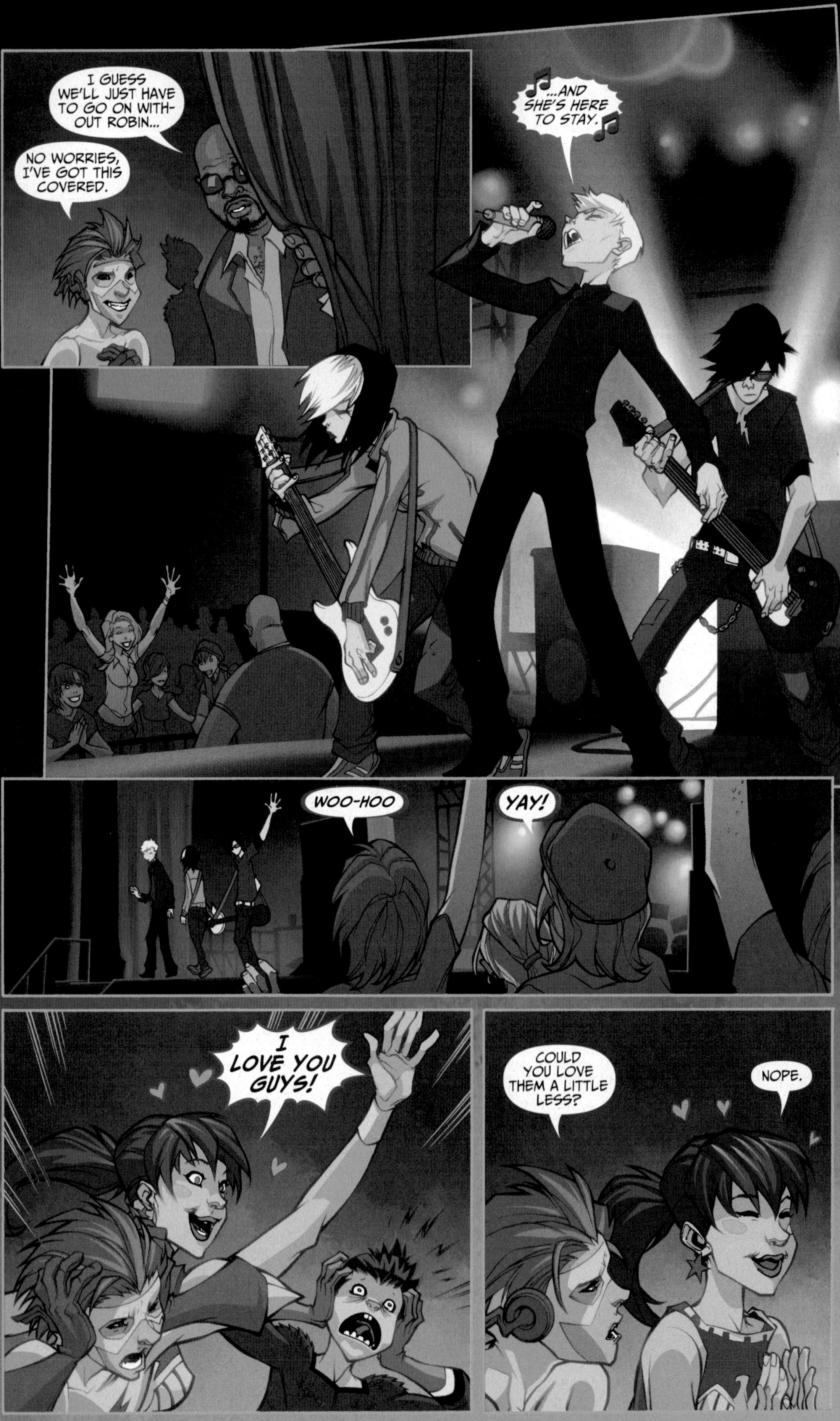
I GUESS WE'LL JUST HAVE TO GO ON WITH-OUT ROBIN...
NO WORRIES, I'VE GOT THIS COVERED.
...AND SHE'S HERE TO STAY.
WOO-HOO
YAY!
I LOVE YOU GUYS!
COULD YOU LOVE THEM A LITTLE LESS?
NOPE.

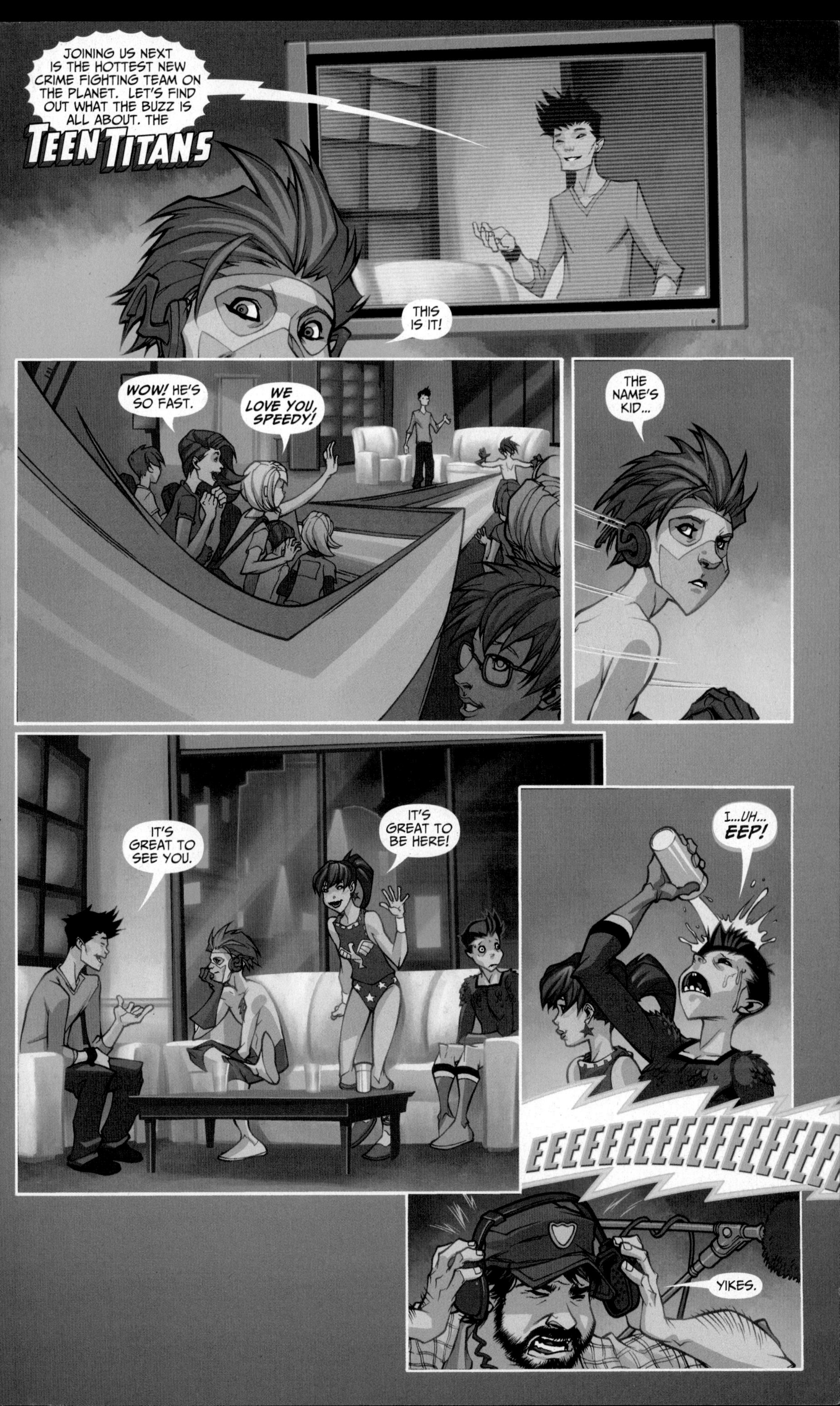

JOINING US NEXT IS THE HOTTEST NEW CRIME FIGHTING TEAM ON THE PLANET. LET'S FIND OUT WHAT THE BUZZ IS ALL ABOUT. THE
TEEN TITANS
THIS IS IT!
WOW! HE'S SO FAST.
WE LOVE YOU, SPEEDY!
THE NAME'S KID...
IT'S GREAT TO SEE YOU.
IT'S GREAT TO BE HERE!
I...UH... EEP!
EEEEEEEEEEEEEEEEEE
YIKES.

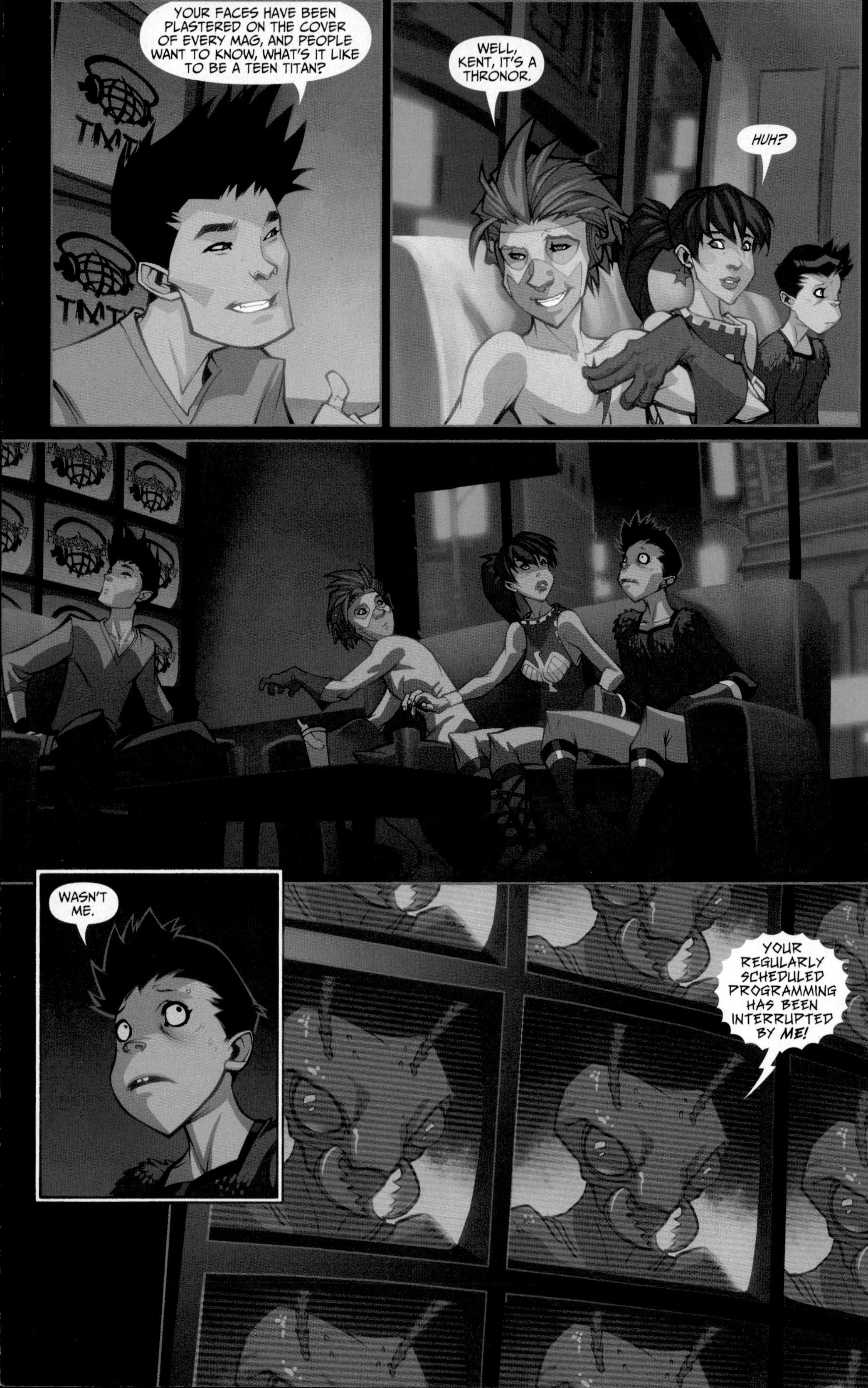
YOUR FACES HAVE BEEN PLASTERED ON THE COVER OF EVERY MAG, AND PEOPLE WANT TO KNOW, WHAT'S IT LIKE TO BE A TEEN TITAN?
WELL, KENT, IT'S A THRONOR.
HUH?
WASN'T ME.
YOUR REGULARLY SCHEDULED PROGRAMMING HAS BEEN INTERRUPTED BY ME!

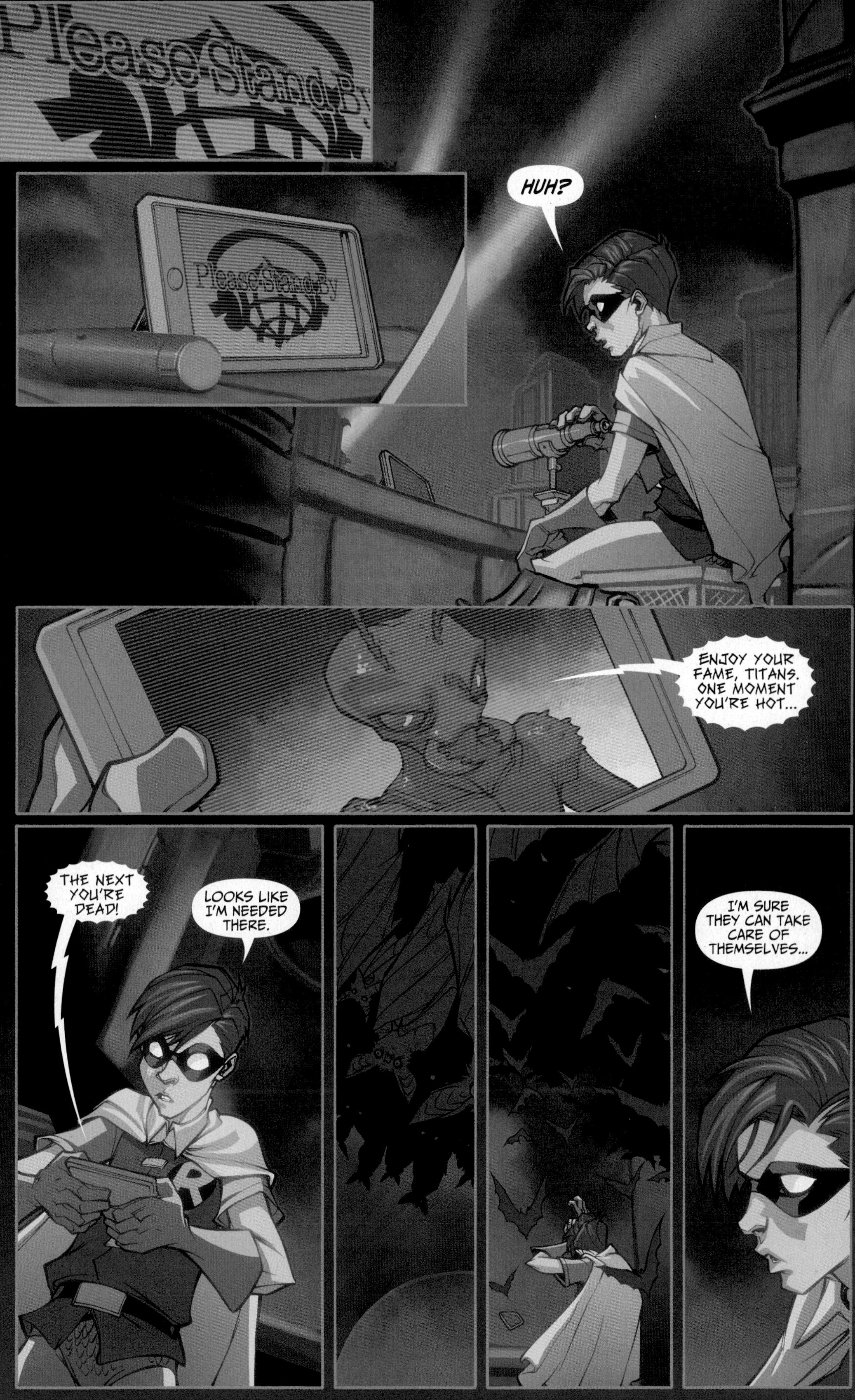
Please Stand By
Please Stand By
HUH?
ENJOY YOUR FAME, TITANS. ONE MOMENT YOU'RE HOT...
THE NEXT YOU'RE DEAD!
LOOKS LIKE I'M NEEDED THERE.
I'M SURE THEY CAN TAKE CARE OF THEMSELVES...

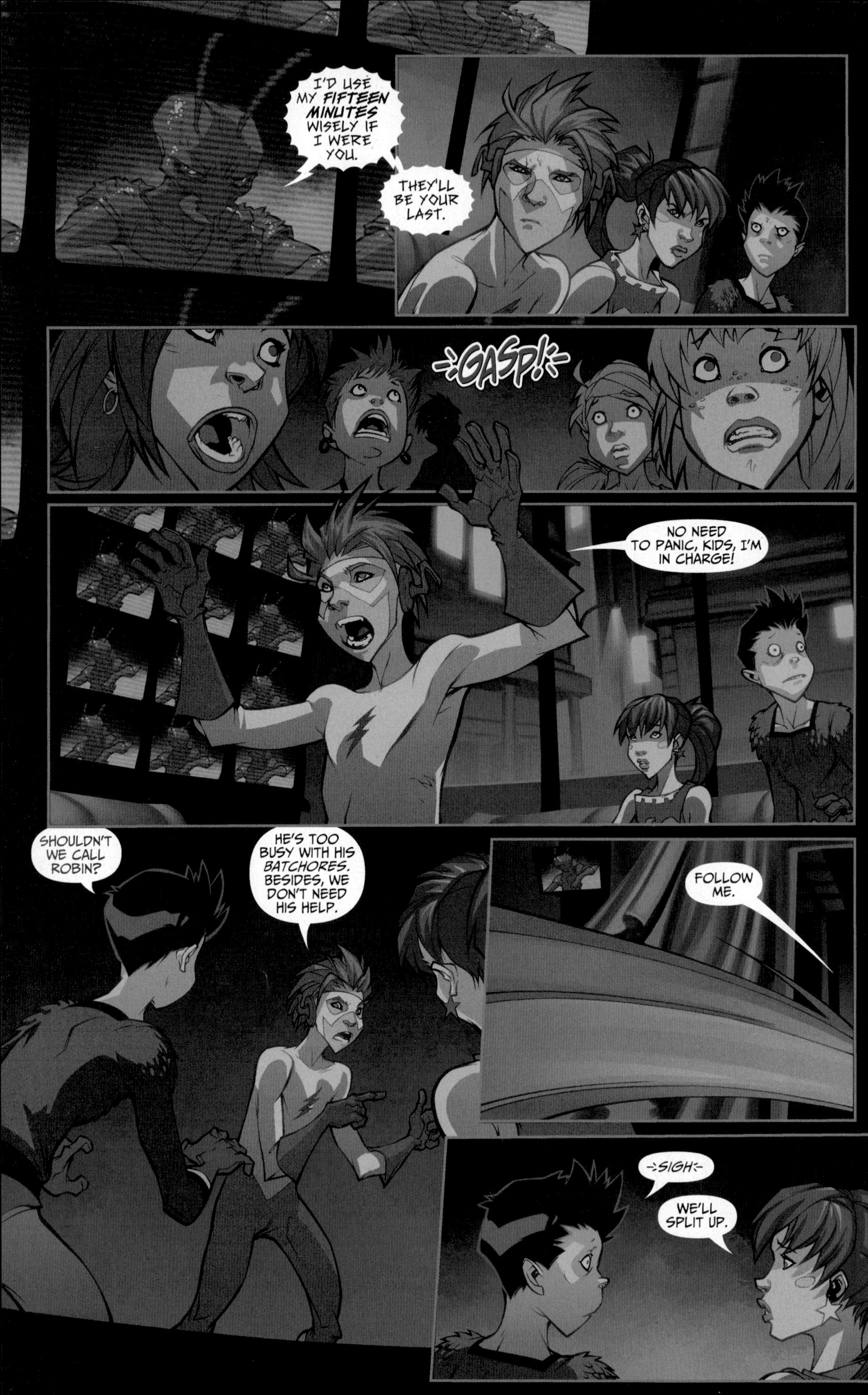
I'D USE MY FIFTEEN MINUTES WISELY IF I WERE YOU.
THEY'LL BE YOUR LAST.
-GASP!-
NO NEED TO PANIC, KIDS, I'M IN CHARGE!
SHOULDN'T WE CALL ROBIN?
HE'S TOO BUSY WITH HIS BATCHORES. BESIDES, WE DON'T NEED HIS HELP.
FOLLOW ME.
-SIGH-
WE'LL SPLIT UP.

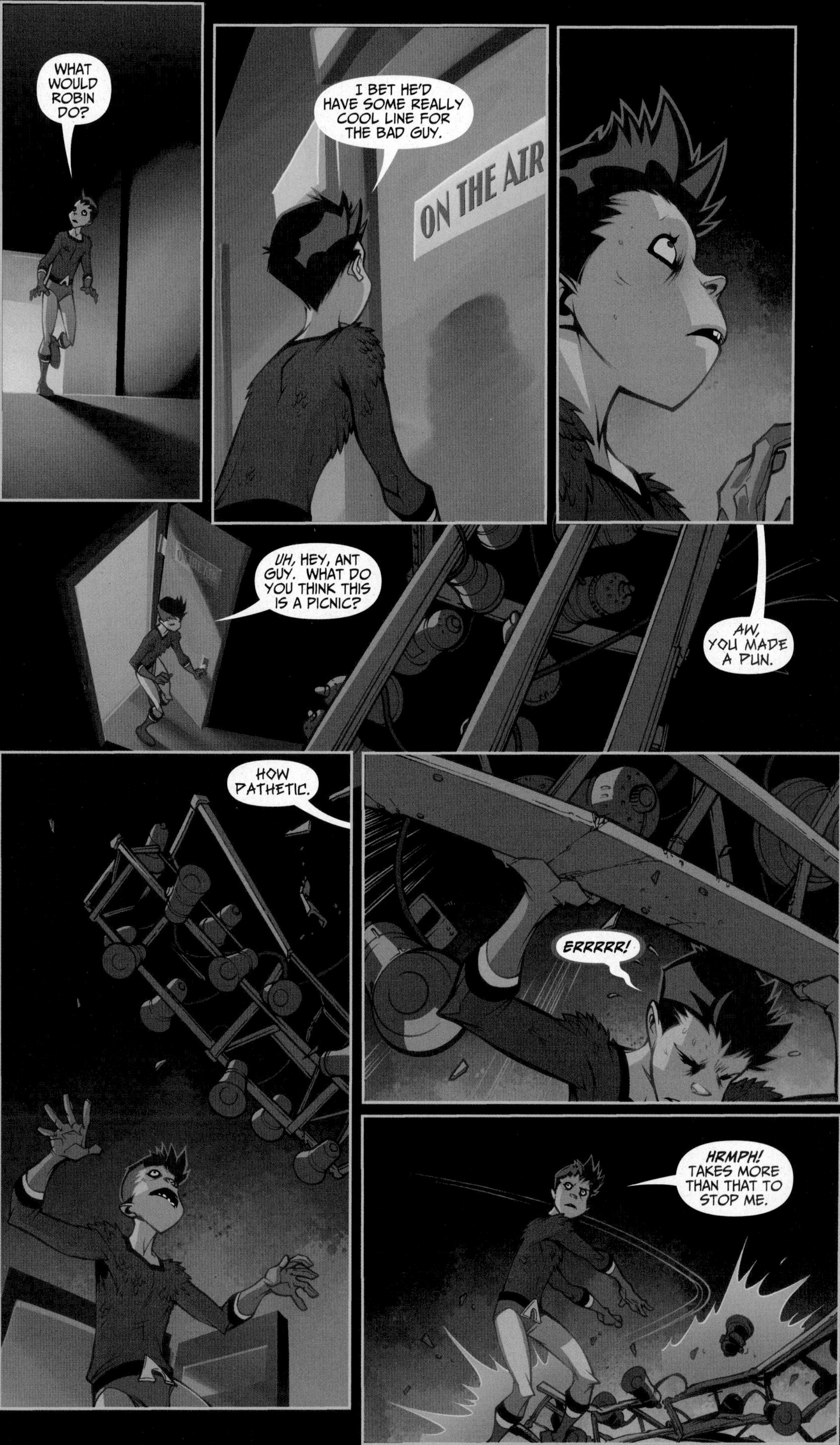

WHAT WOULD ROBIN DO?
I BET HE'D HAVE SOME REALLY COOL LINE FOR THE BAD GUY.
ON THE AIR
UH, HEY, ANT GUY. WHAT DO YOU THINK THIS IS A PICNIC?
AW, YOU MADE A PUN.
HOW PATHETIC.
ERRRRR!
HRMPH! TAKES MORE THAN THAT TO STOP ME.

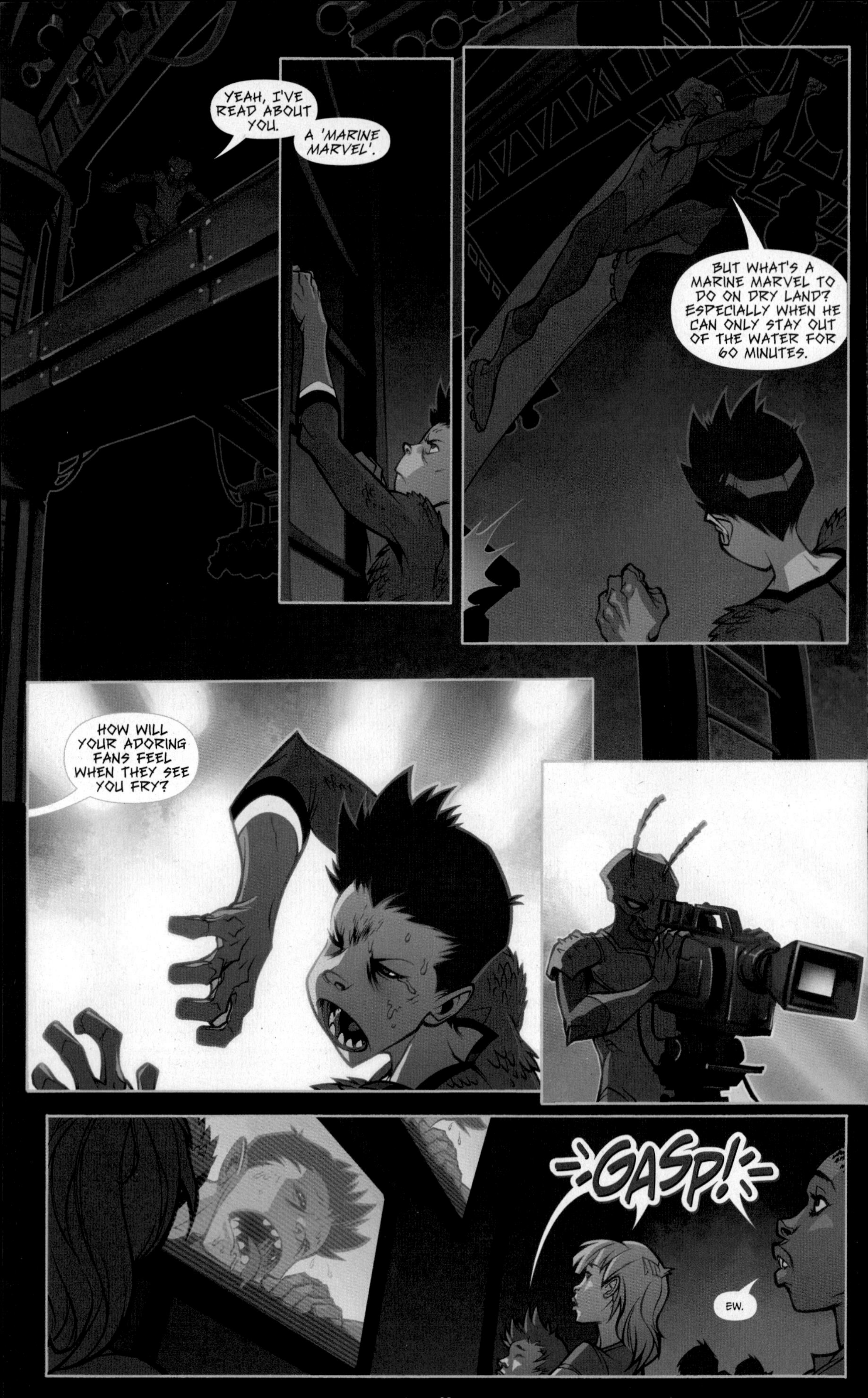
YEAH, I'VE READ ABOUT YOU.
A 'MARINE MARVEL'.
BUT WHAT'S A MARINE MARVEL TO DO ON DRY LAND? ESPECIALLY WHEN HE CAN ONLY STAY OUT OF THE WATER FOR 60 MINUTES.
HOW WILL YOUR ADORING FANS FEEL WHEN THEY SEE YOU FRY?
GASP!
EW.

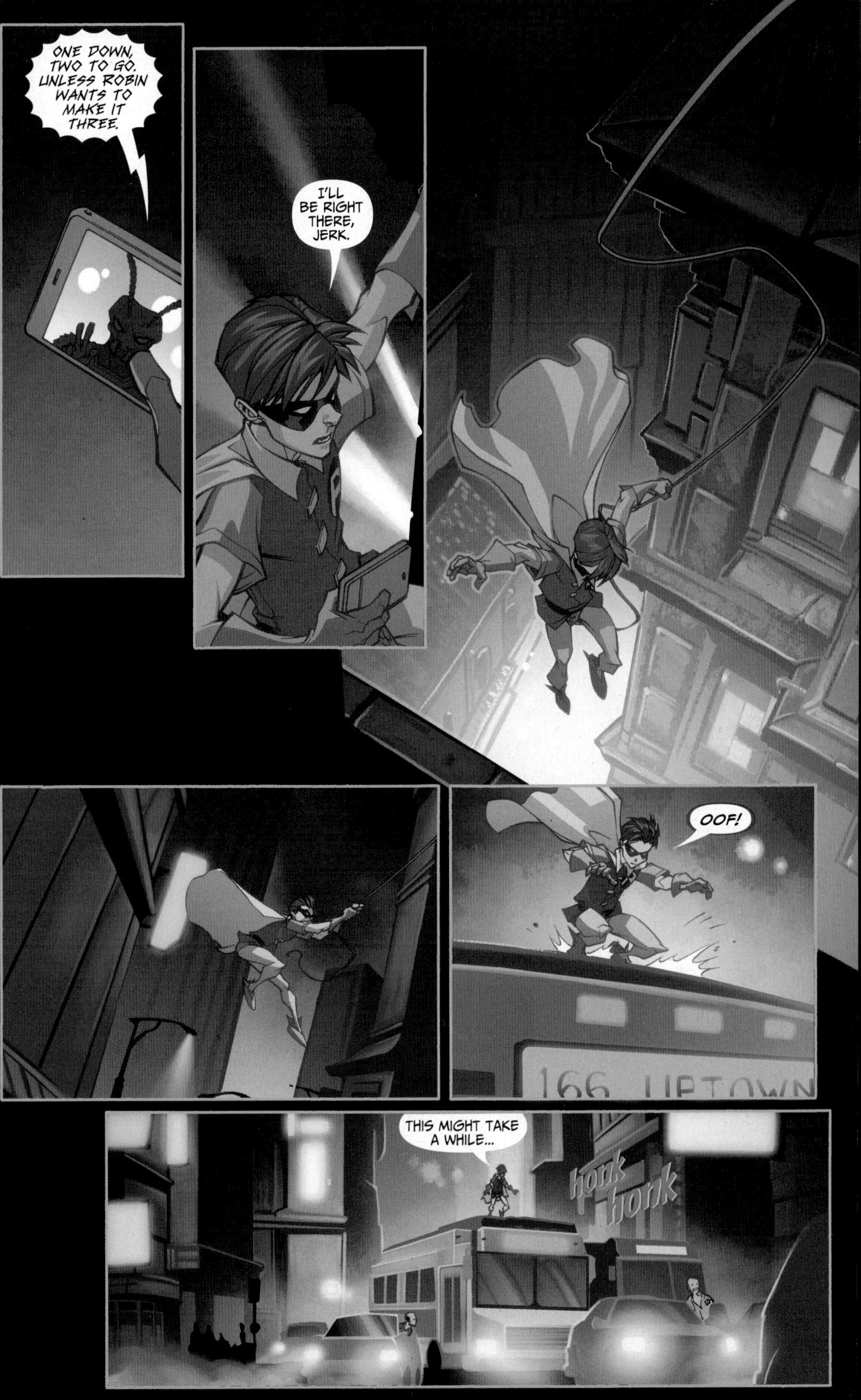
ONE DOWN, TWO TO GO. UNLESS ROBIN WANTS TO MAKE IT THREE.
I'LL BE RIGHT THERE, JERK.
OOF!
166 UPTOWN
THIS MIGHT TAKE A WHILE...
honk
honk

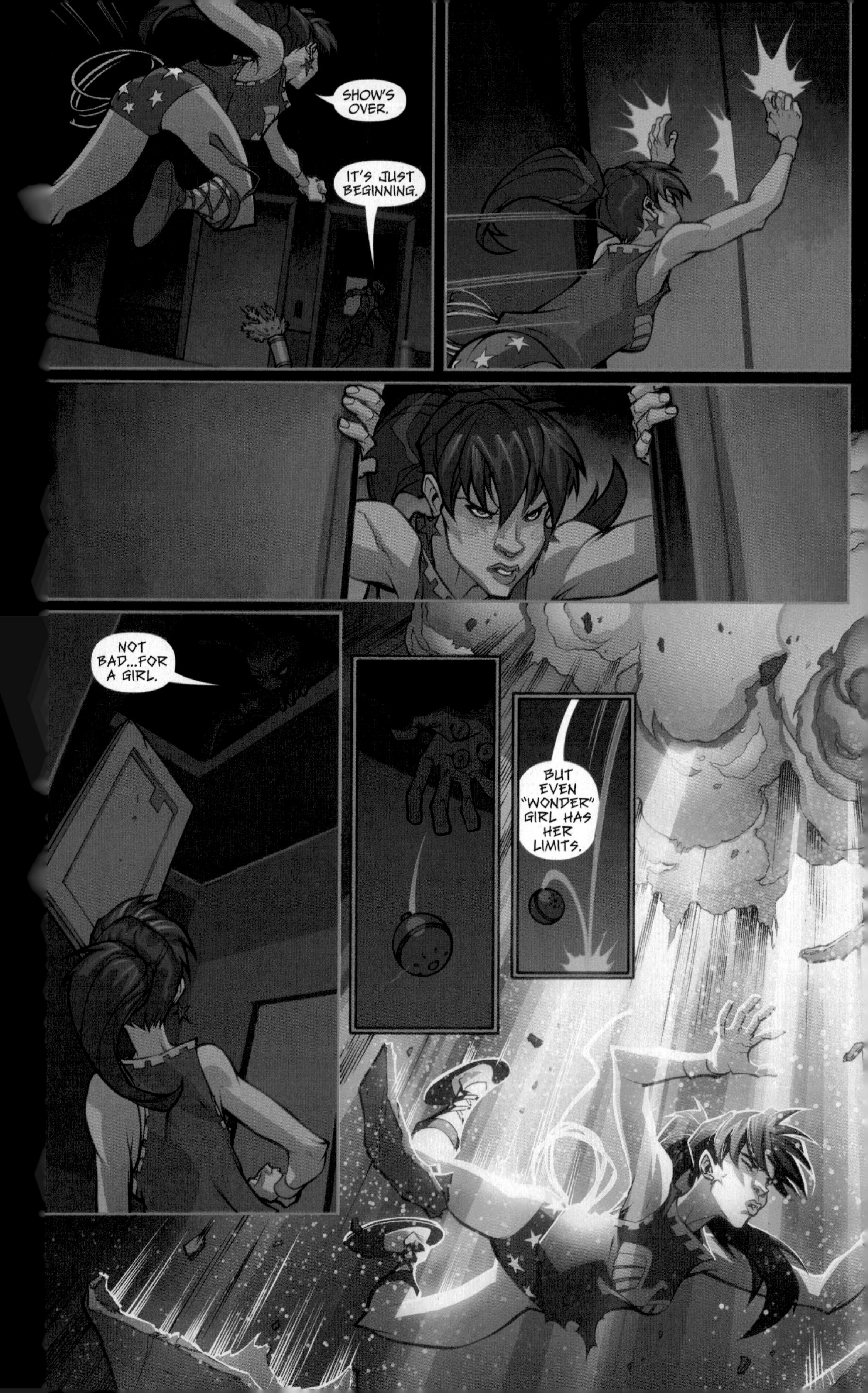
SHOW'S OVER.
IT'S JUST BEGINNING.
NOT BAD...FOR A GIRL.
BUT EVEN "WONDER" GIRL HAS HER LIMITS.

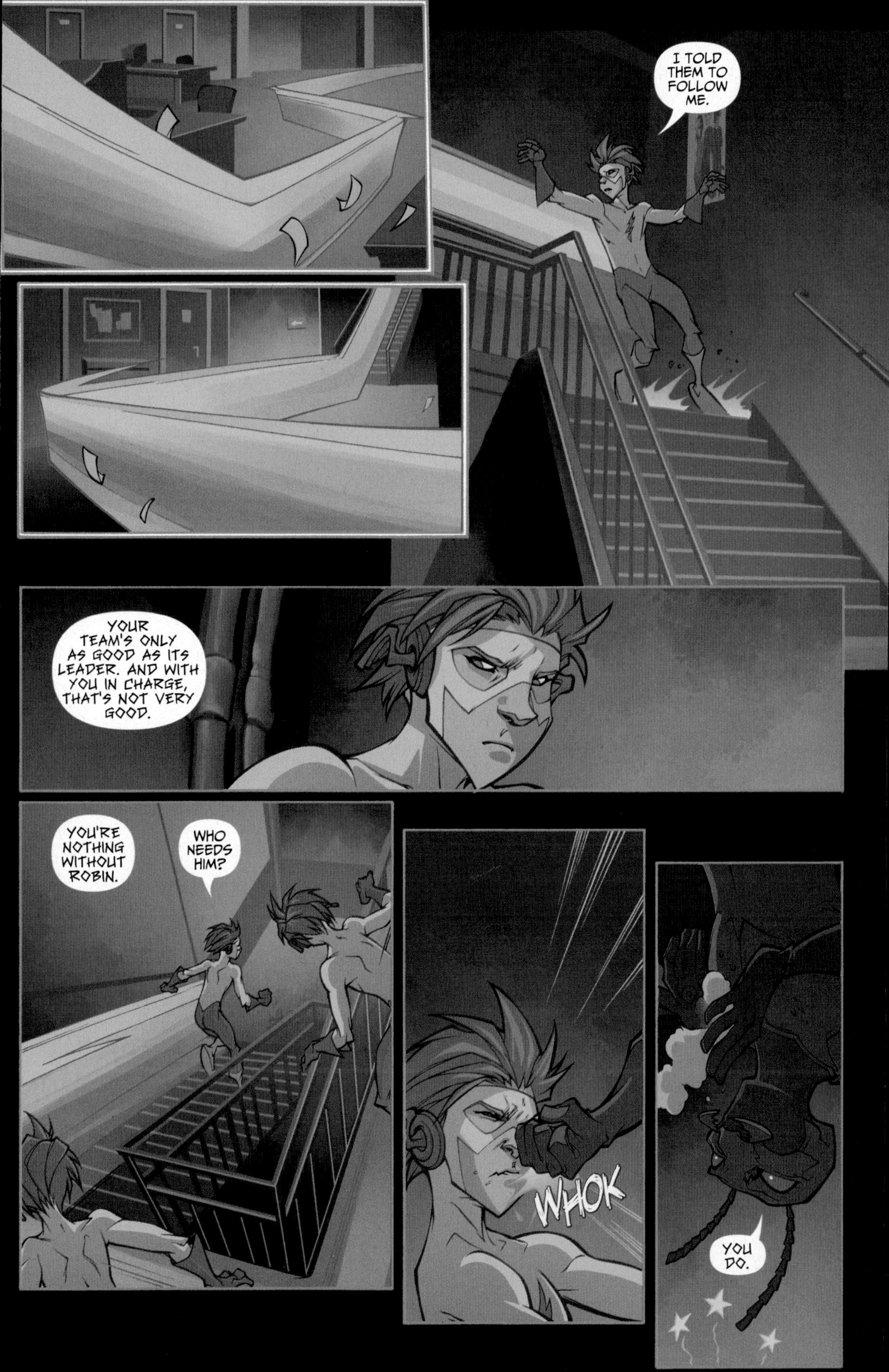
I TOLD THEM TO FOLLOW ME.
YOUR TEAM'S ONLY AS GOOD AS ITS LEADER. AND WITH YOU IN CHARGE, THAT'S NOT VERY GOOD.
YOU'RE NOTHING WITHOUT ROBIN.
WHO NEEDS HIM?
WHOK
YOU DO.

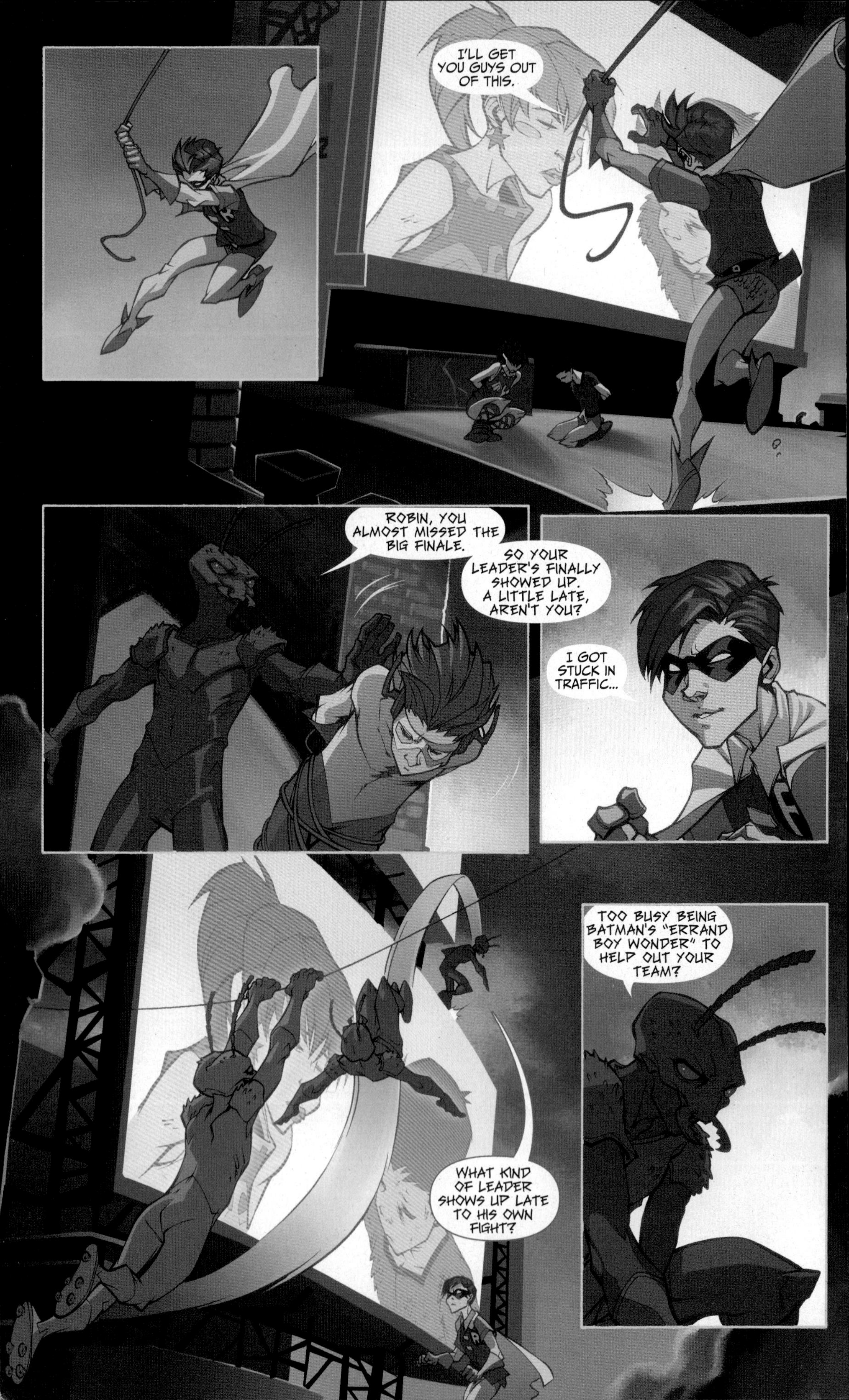
I'LL GET YOU GUYS OUT OF THIS.
ROBIN, YOU ALMOST MISSED THE BIG FINALE.
SO YOUR LEADER'S FINALLY SHOWED UP. A LITTLE LATE, AREN'T YOU?
I GOT STUCK IN TRAFFIC...
TOO BUSY BEING BATMAN'S "ERRAND BOY WONDER" TO HELP OUT YOUR TEAM?
WHAT KIND OF LEADER SHOWS UP LATE TO HIS OWN FIGHT?

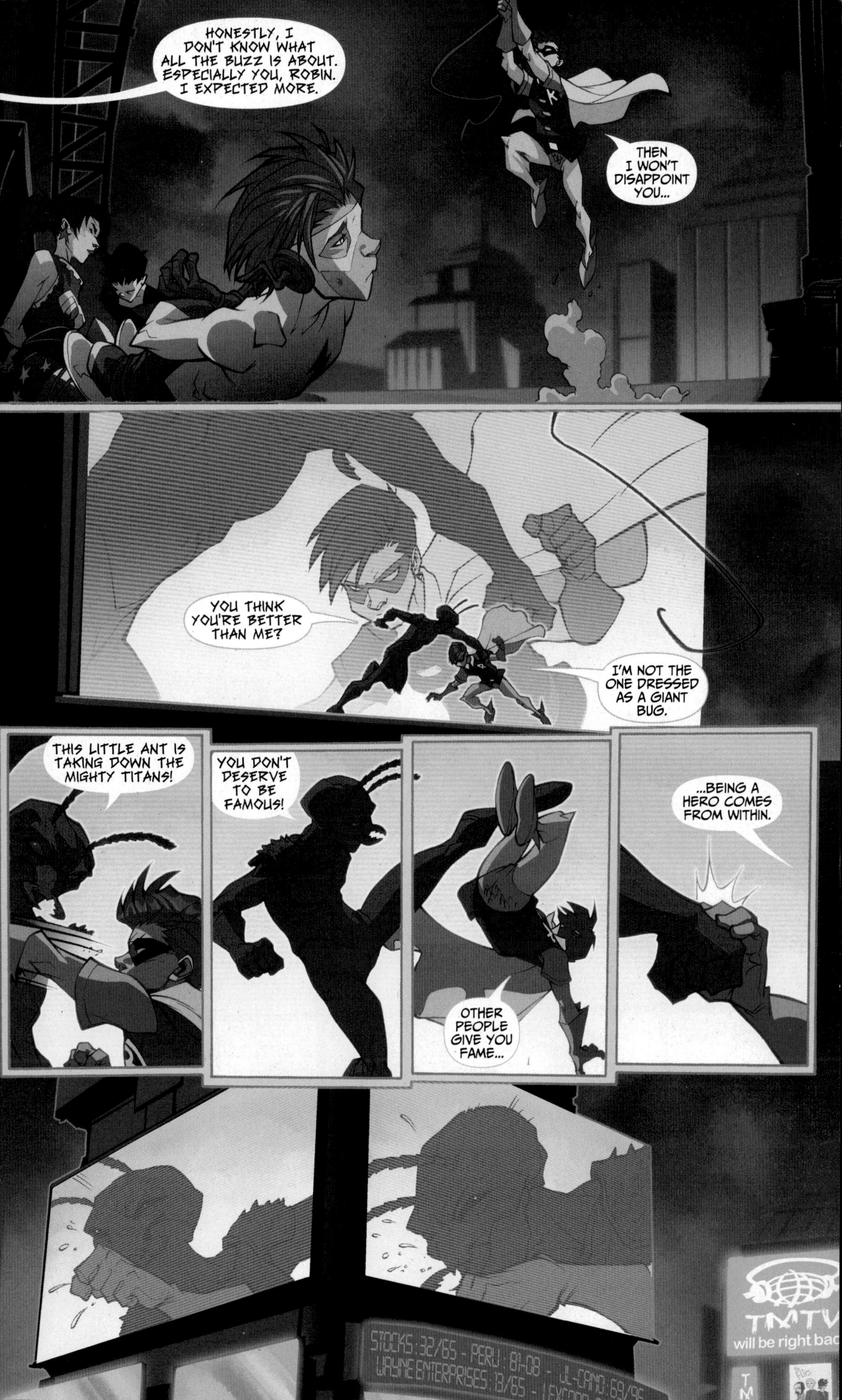
HONESTLY, I DON'T KNOW WHAT ALL THE BUZZ IS ABOUT. ESPECIALLY YOU, ROBIN. I EXPECTED MORE.
THEN I WON'T DISAPPOINT YOU...
YOU THINK YOU'RE BETTER THAN ME?
I'M NOT THE ONE DRESSED AS A GIANT BUG.
THIS LITTLE ANT IS TAKING DOWN THE MIGHTY TITANS!
YOU DON'T DESERVE TO BE FAMOUS!
OTHER PEOPLE GIVE YOU FAME...
...BEING A HERO COMES FROM WITHIN.
STOCKS: 32/65 - PERU: 81-08 - JL-CAND: 69/95
WAYNE ENTERPRISES: 13/65
TMTV
will be right bac

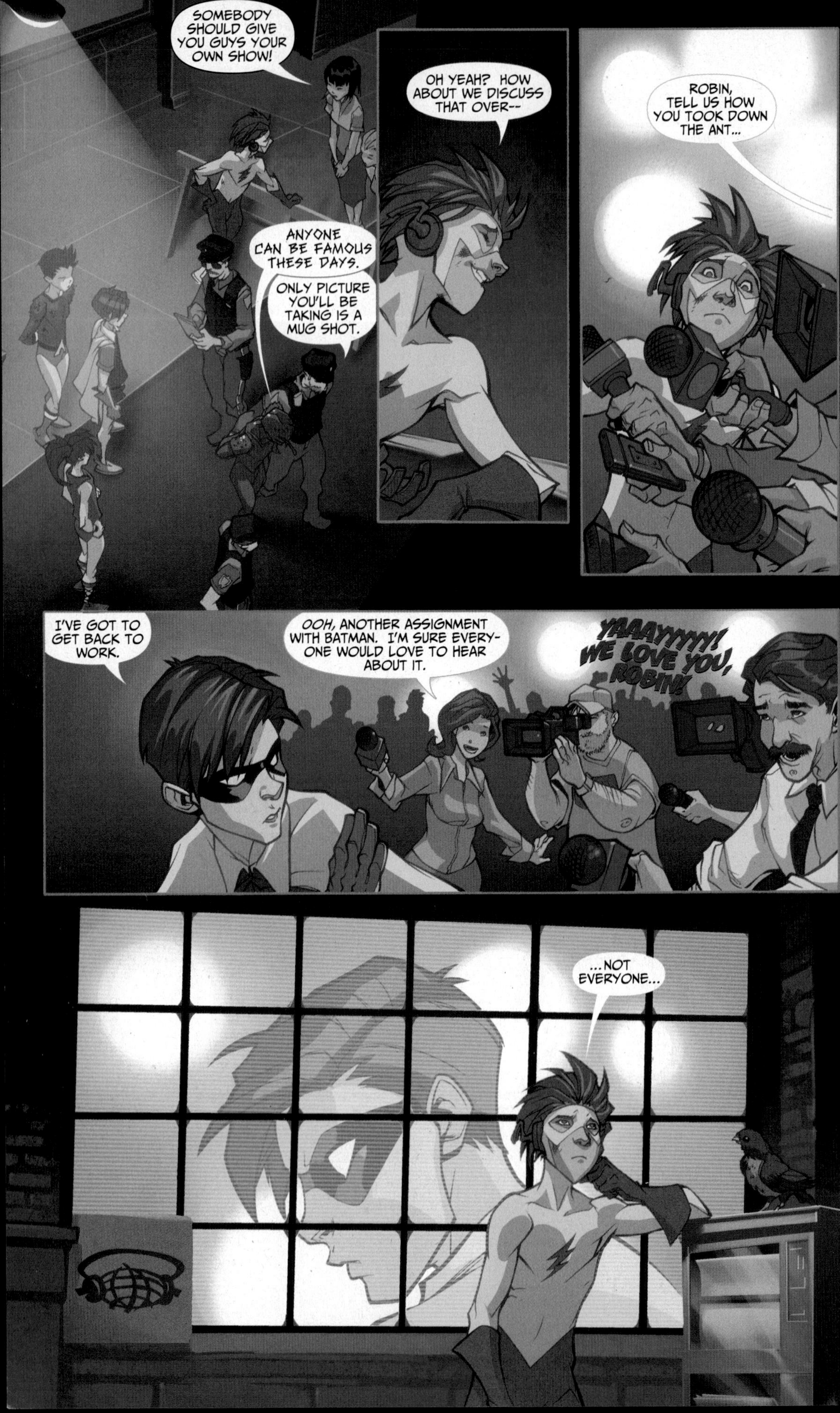
SOMEBODY SHOULD GIVE YOU GUYS YOUR OWN SHOW!
OH YEAH? HOW ABOUT WE DISCUSS THAT OVER--
ROBIN, TELL US HOW YOU TOOK DOWN THE ANT...
ANYONE CAN BE FAMOUS THESE DAYS.
ONLY PICTURE YOU'LL BE TAKING IS A MUG SHOT.
I'VE GOT TO GET BACK TO WORK.
OOH, ANOTHER ASSIGNMENT WITH BATMAN. I'M SURE EVERY-ONE WOULD LOVE TO HEAR ABOUT IT.
YAAAYYYYY! WE LOVE YOU, ROBIN!
...NOT EVERYONE...

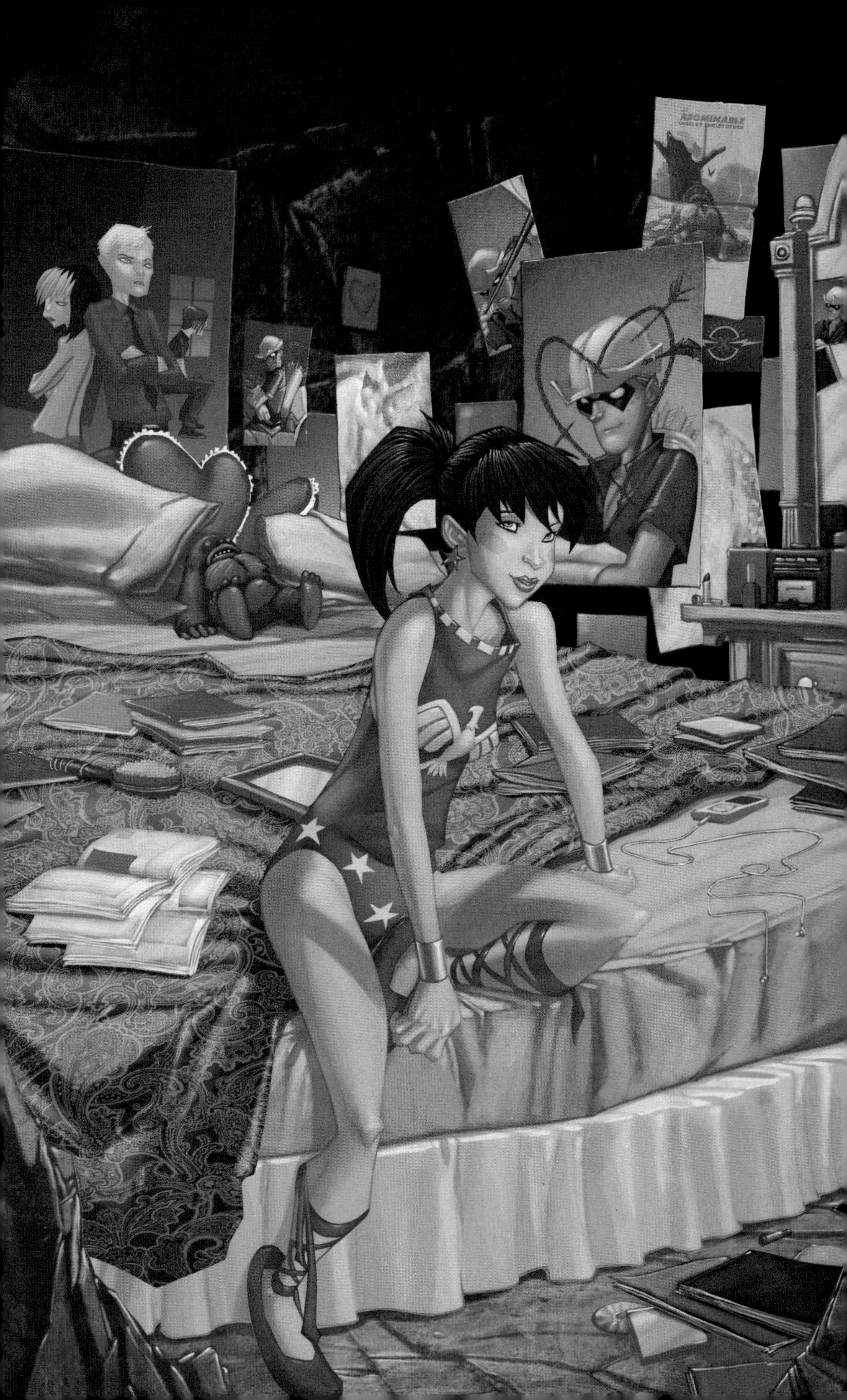
ABOMINABLE
CHARLES CHRISTOPHER

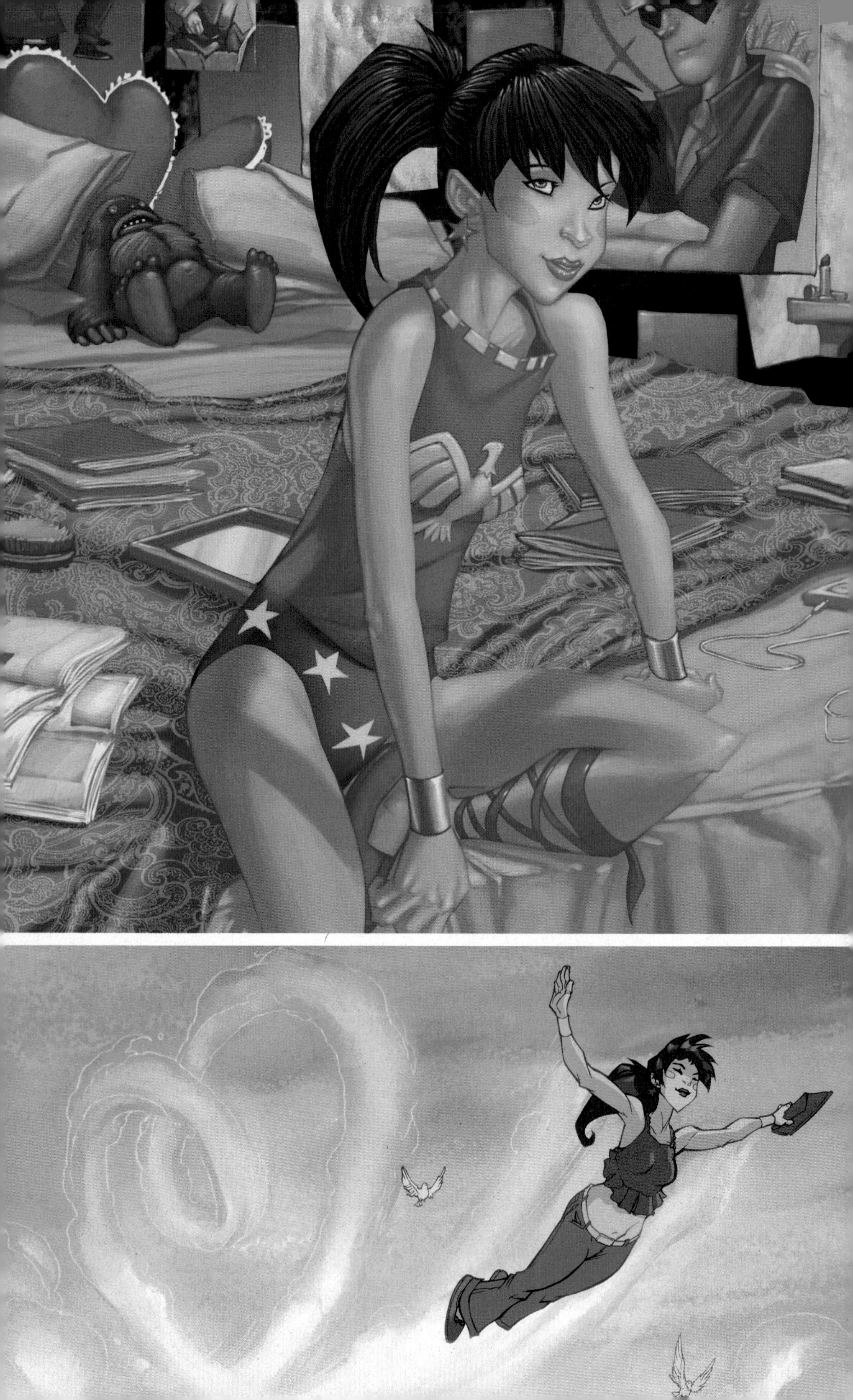

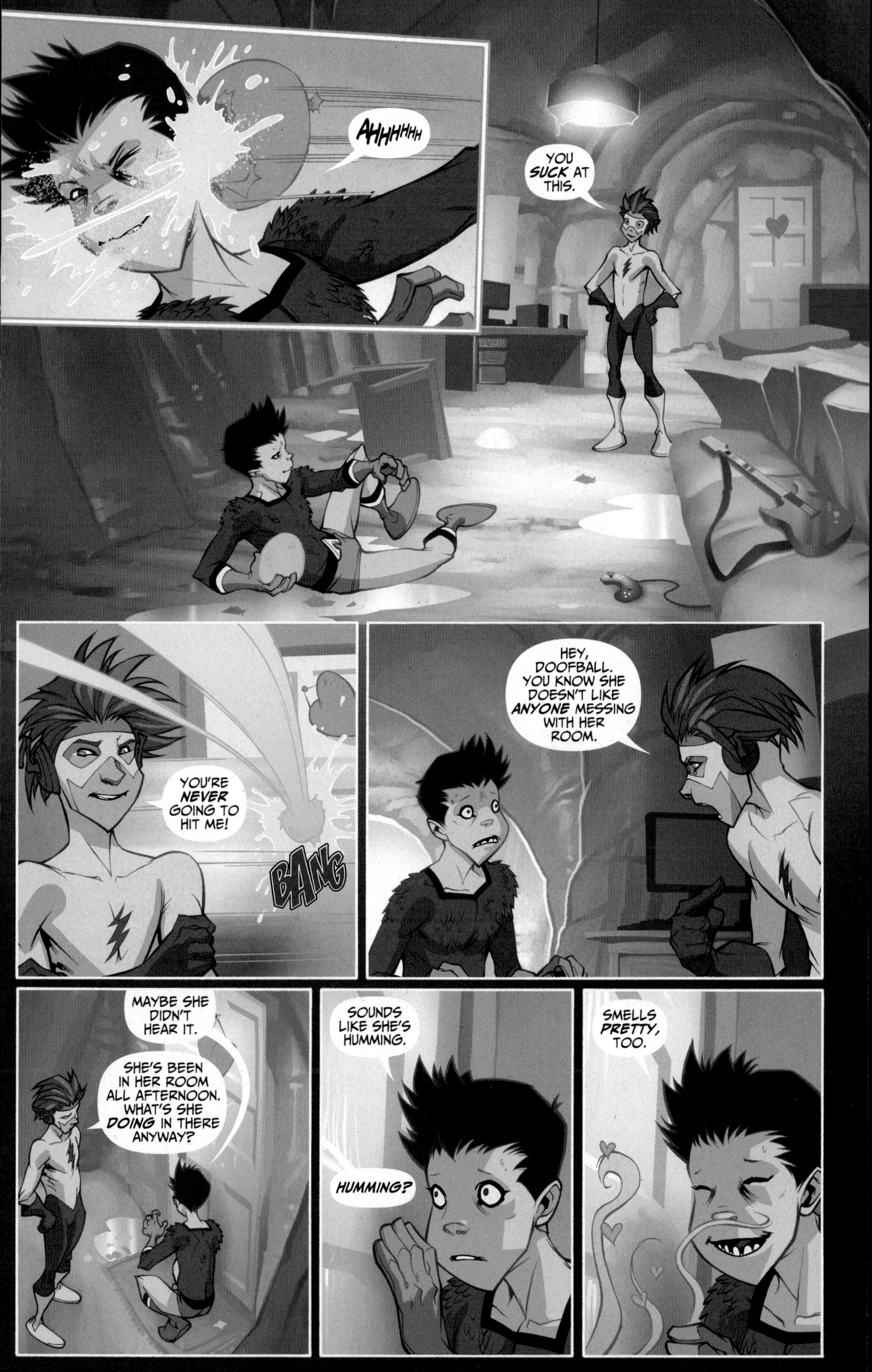
AHHHHHH
YOU SUCK AT THIS.
YOU'RE NEVER GOING TO HIT ME!
BANG
HEY, DOOFBALL. YOU KNOW SHE DOESN'T LIKE ANYONE MESSING WITH HER ROOM.
MAYBE SHE DIDN'T HEAR IT.
SHE'S BEEN IN HER ROOM ALL AFTERNOON. WHAT'S SHE DOING IN THERE ANYWAY?
SOUNDS LIKE SHE'S HUMMING.
HUMMING?
SMELLS PRETTY, TOO.

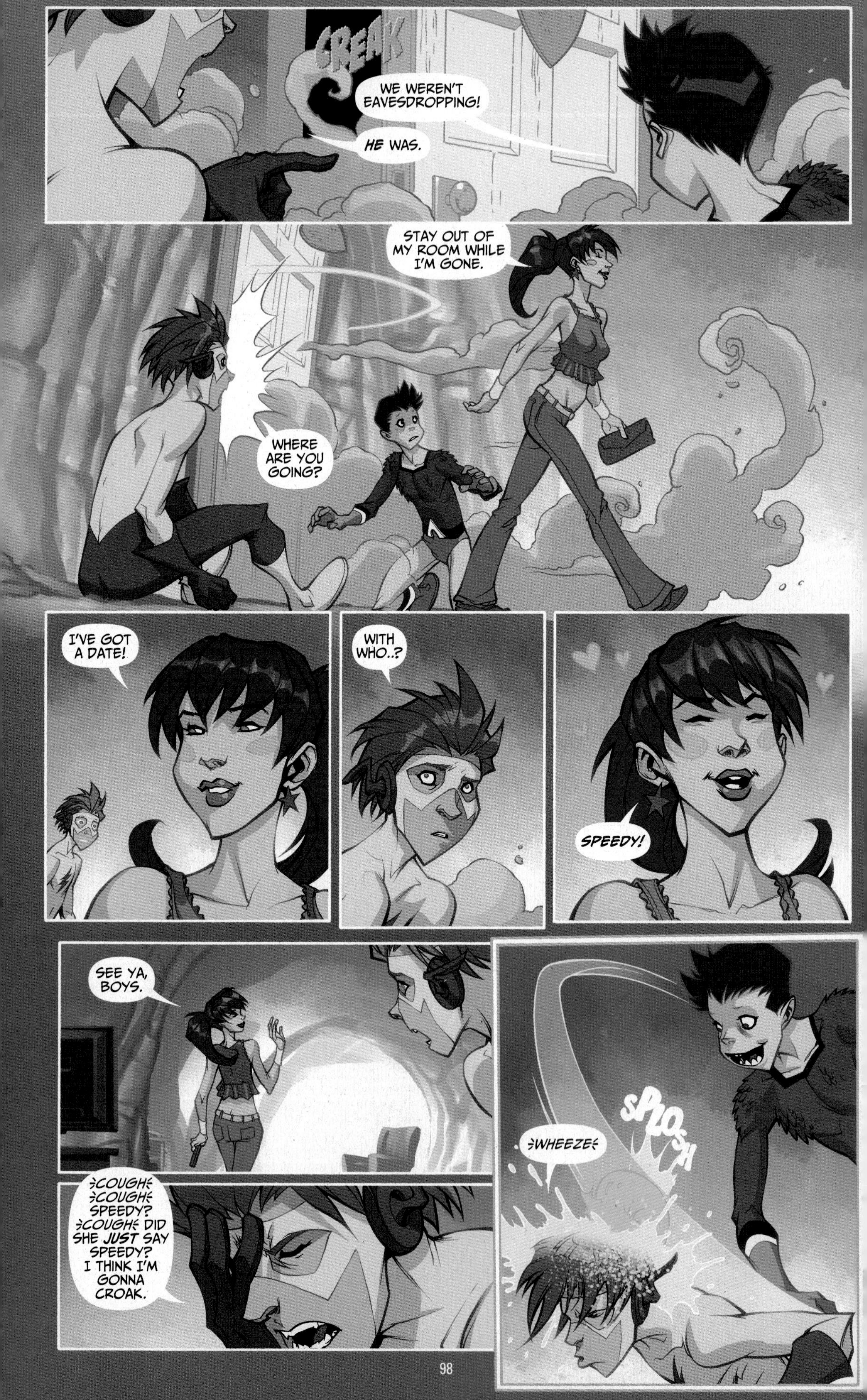

CREAK
WE WEREN'T EAVESDROPPING!
HE WAS.
STAY OUT OF MY ROOM WHILE I'M GONE.
WHERE ARE YOU GOING?
I'VE GOT A DATE!
WITH WHO..?
SPEEDY!
SEE YA, BOYS.
COUGH *COUGH* SPEEDY? *COUGH* DID SHE JUST SAY SPEEDY? I THINK I'M GONNA CROAK.
WHEEZE
SPLOSH

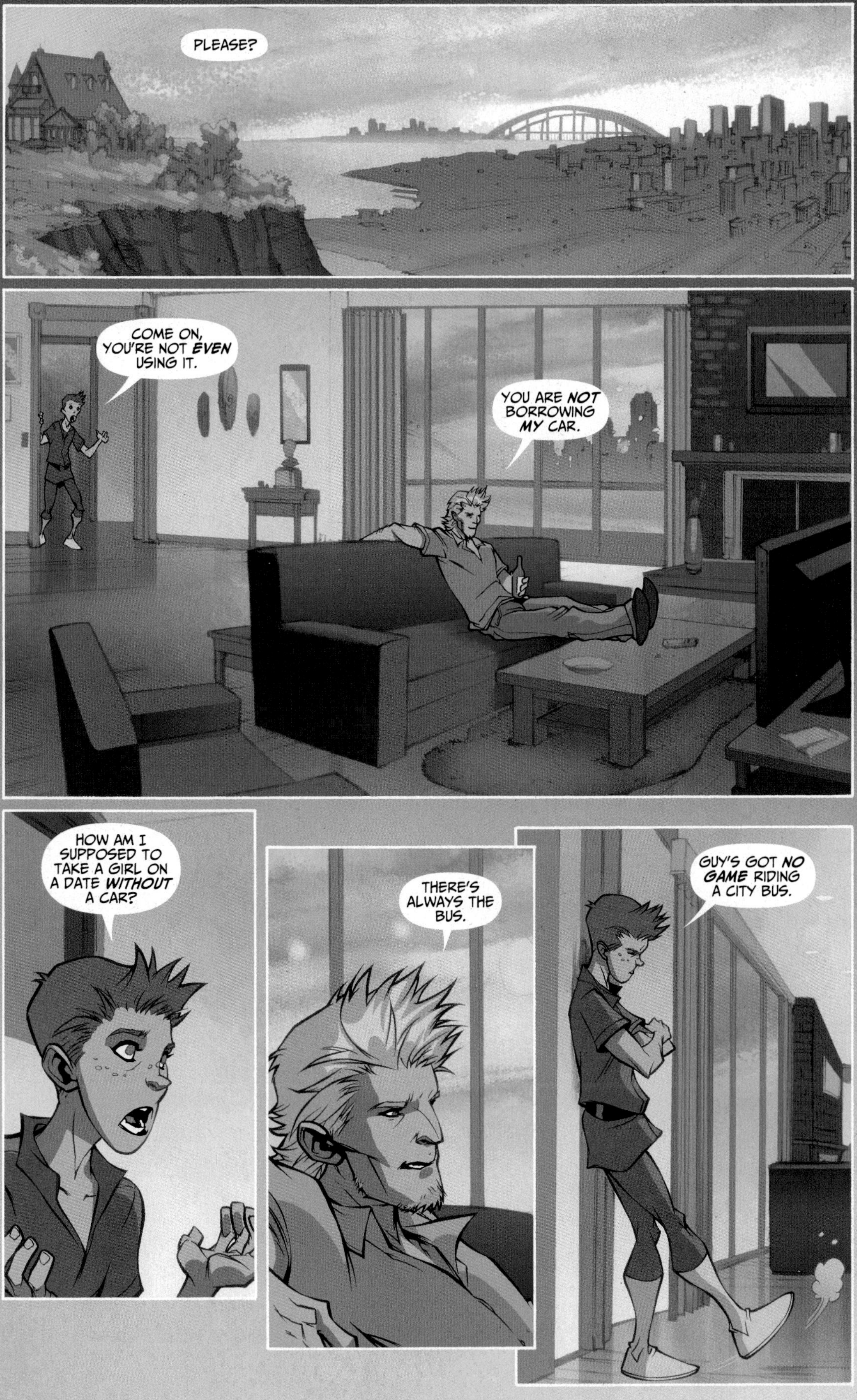
PLEASE?
COME ON, YOU'RE NOT EVEN USING IT.
YOU ARE NOT BORROWING MY CAR.
HOW AM I SUPPOSED TO TAKE A GIRL ON A DATE WITHOUT A CAR?
THERE'S ALWAYS THE BUS.
GUY'S GOT NO GAME RIDING A CITY BUS.

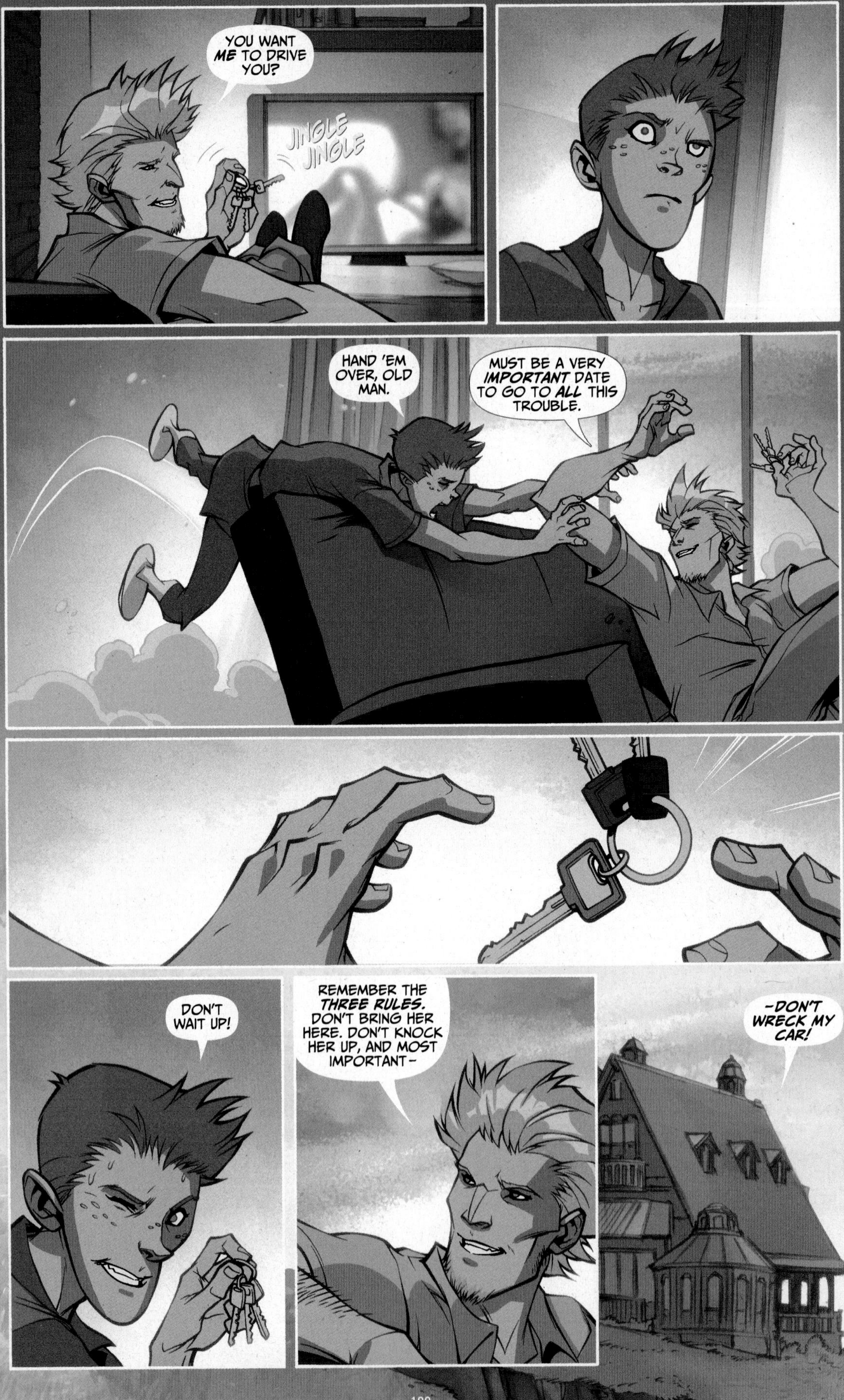
YOU WANT ME TO DRIVE YOU?
JINGLE JINGLE
HAND 'EM OVER, OLD MAN.
MUST BE A VERY IMPORTANT DATE TO GO TO ALL THIS TROUBLE.
DON'T WAIT UP!
REMEMBER THE THREE RULES. DON'T BRING HER HERE. DON'T KNOCK HER UP, AND MOST IMPORTANT–
–DON'T WRECK MY CAR!

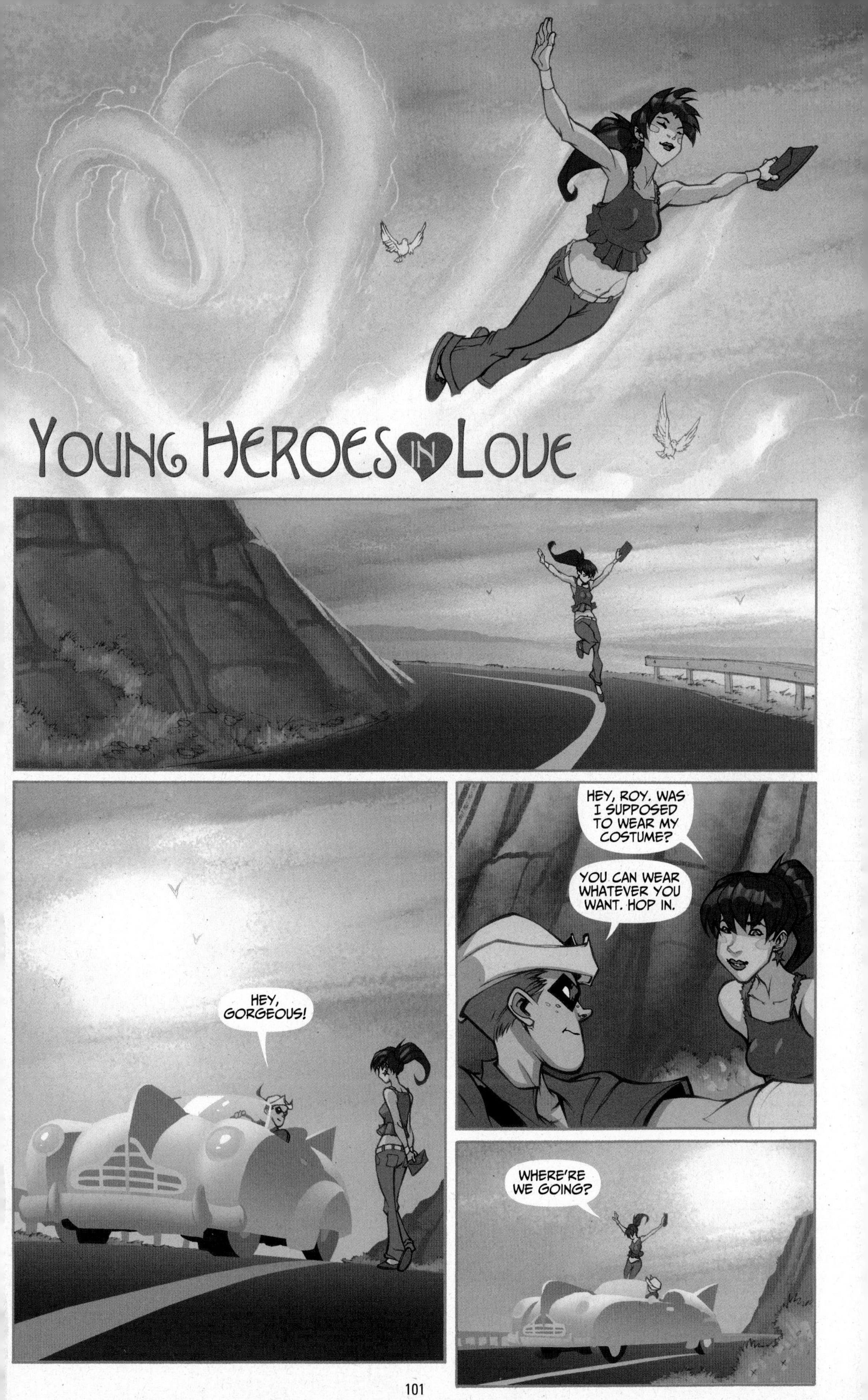
YOUNG HEROES IN LOVE
HEY, GORGEOUS!
HEY, ROY. WAS I SUPPOSED TO WEAR MY COSTUME?
YOU CAN WEAR WHATEVER YOU WANT. HOP IN.
WHERE'RE WE GOING?

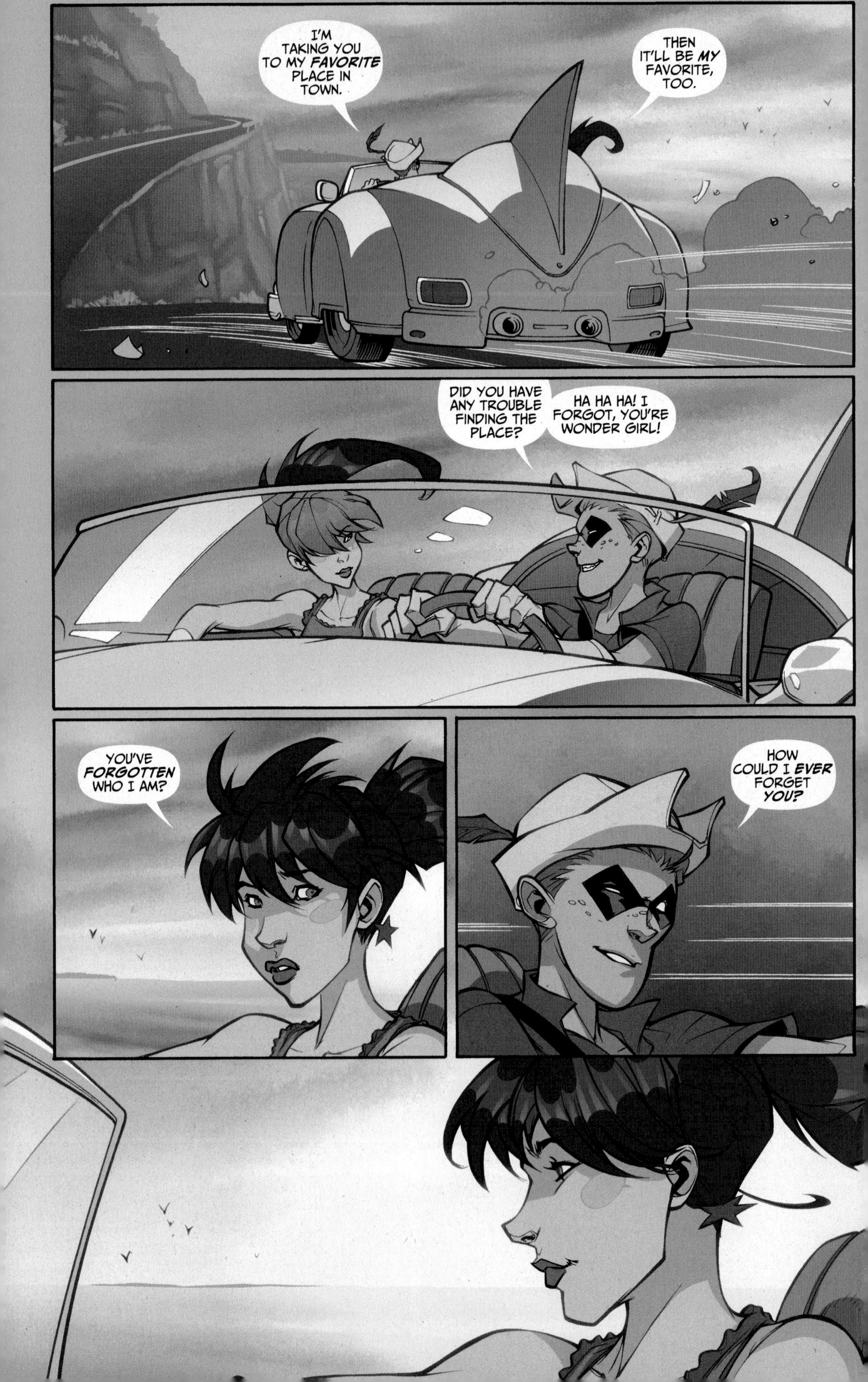
I'M TAKING YOU TO MY FAVORITE PLACE IN TOWN.
THEN IT'LL BE MY FAVORITE, TOO.
DID YOU HAVE ANY TROUBLE FINDING THE PLACE?
HA HA HA! I FORGOT, YOU'RE WONDER GIRL!
YOU'VE FORGOTTEN WHO I AM?
HOW COULD I EVER FORGET YOU?

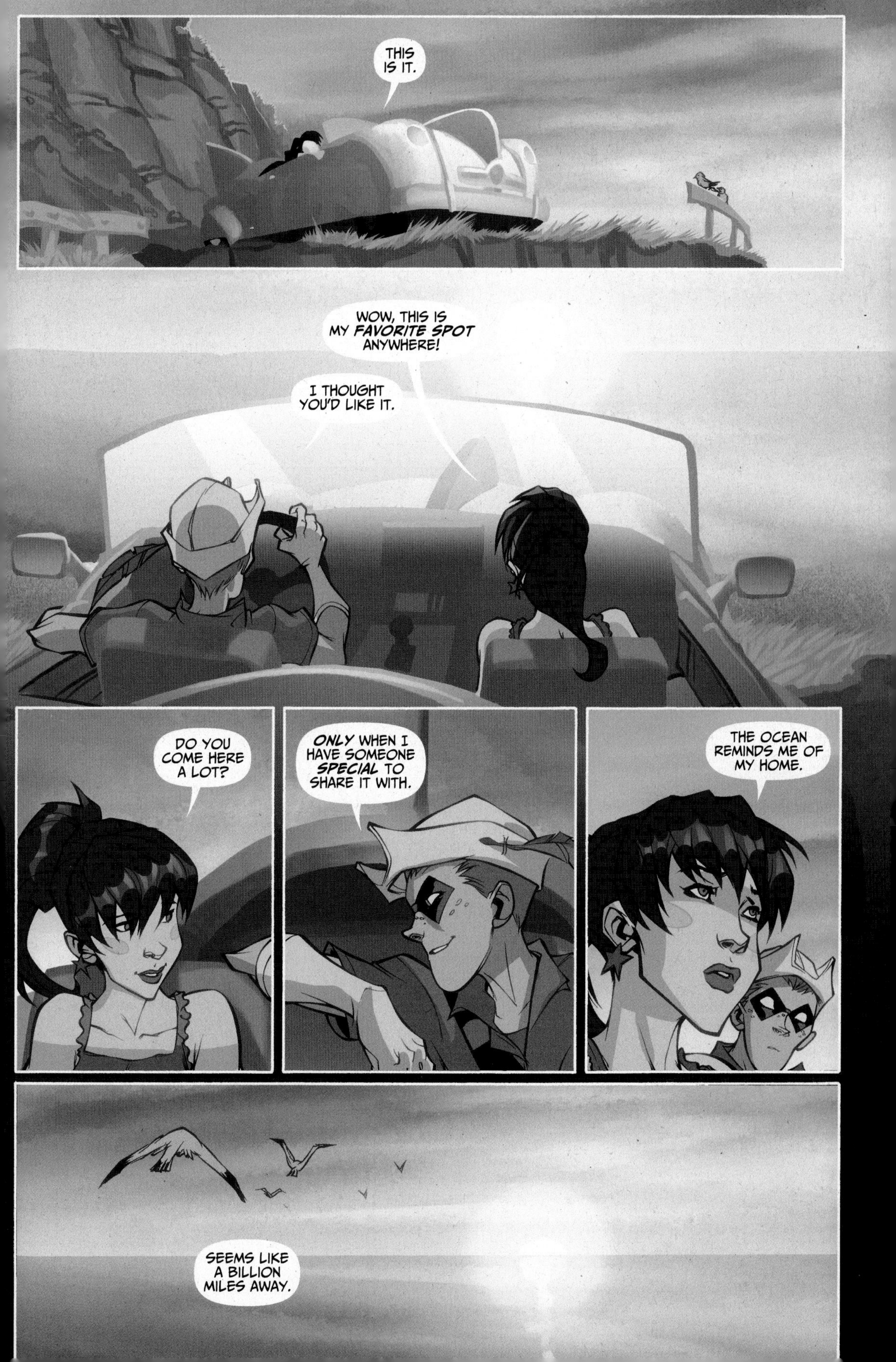
THIS IS IT.
WOW, THIS IS MY FAVORITE SPOT ANYWHERE!
I THOUGHT YOU'D LIKE IT.
DO YOU COME HERE A LOT?
ONLY WHEN I HAVE SOMEONE SPECIAL TO SHARE IT WITH.
THE OCEAN REMINDS ME OF MY HOME.
SEEMS LIKE A BILLION MILES AWAY.

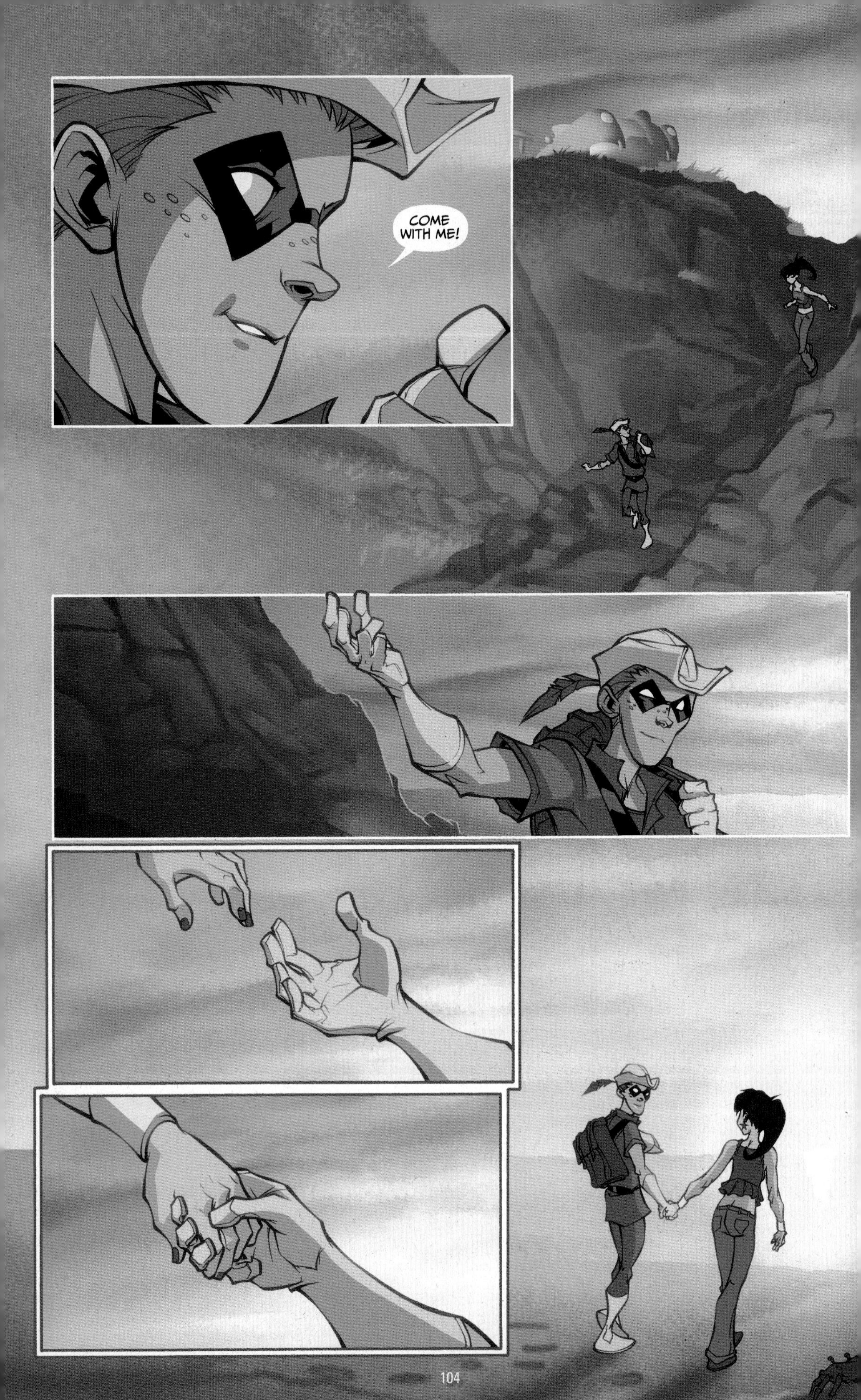
COME WITH ME!

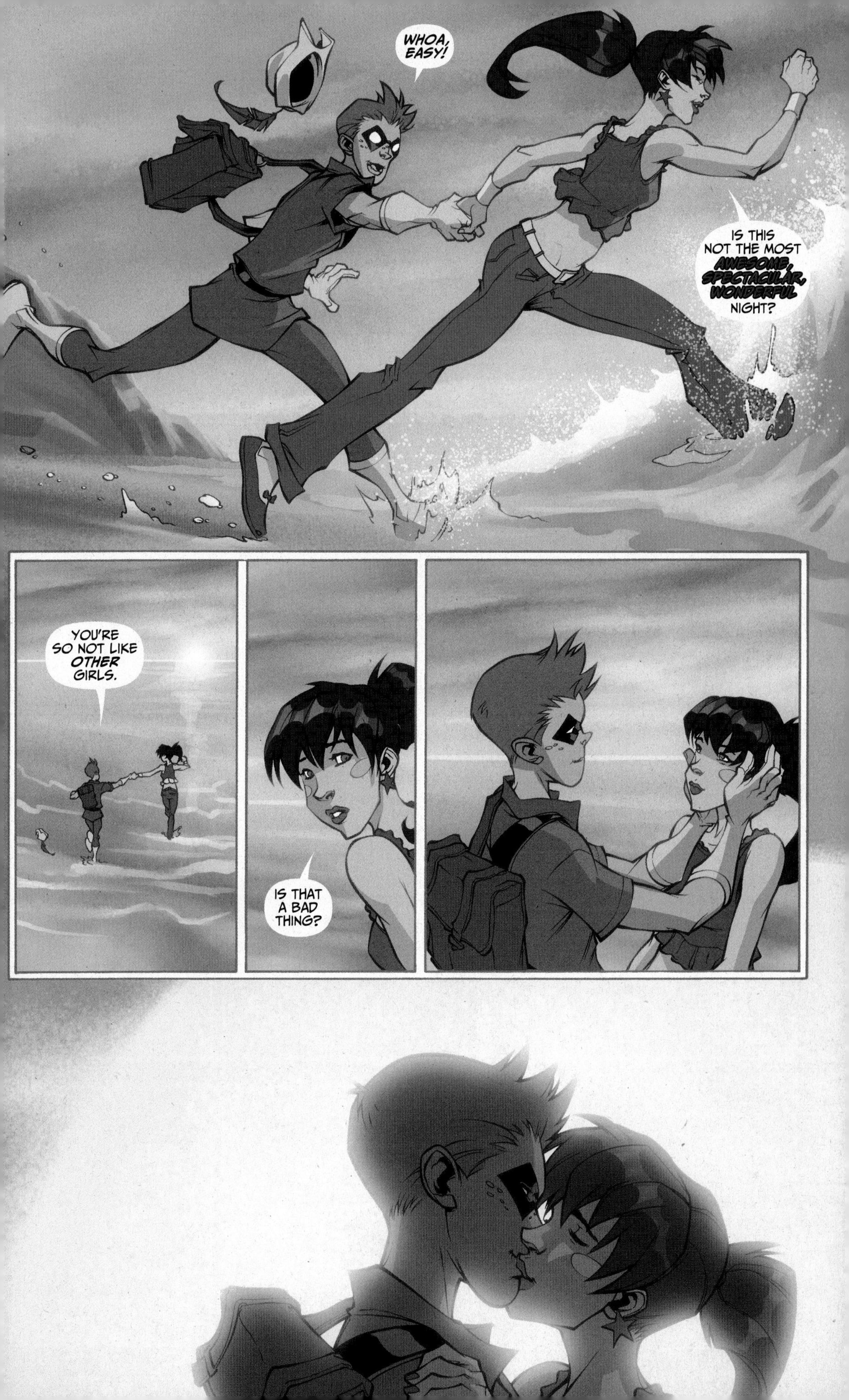
WHOA, EASY!
IS THIS NOT THE MOST AWESOME, SPECTACULAR, WONDERFUL NIGHT?
YOU'RE SO NOT LIKE OTHER GIRLS.
IS THAT A BAD THING?

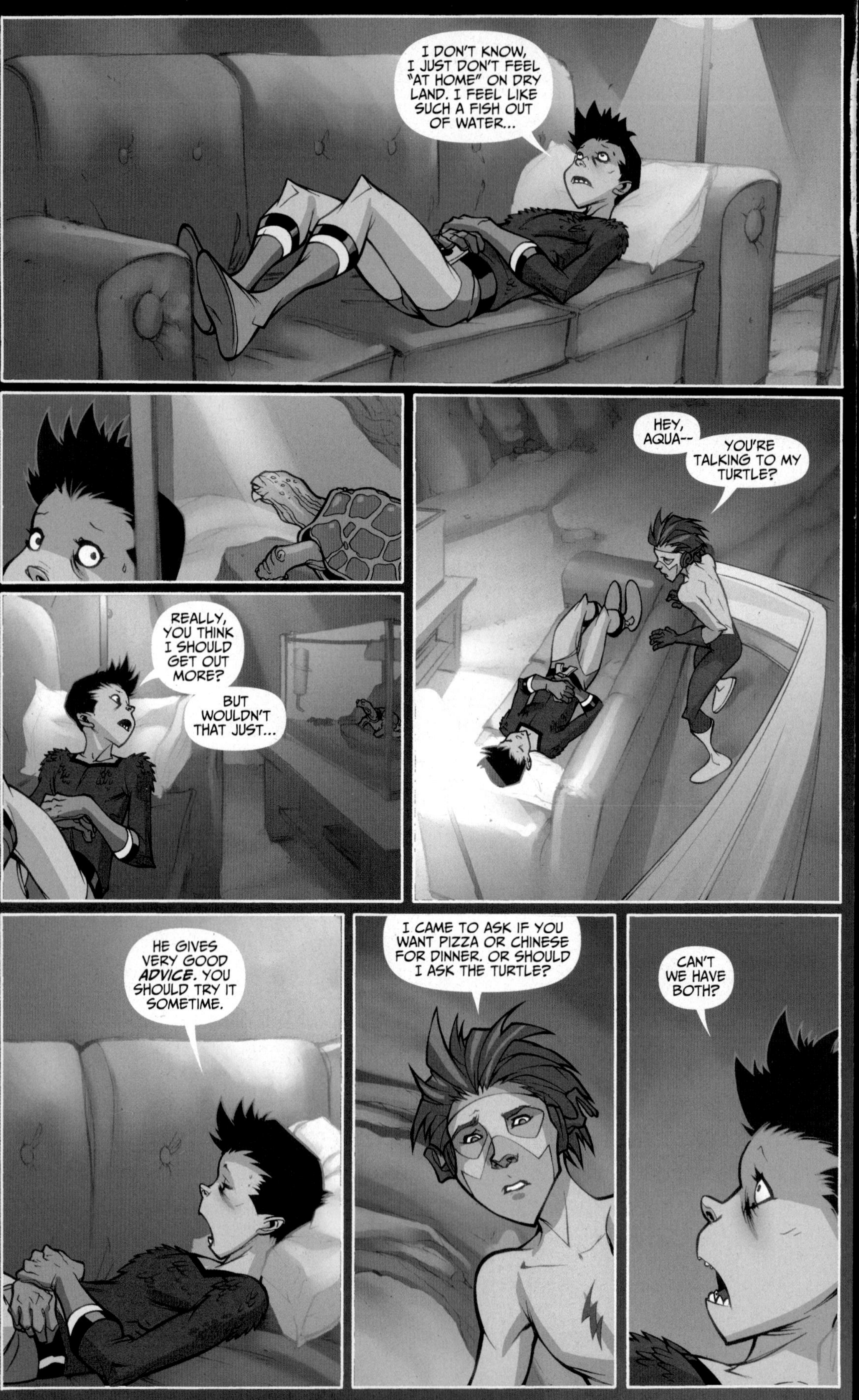
I DON'T KNOW, I JUST DON'T FEEL "AT HOME" ON DRY LAND. I FEEL LIKE SUCH A FISH OUT OF WATER...
REALLY, YOU THINK I SHOULD GET OUT MORE?
BUT WOULDN'T THAT JUST...
HEY, AQUA--
YOU'RE TALKING TO MY TURTLE?
HE GIVES VERY GOOD ***ADVICE.*** YOU SHOULD TRY IT SOMETIME.
I CAME TO ASK IF YOU WANT PIZZA OR CHINESE FOR DINNER. OR SHOULD I ASK THE TURTLE?
CAN'T WE HAVE BOTH?

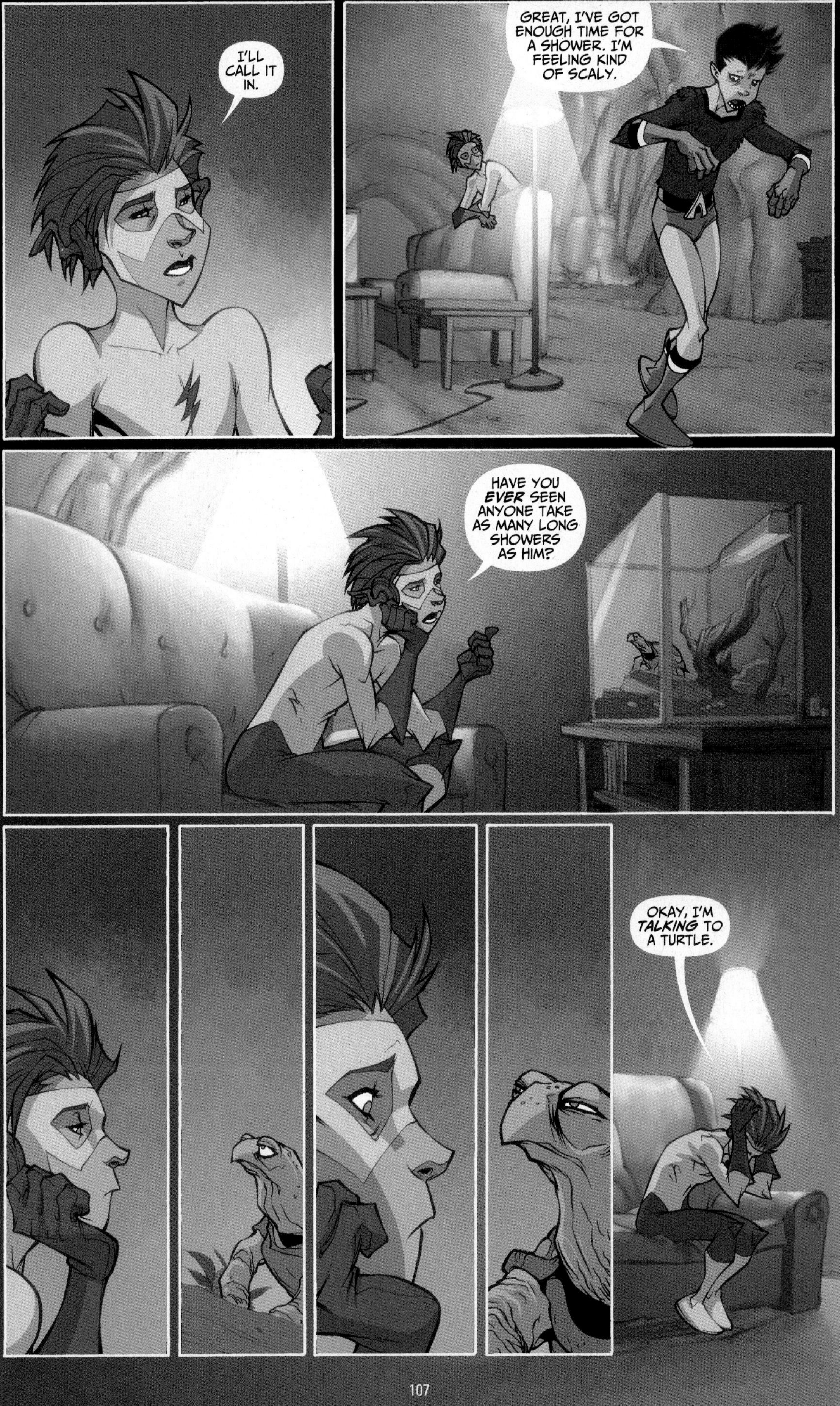
I'LL CALL IT IN.
GREAT, I'VE GOT ENOUGH TIME FOR A SHOWER. I'M FEELING KIND OF SCALY.
HAVE YOU EVER SEEN ANYONE TAKE AS MANY LONG SHOWERS AS HIM?
OKAY, I'M TALKING TO A TURTLE.

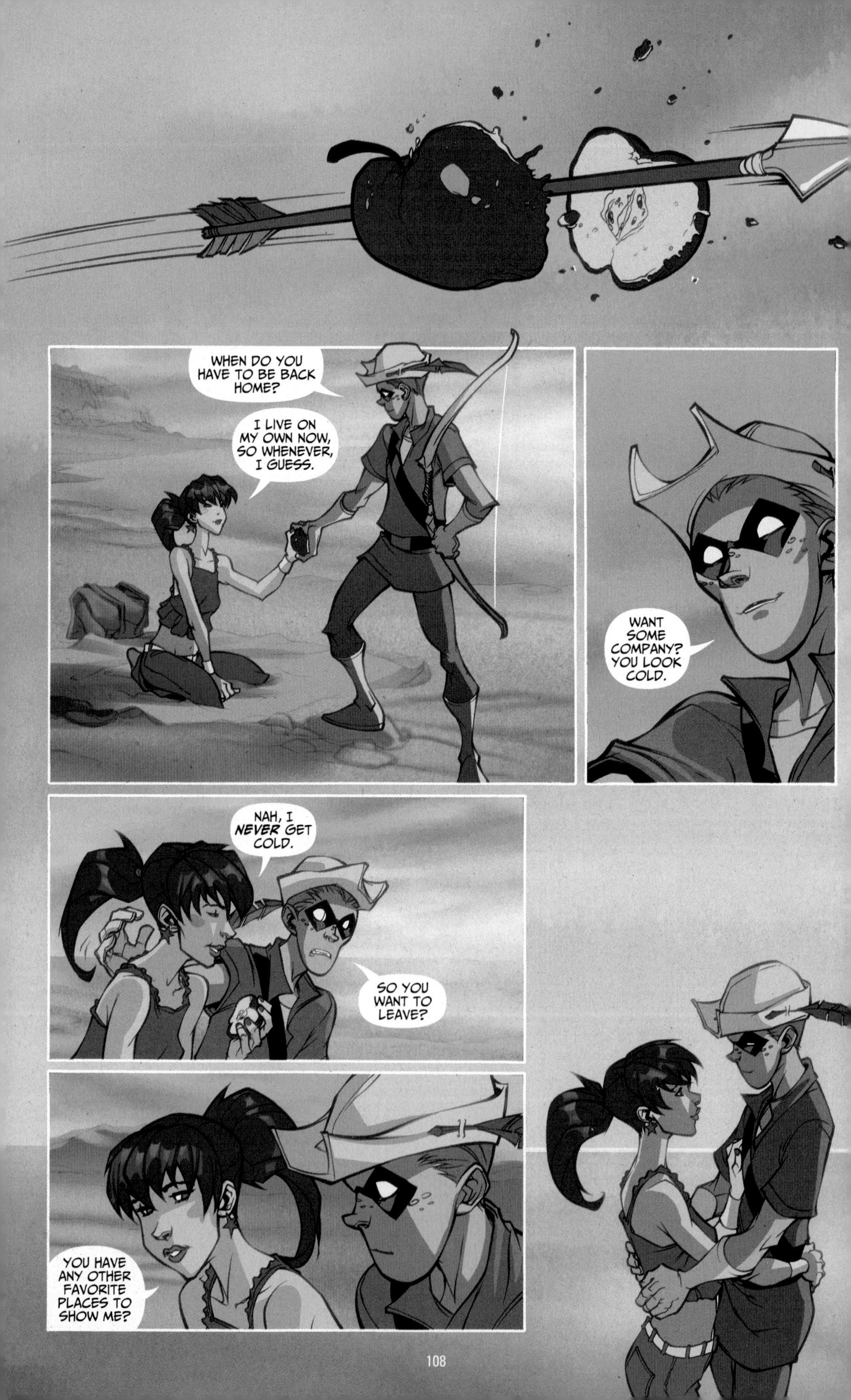
WHEN DO YOU HAVE TO BE BACK HOME?
I LIVE ON MY OWN NOW, SO WHENEVER, I GUESS.
WANT SOME COMPANY? YOU LOOK COLD.
NAH, I NEVER GET COLD.
SO YOU WANT TO LEAVE?
YOU HAVE ANY OTHER FAVORITE PLACES TO SHOW ME?

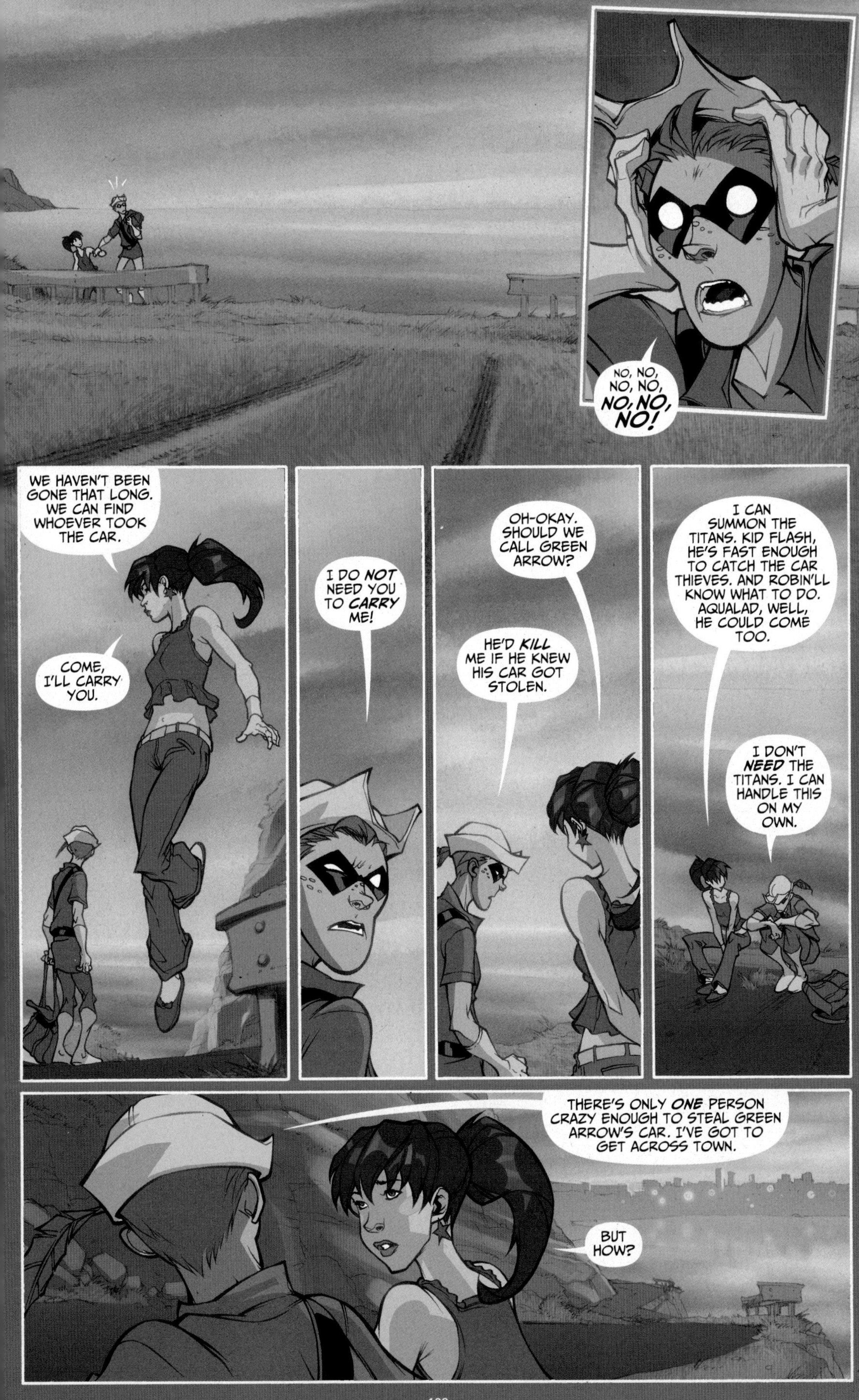
NO, NO, NO, NO, NO, NO, NO!
WE HAVEN'T BEEN GONE THAT LONG. WE CAN FIND WHOEVER TOOK THE CAR.
COME, I'LL CARRY YOU.
I DO NOT NEED YOU TO CARRY ME!
OH-OKAY. SHOULD WE CALL GREEN ARROW?
HE'D KILL ME IF HE KNEW HIS CAR GOT STOLEN.
I CAN SUMMON THE TITANS. KID FLASH, HE'S FAST ENOUGH TO CATCH THE CAR THIEVES. AND ROBIN'LL KNOW WHAT TO DO. AQUALAD, WELL, HE COULD COME TOO.
I DON'T NEED THE TITANS. I CAN HANDLE THIS ON MY OWN.
THERE'S ONLY ONE PERSON CRAZY ENOUGH TO STEAL GREEN ARROW'S CAR. I'VE GOT TO GET ACROSS TOWN.
BUT HOW?

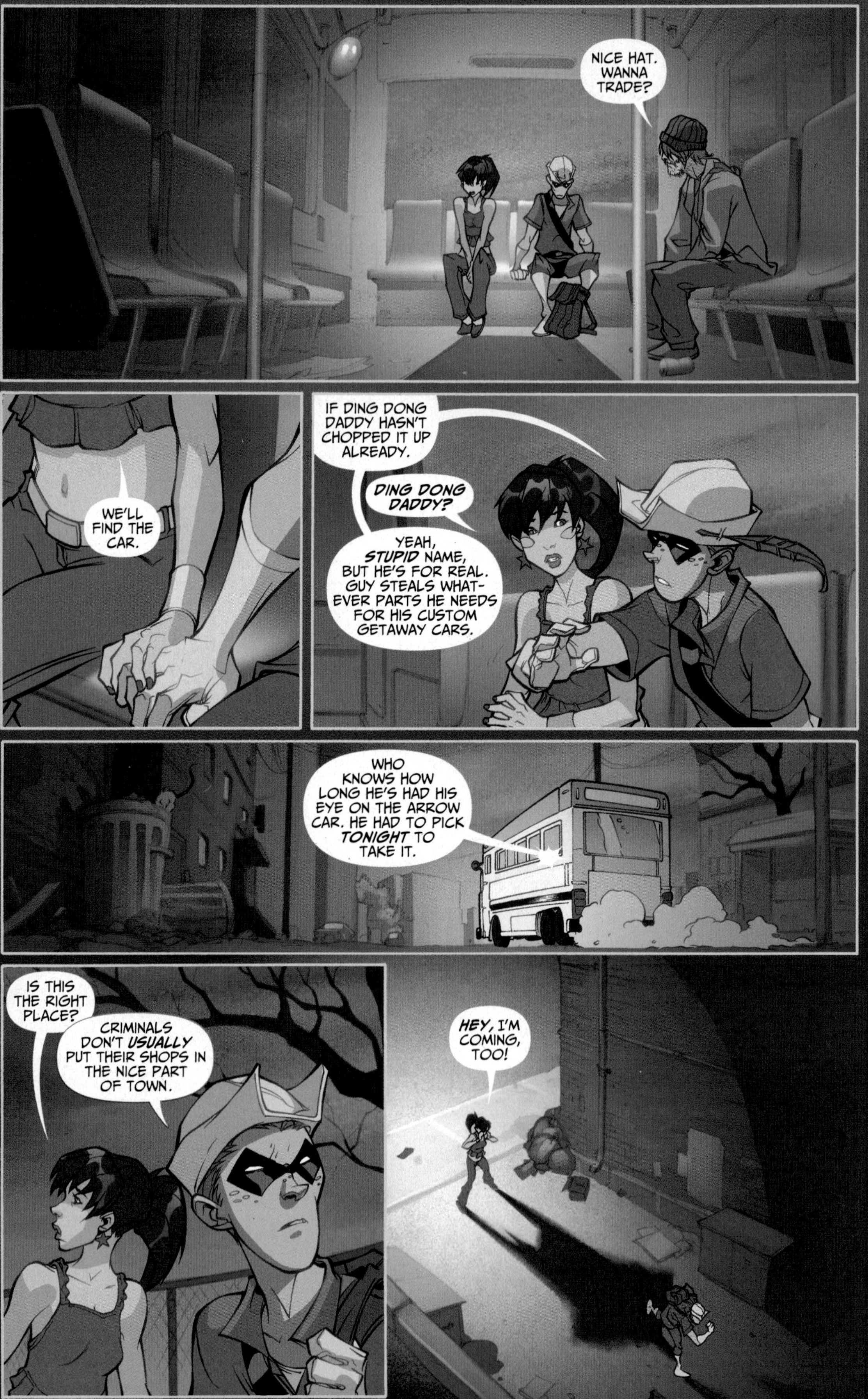
NICE HAT. WANNA TRADE?
WE'LL FIND THE CAR.
IF DING DONG DADDY HASN'T CHOPPED IT UP ALREADY.
DING DONG DADDY?
YEAH, STUPID NAME, BUT HE'S FOR REAL. GUY STEALS WHATEVER PARTS HE NEEDS FOR HIS CUSTOM GETAWAY CARS.
WHO KNOWS HOW LONG HE'S HAD HIS EYE ON THE ARROW CAR. HE HAD TO PICK TONIGHT TO TAKE IT.
IS THIS THE RIGHT PLACE?
CRIMINALS DON'T USUALLY PUT THEIR SHOPS IN THE NICE PART OF TOWN.
HEY, I'M COMING, TOO!

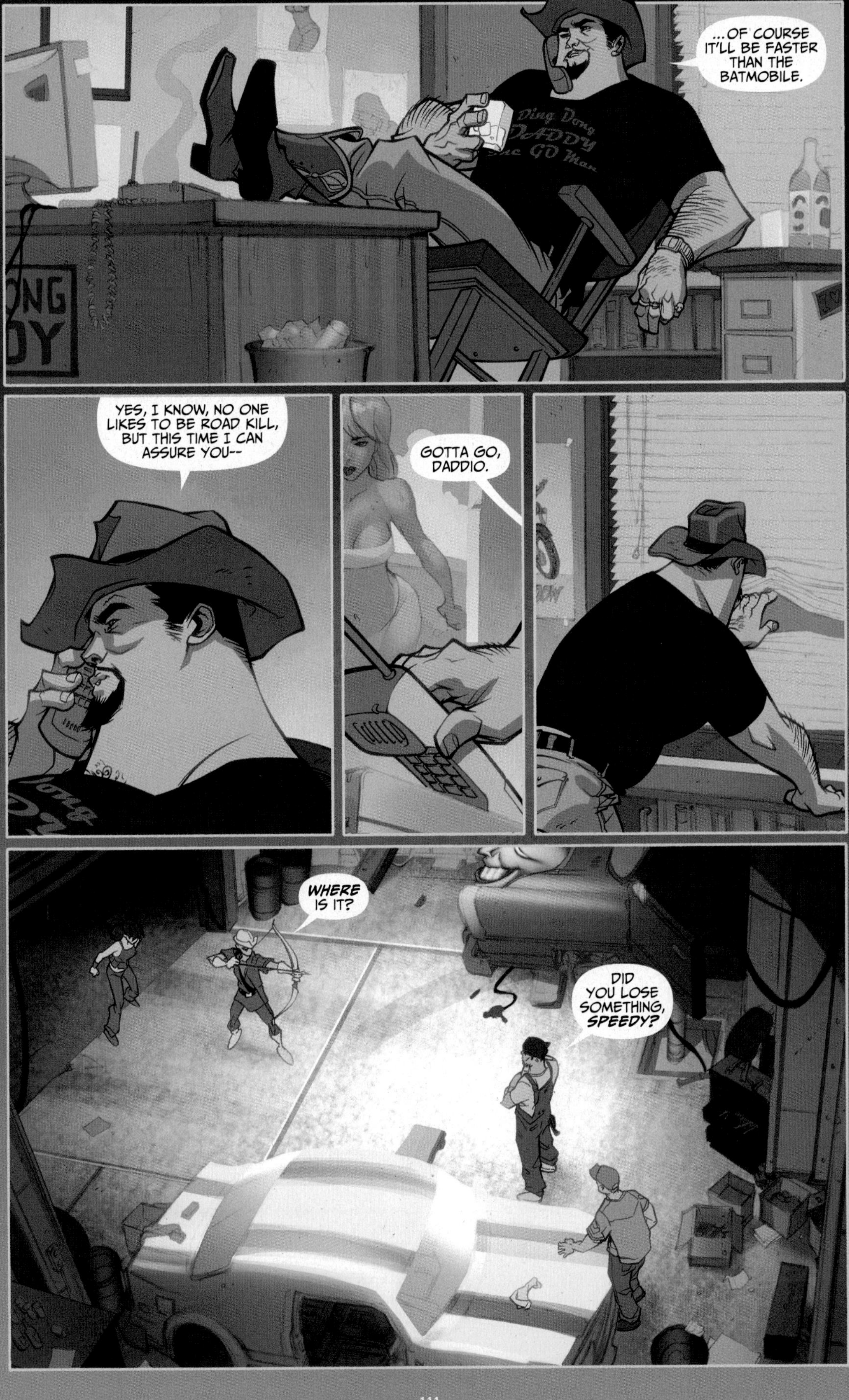
...OF COURSE IT'LL BE FASTER THAN THE BATMOBILE.
Ding Dong DADDY The GO Man
YES, I KNOW, NO ONE LIKES TO BE ROAD KILL, BUT THIS TIME I CAN ASSURE YOU--
GOTTA GO, DADDIO.
WHERE IS IT?
DID YOU LOSE SOMETHING, SPEEDY?

WE'VE COME FOR THE ARROW CAR.

OOOH, HE BROUGHT HIS LITTLE GIRLFRIEND. SHE GONNA *PROTECT* YOU?

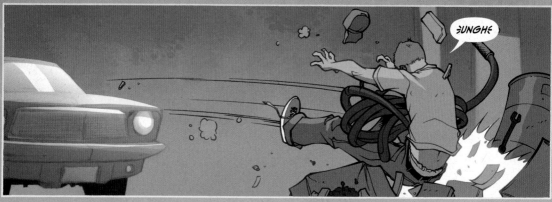

≤UNGH≥

LOOKS LIKE YOU'RE THE ONE WHO *NEEDS* PROTECTING.

NOBODY STEALS THE ARROW CAR.

≤GROANS≥

WHERE. IS. IT?

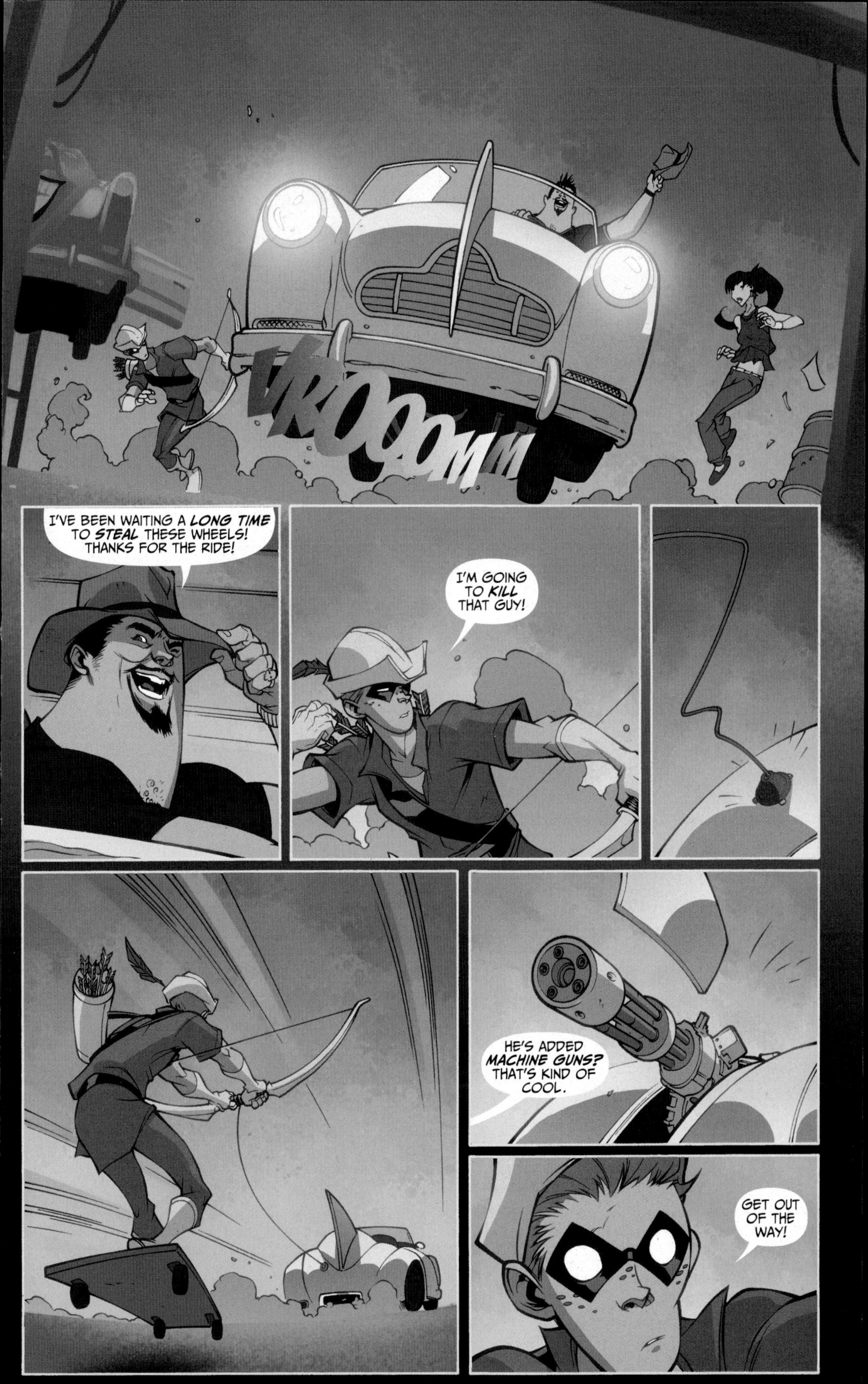

VROOOMM
I'VE BEEN WAITING A LONG TIME TO STEAL THESE WHEELS! THANKS FOR THE RIDE!
I'M GOING TO KILL THAT GUY!
HE'S ADDED MACHINE GUNS? THAT'S KIND OF COOL.
GET OUT OF THE WAY!

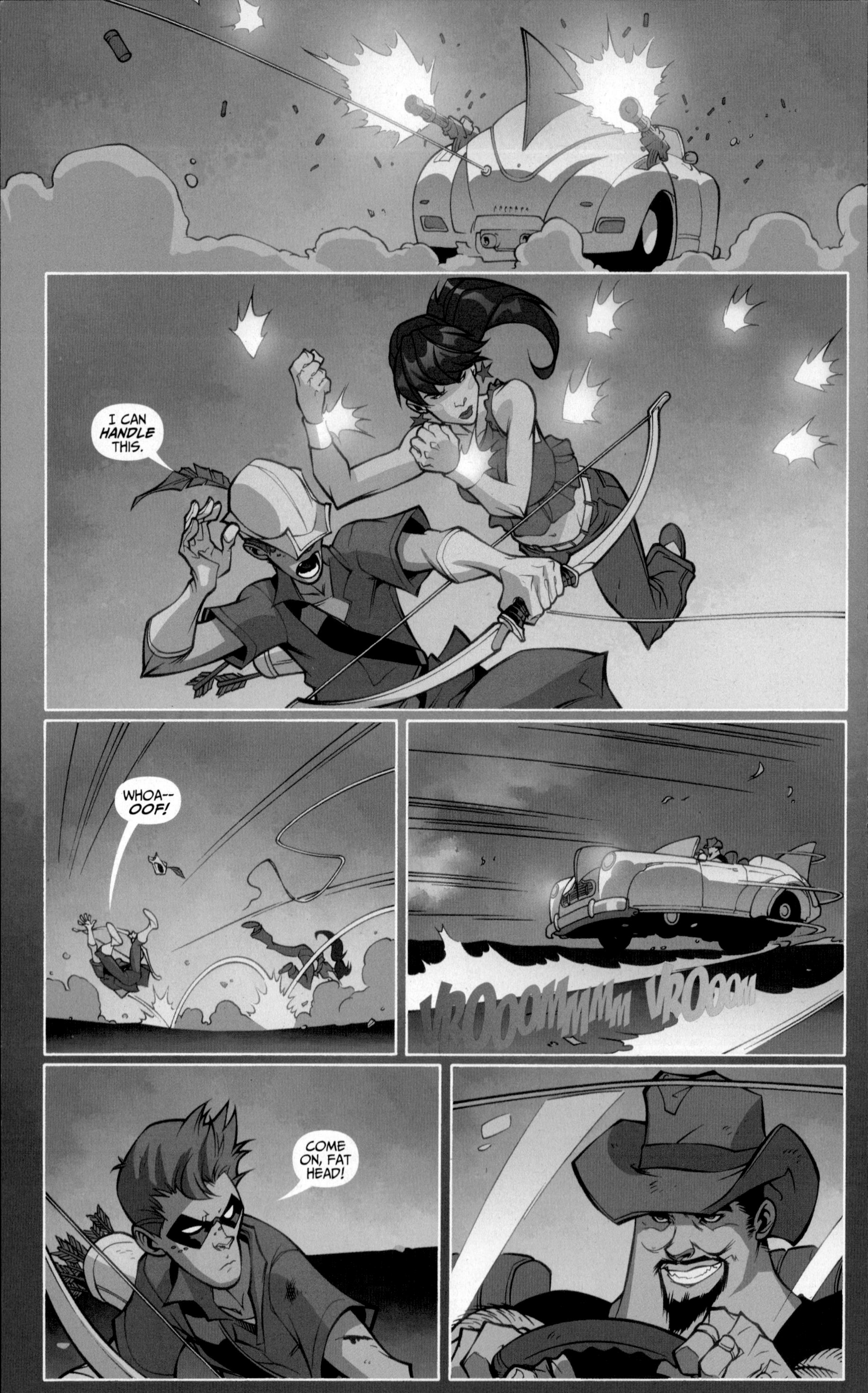
I CAN *HANDLE* THIS.
WHOA-- *OOF!*
VROOOMMMM VROOOM
COME ON, FAT HEAD!

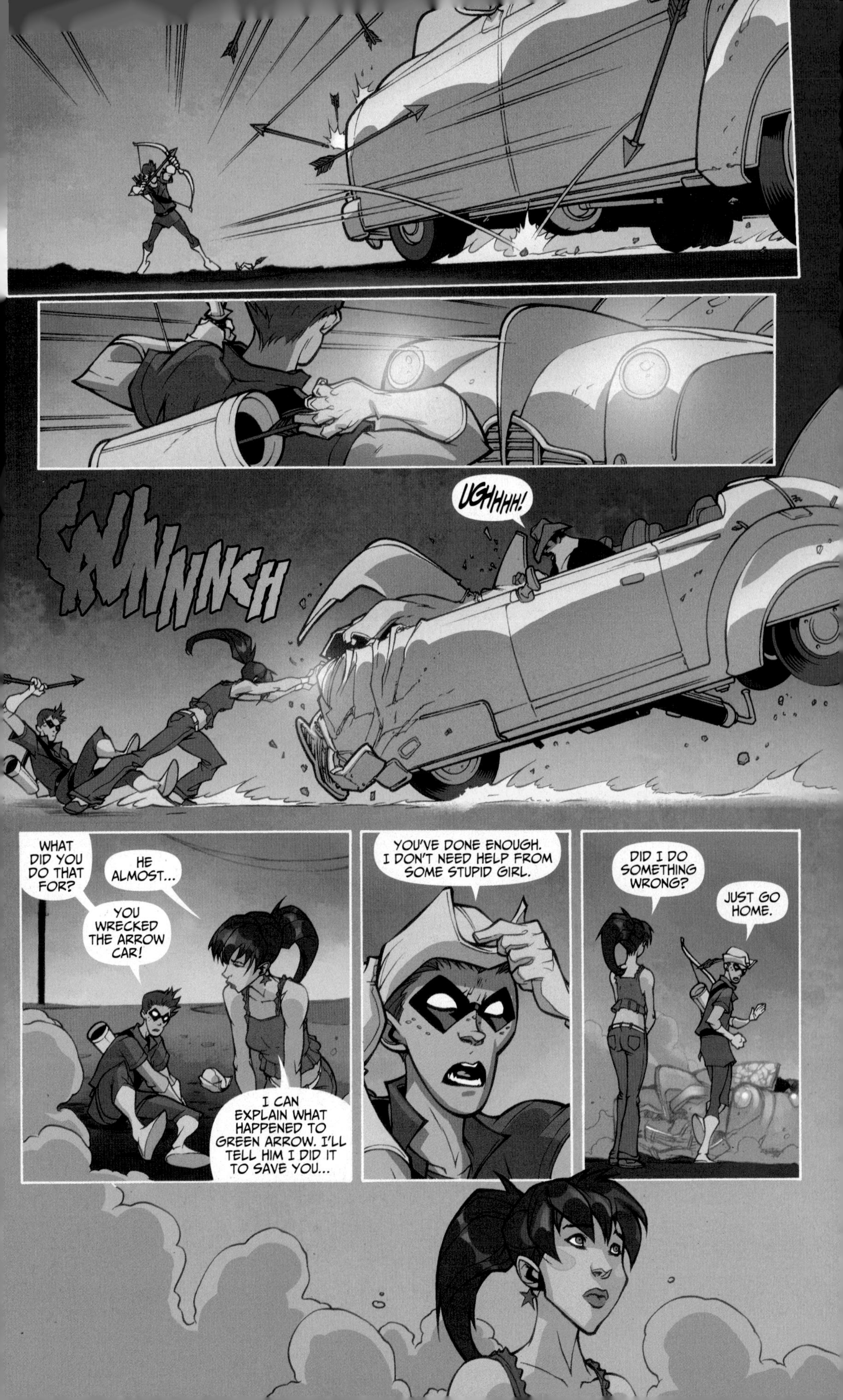

UGHHHH!
SKUNNNCH
WHAT DID YOU DO THAT FOR?
HE ALMOST...
YOU WRECKED THE ARROW CAR!
I CAN EXPLAIN WHAT HAPPENED TO GREEN ARROW. I'LL TELL HIM I DID IT TO SAVE YOU...
YOU'VE DONE ENOUGH. I DON'T NEED HELP FROM SOME STUPID GIRL.
DID I DO SOMETHING WRONG?
JUST GO HOME.

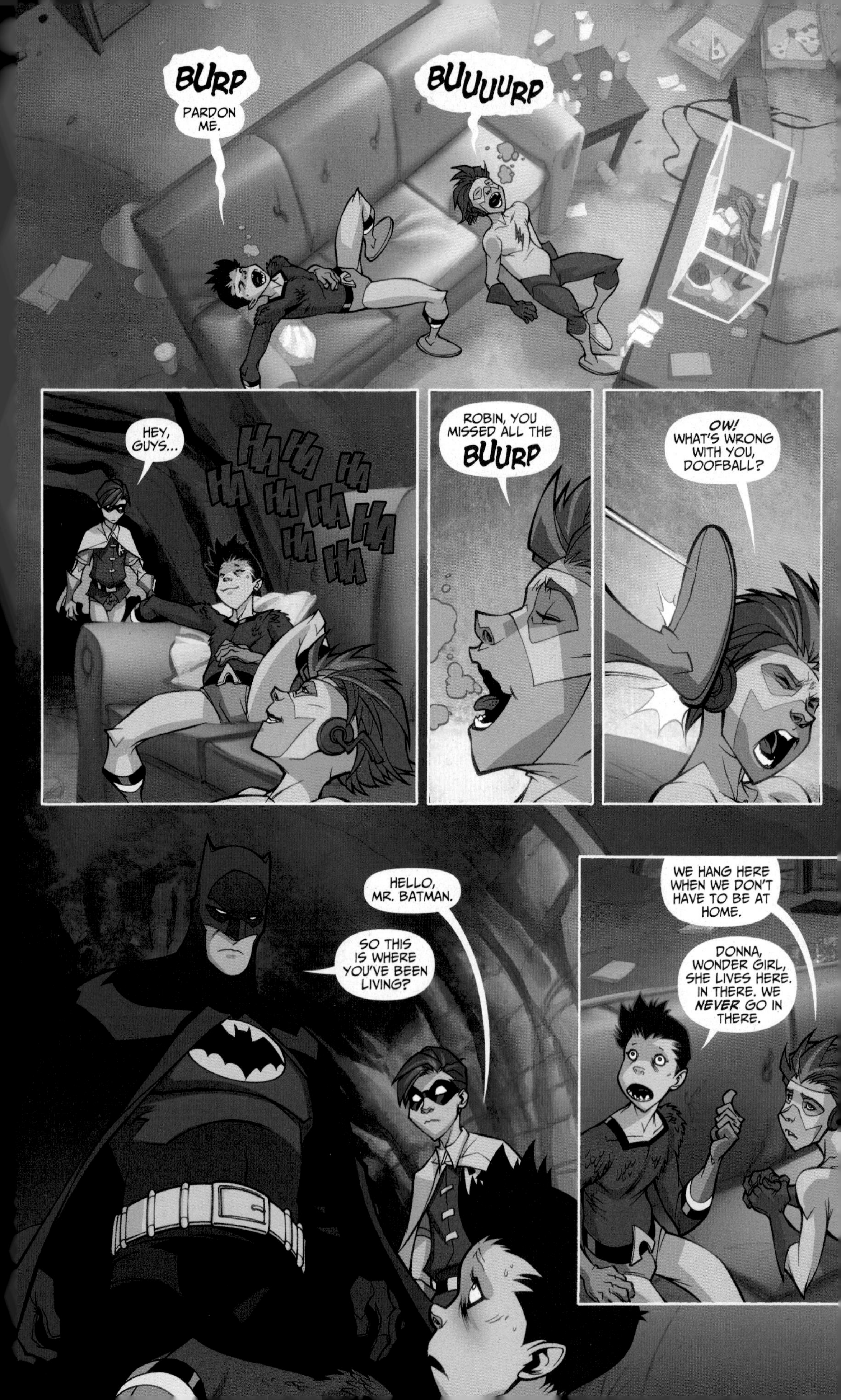
BURP
PARDON ME.
BUUUURP
HEY, GUYS...
HA HA HA HA HA HA HA HA HA HA
ROBIN, YOU MISSED ALL THE BUURP
OW! WHAT'S WRONG WITH YOU, DOOFBALL?
HELLO, MR. BATMAN.
SO THIS IS WHERE YOU'VE BEEN LIVING?
WE HANG HERE WHEN WE DON'T HAVE TO BE AT HOME.
DONNA, WONDER GIRL, SHE LIVES HERE. IN THERE. WE NEVER GO IN THERE.

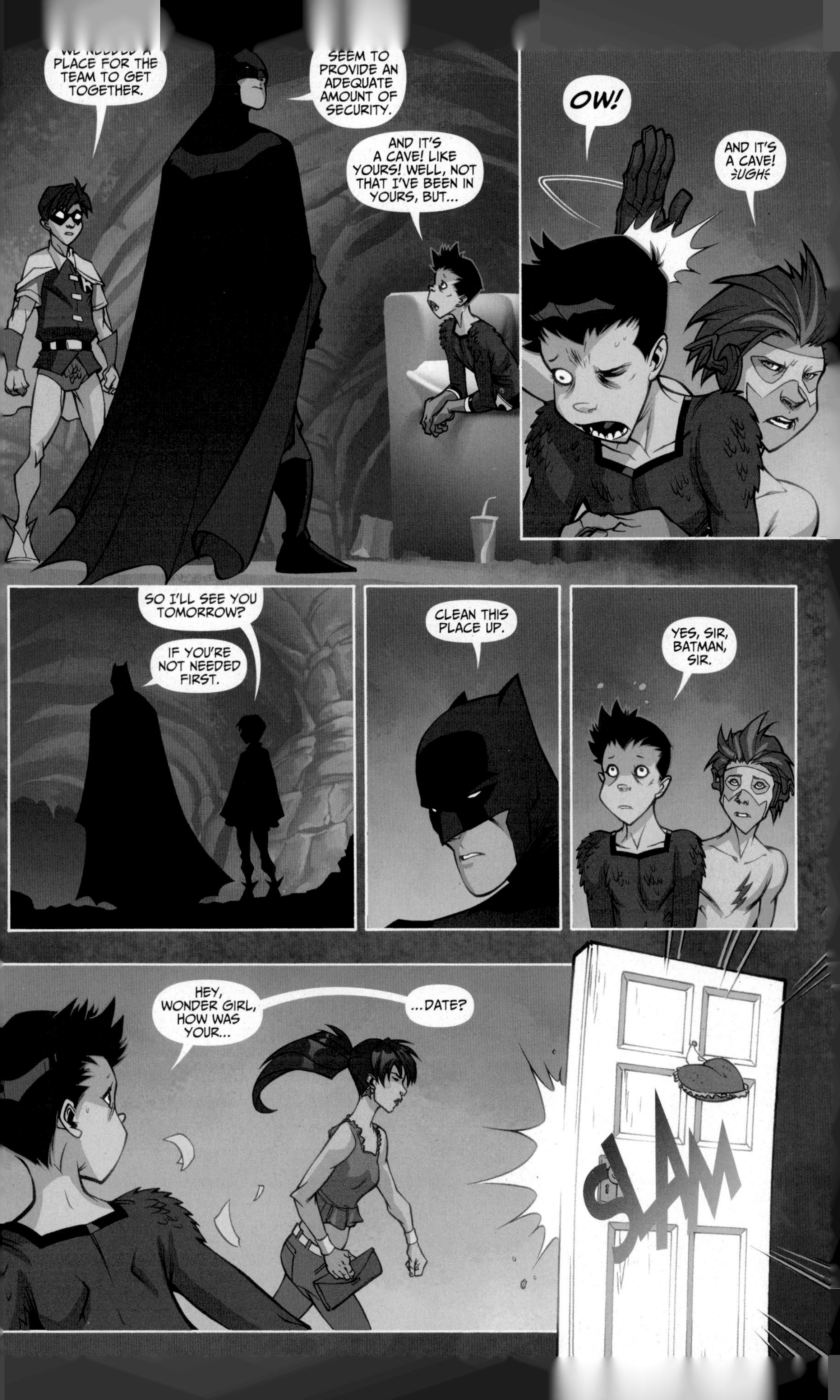
PLACE FOR THE TEAM TO GET TOGETHER.
SEEM TO PROVIDE AN ADEQUATE AMOUNT OF SECURITY.
AND IT'S A CAVE! LIKE YOURS! WELL, NOT THAT I'VE BEEN IN YOURS, BUT...
OW!
AND IT'S A CAVE! UGH
SO I'LL SEE YOU TOMORROW?
IF YOU'RE NOT NEEDED FIRST.
CLEAN THIS PLACE UP.
YES, SIR, BATMAN, SIR.
HEY, WONDER GIRL, HOW WAS YOUR...
...DATE?
SLAM

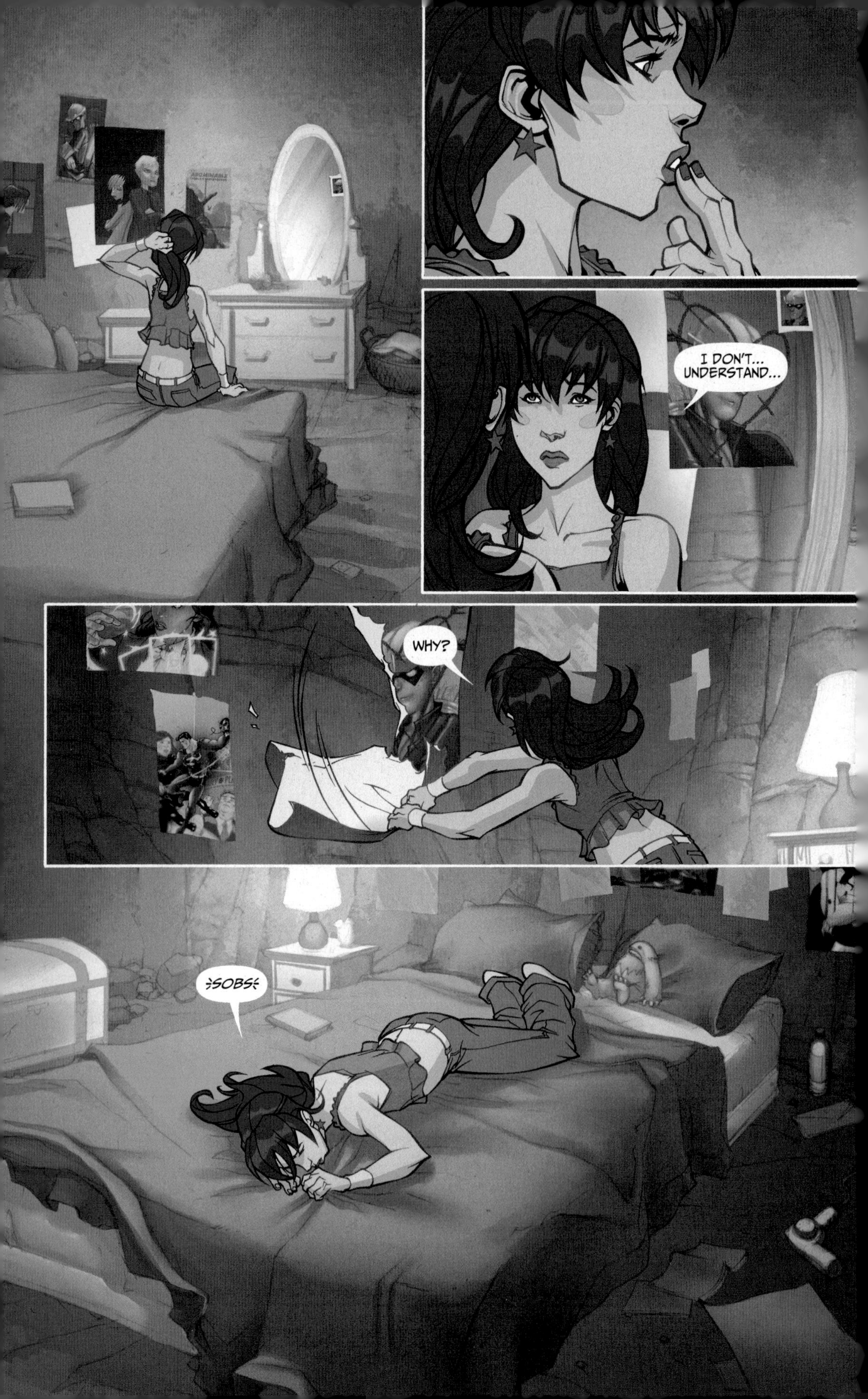
I DON'T... UNDERSTAND...
WHY?
SOBS

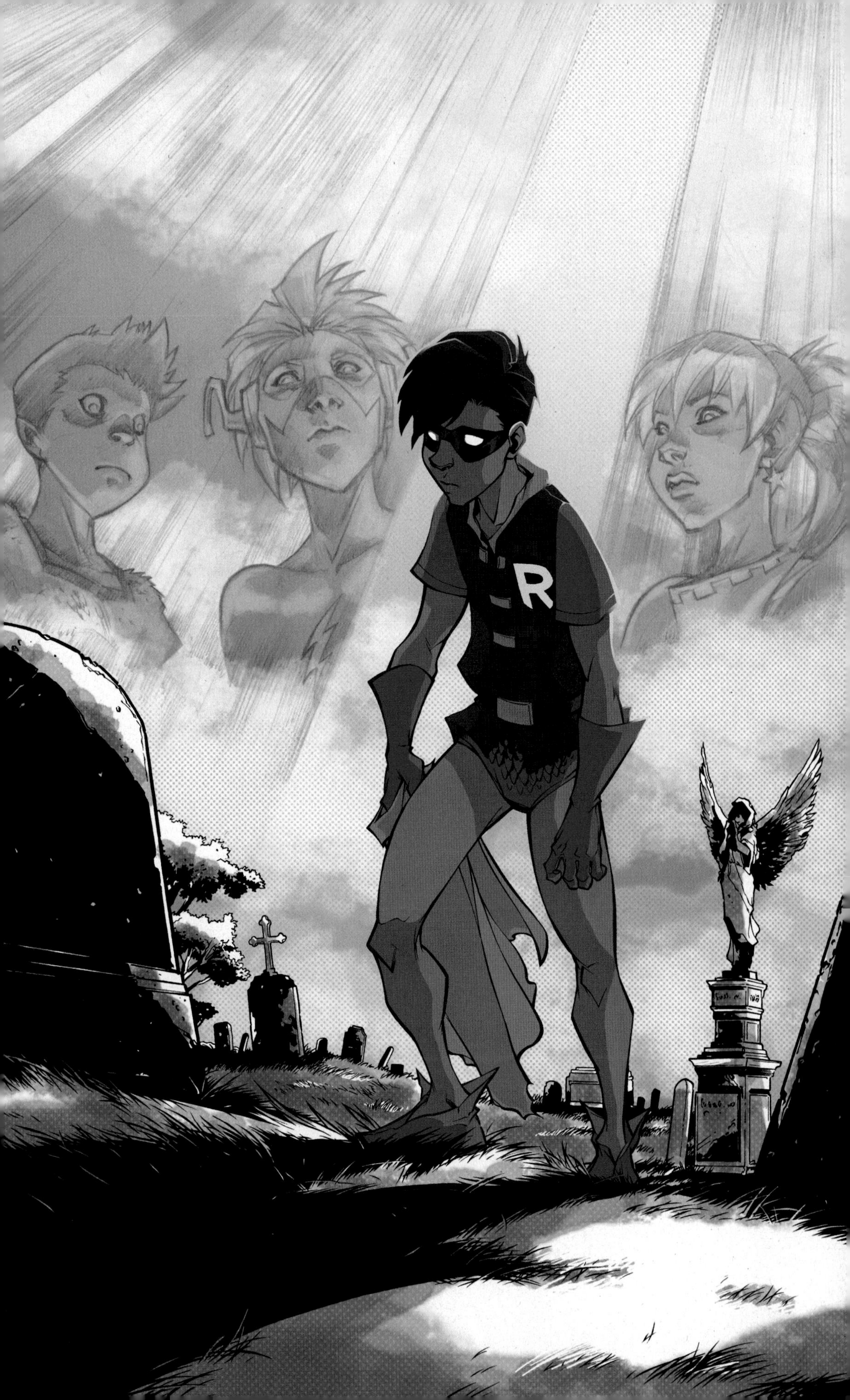

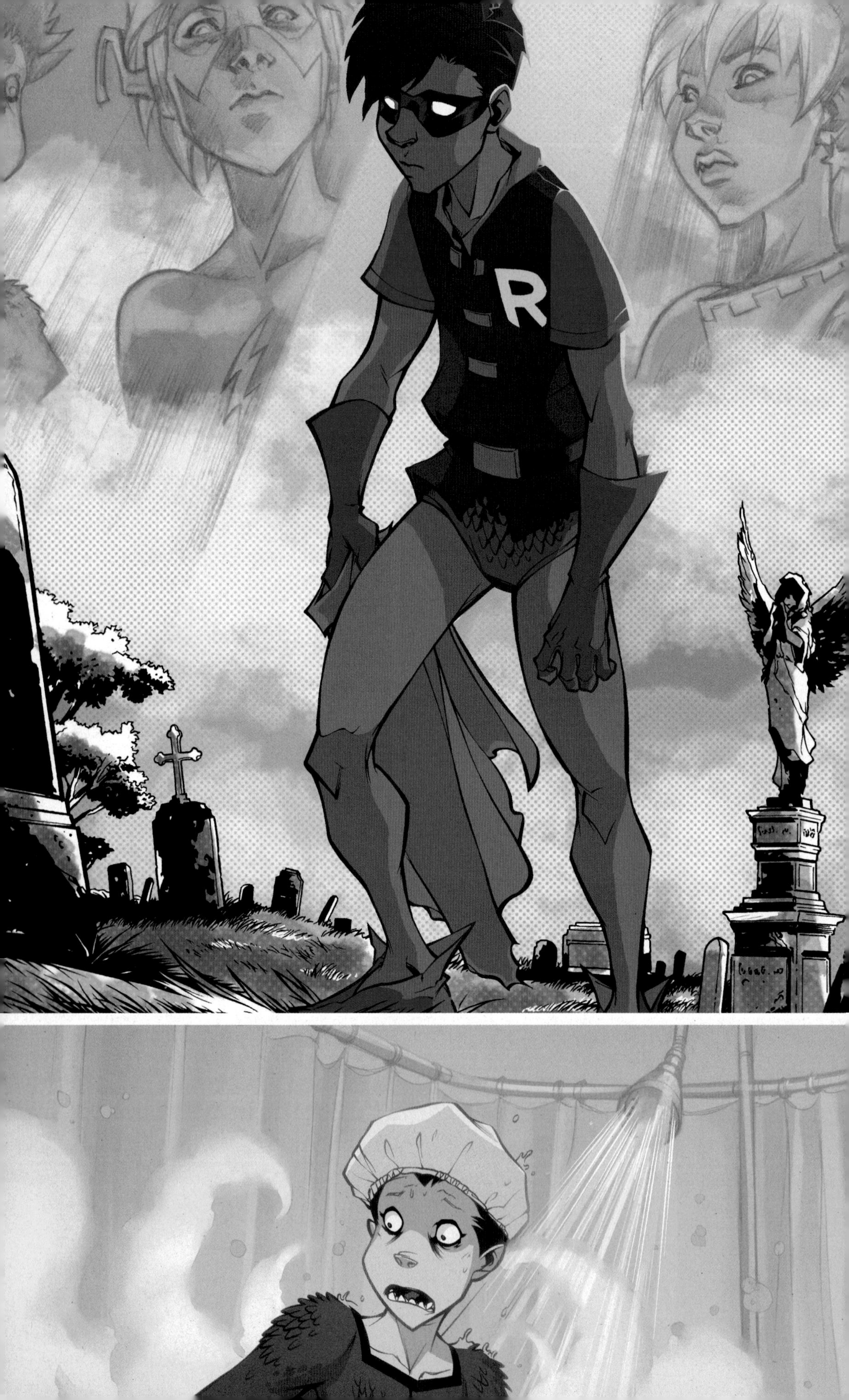

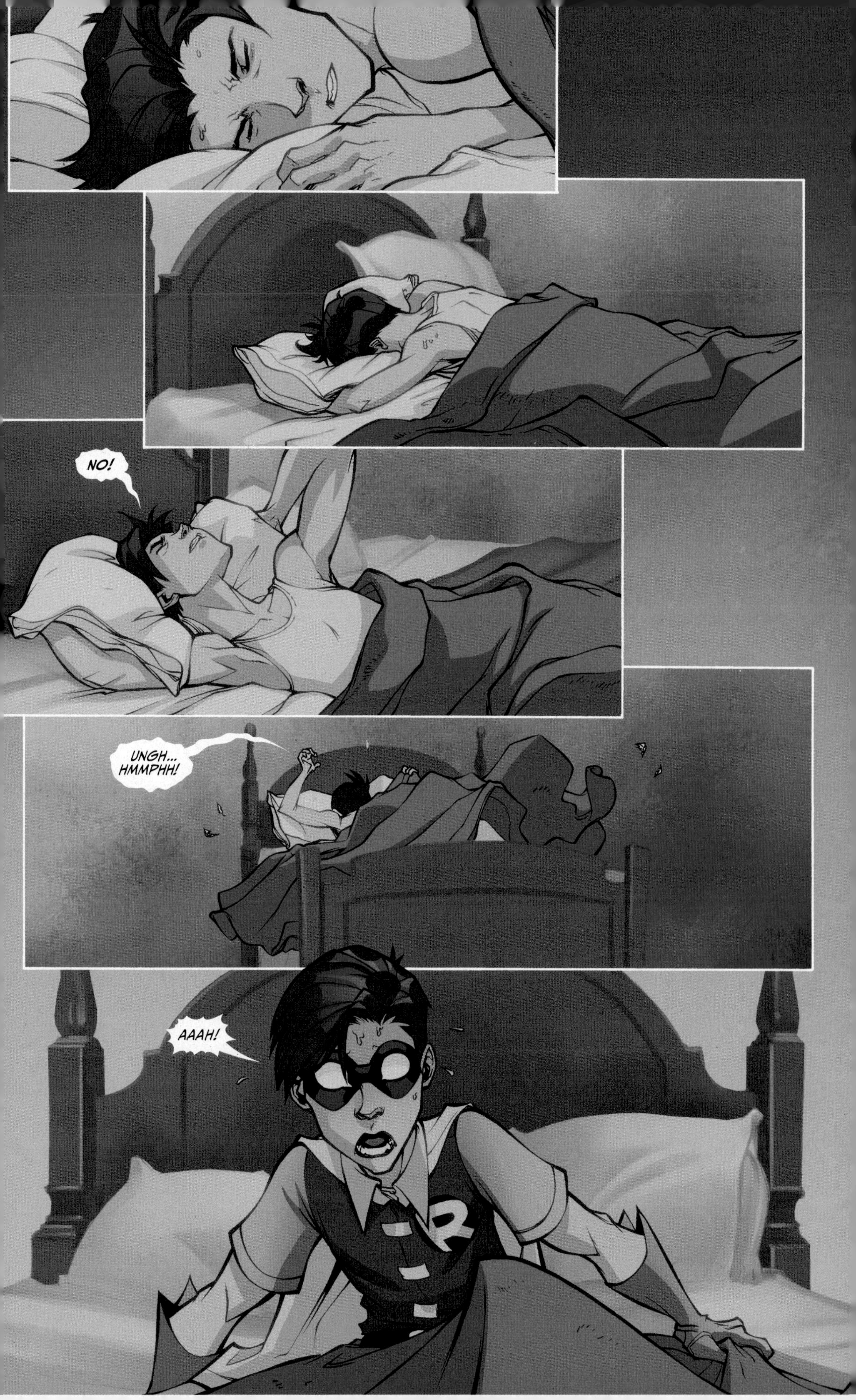
NO!
UNGH... HMMPHH!
AAAH!

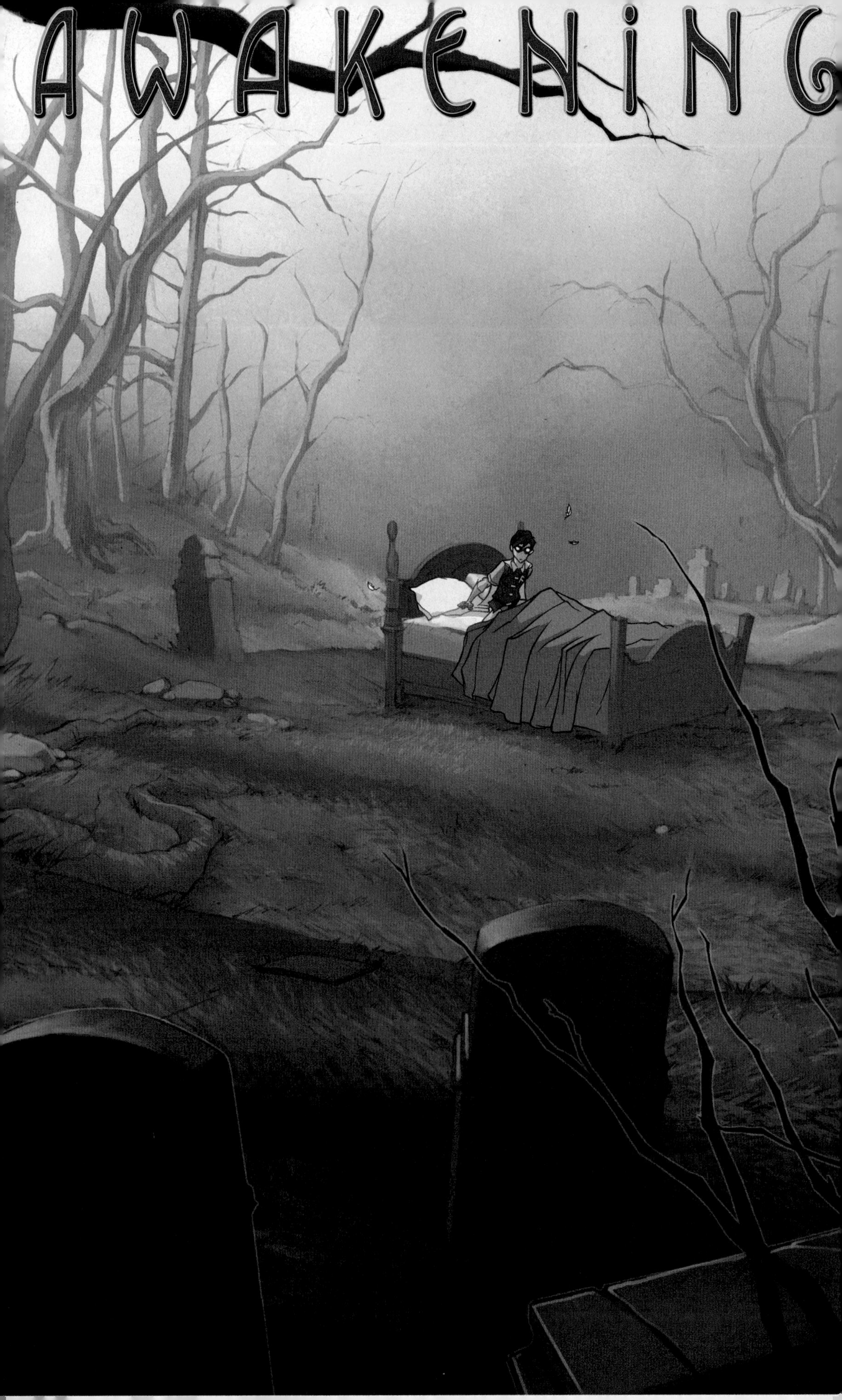
AWAKENING

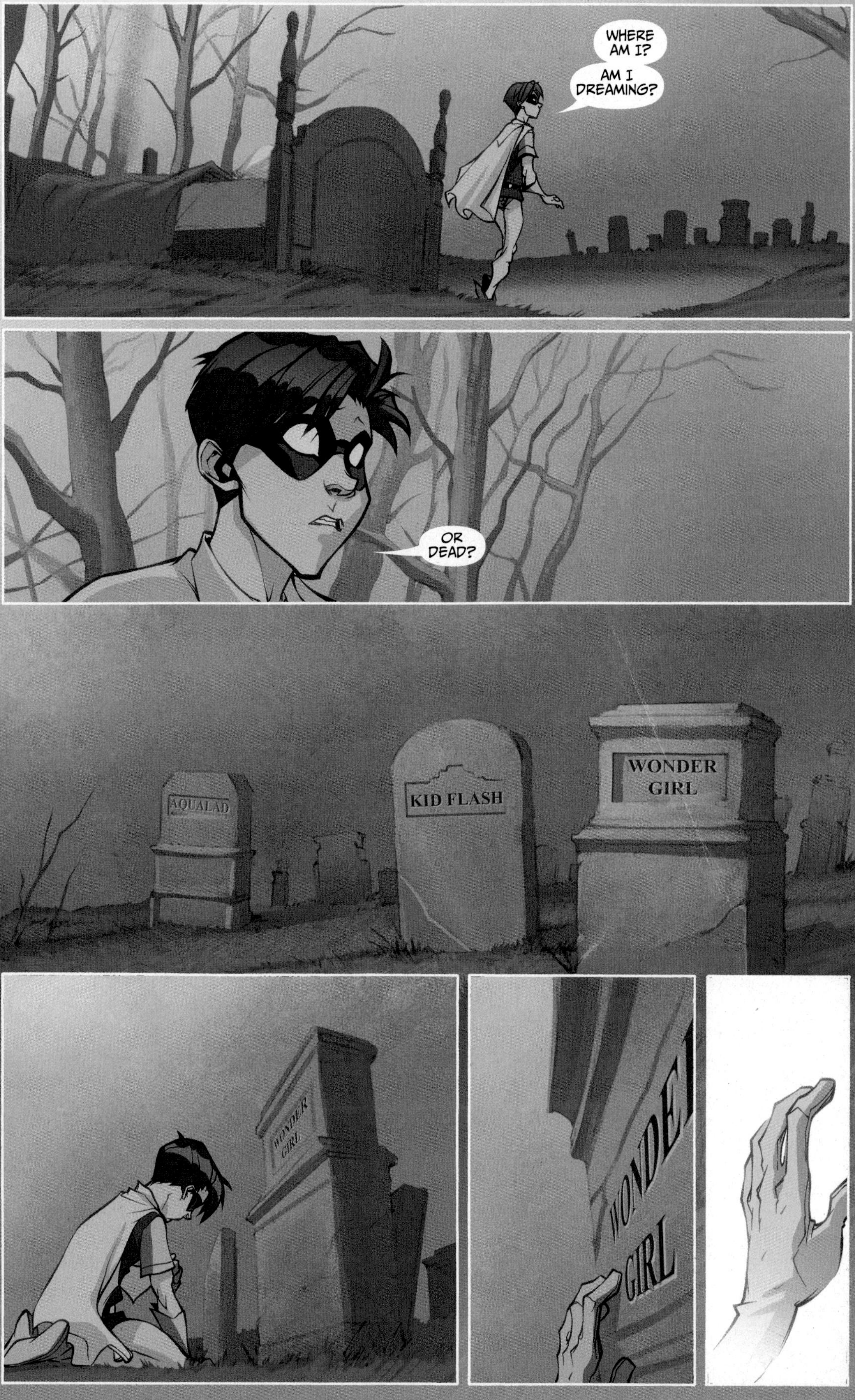
WHERE AM I?
AM I DREAMING?
OR DEAD?
AQUALAD
KID FLASH
WONDER GIRL
WONDER GIRL
WONDER GIRL

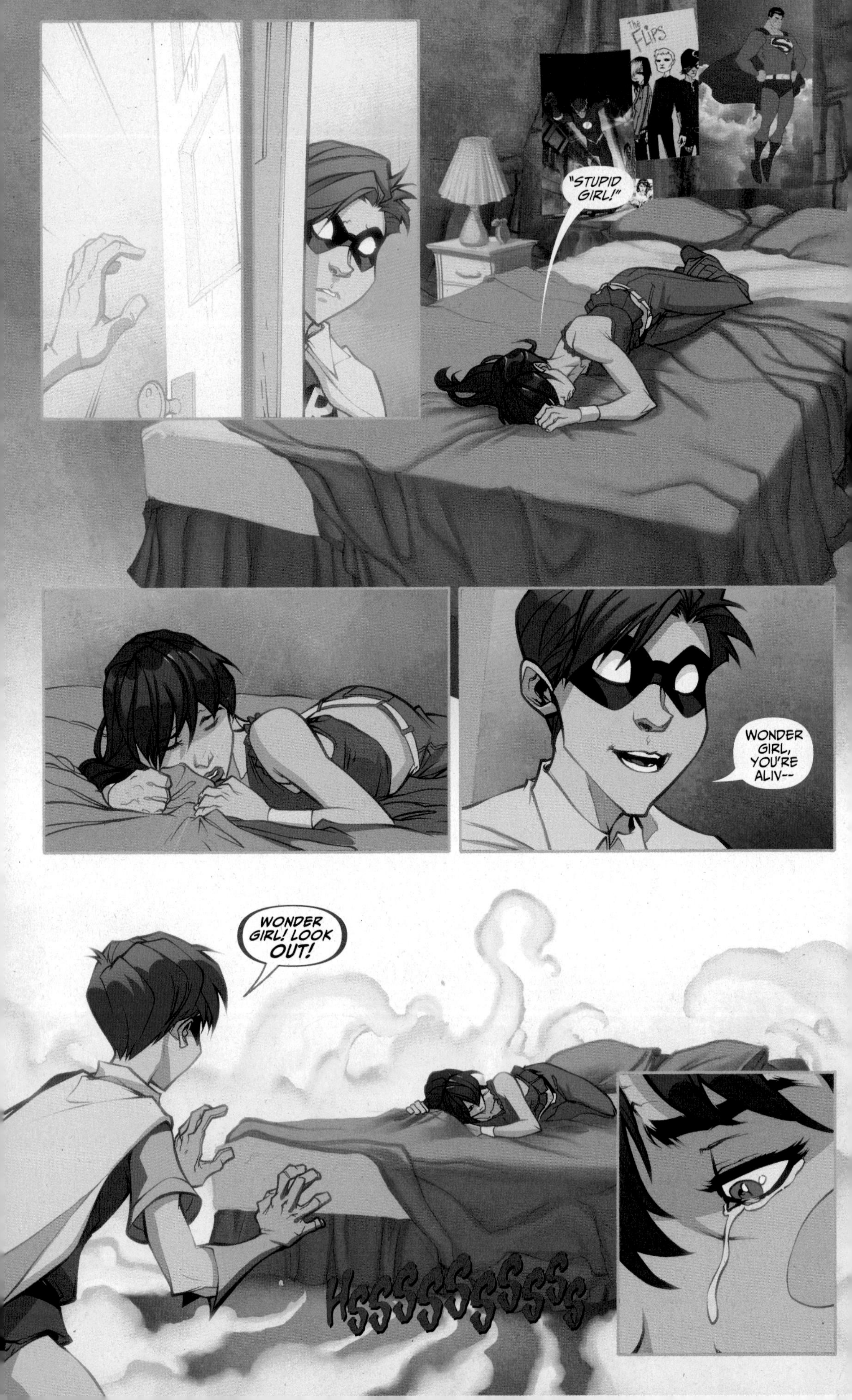
"STUPID GIRL!"
WONDER GIRL, YOU'RE ALIV--
WONDER GIRL! LOOK OUT!
HSSSSSSSSSS

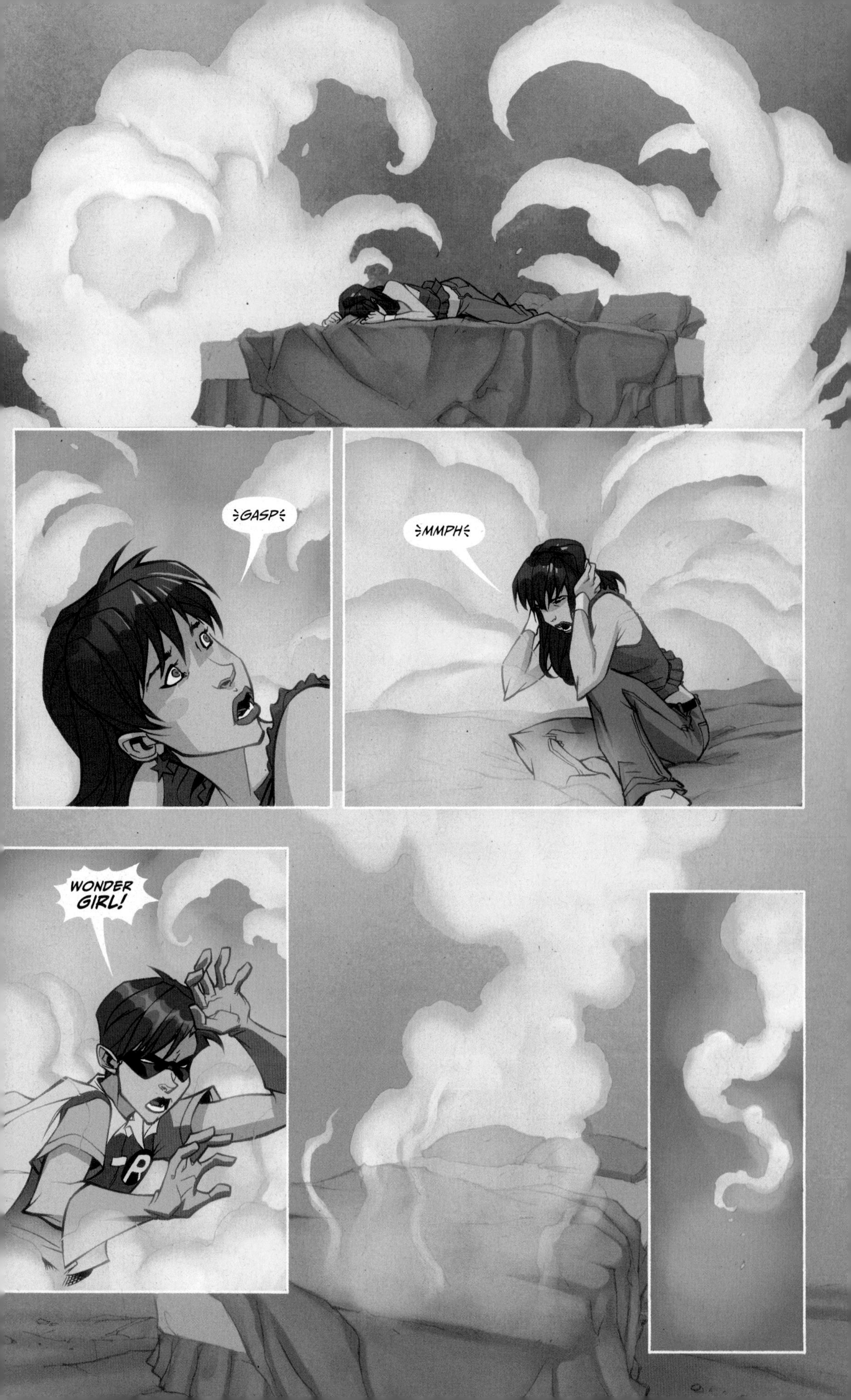
GASP
MMPH
WONDER GIRL!

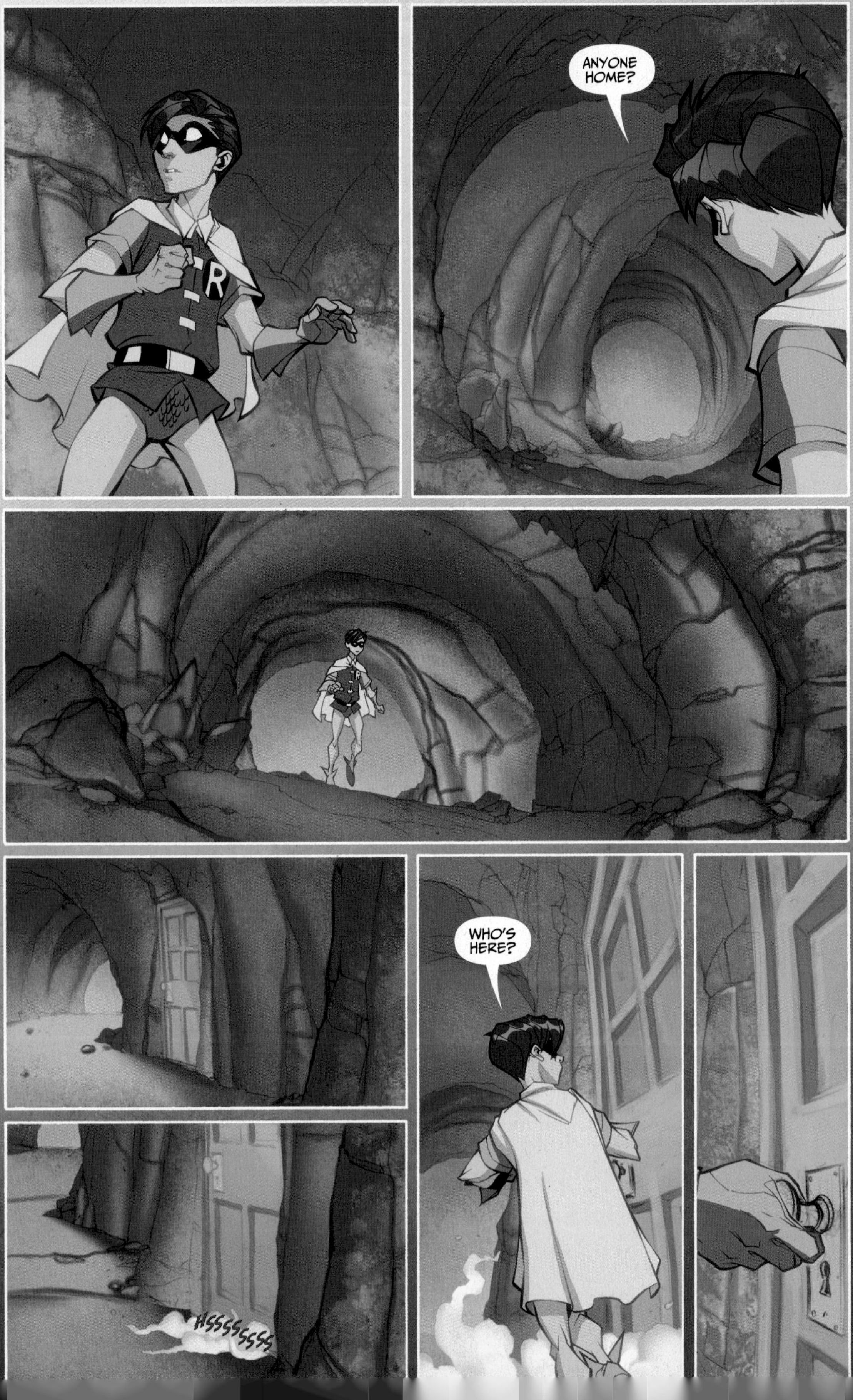
ANYONE HOME?
WHO'S HERE?
HSSSSSSSS

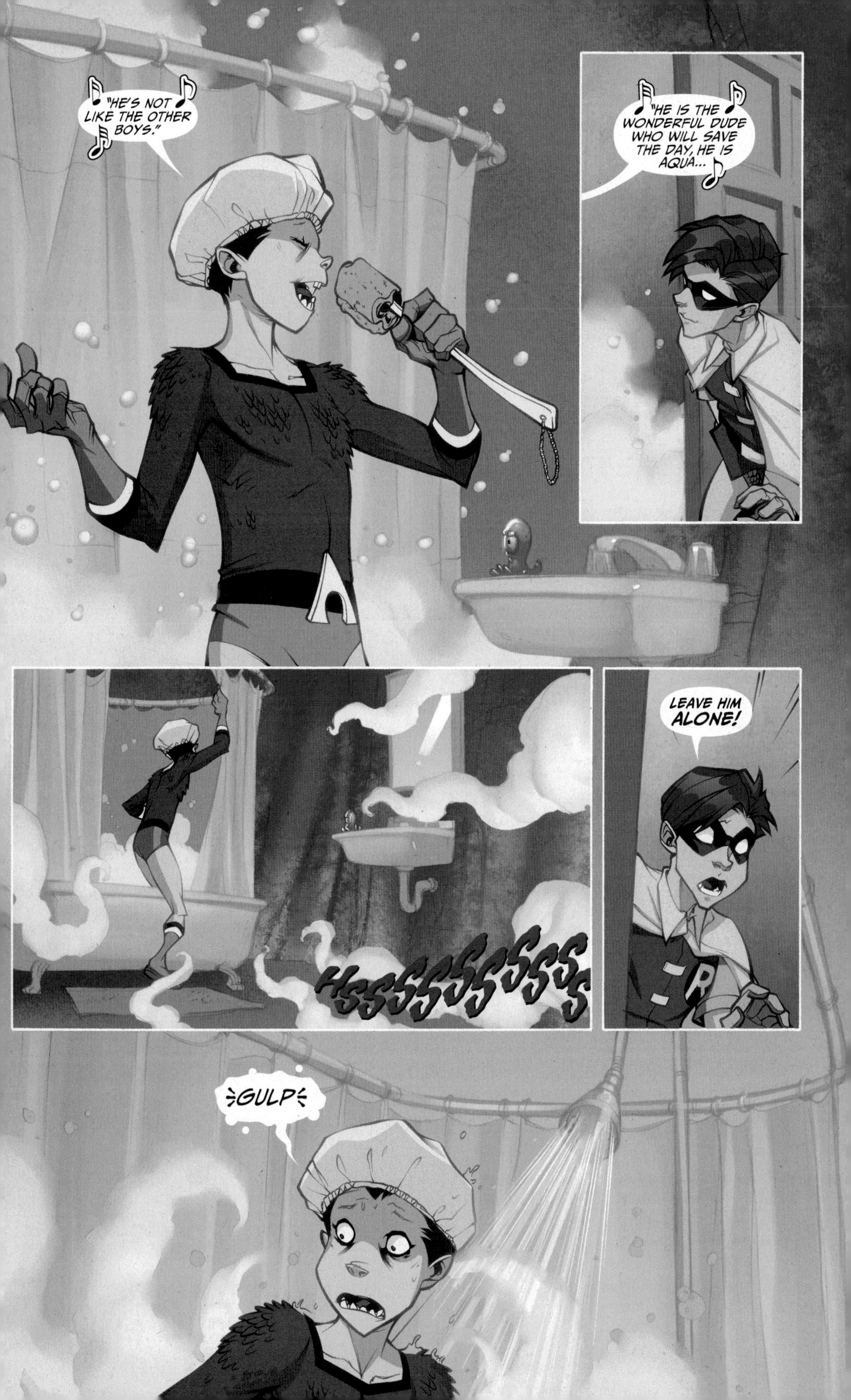
"HE'S NOT LIKE THE OTHER BOYS."
"HE IS THE WONDERFUL DUDE WHO WILL SAVE THE DAY, HE IS AQUA...
HSSSSSSSSSS
LEAVE HIM ALONE!
GULP

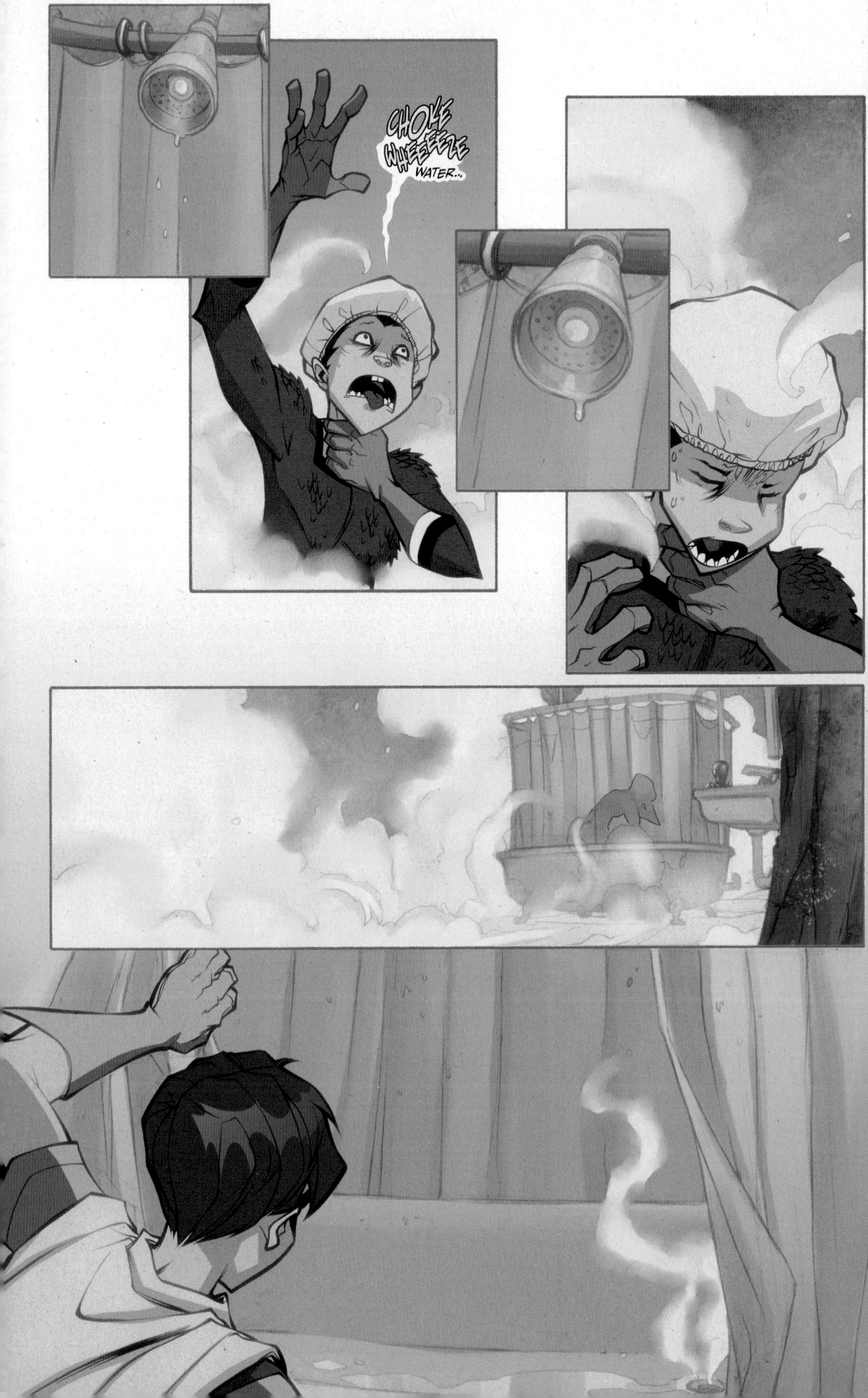
CHOKE
WHEEEEEZE
WATER...

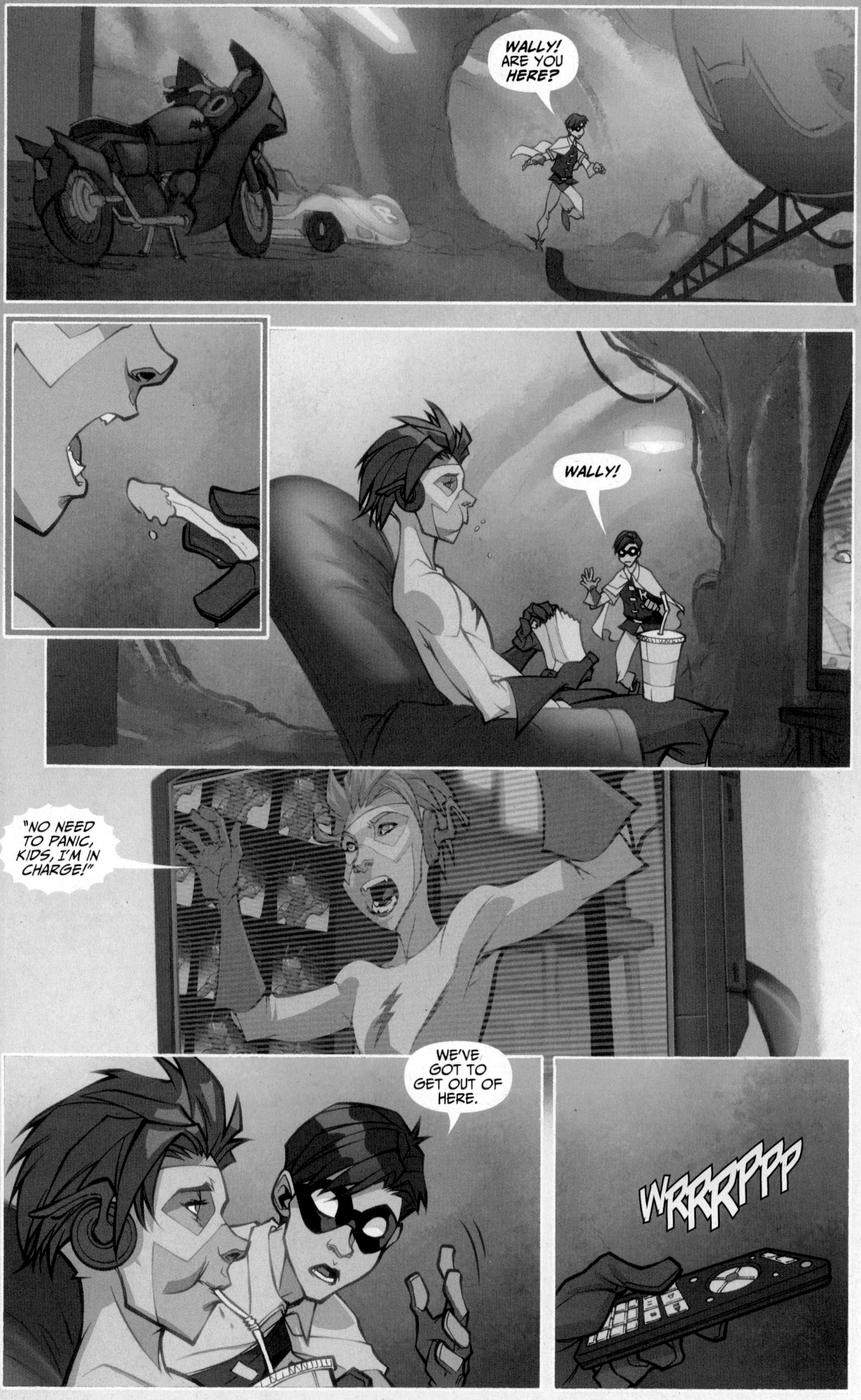
WALLY! ARE YOU HERE?
WALLY!
"NO NEED TO PANIC, KIDS, I'M IN CHARGE!"
WE'VE GOT TO GET OUT OF HERE.
WRRRPPP

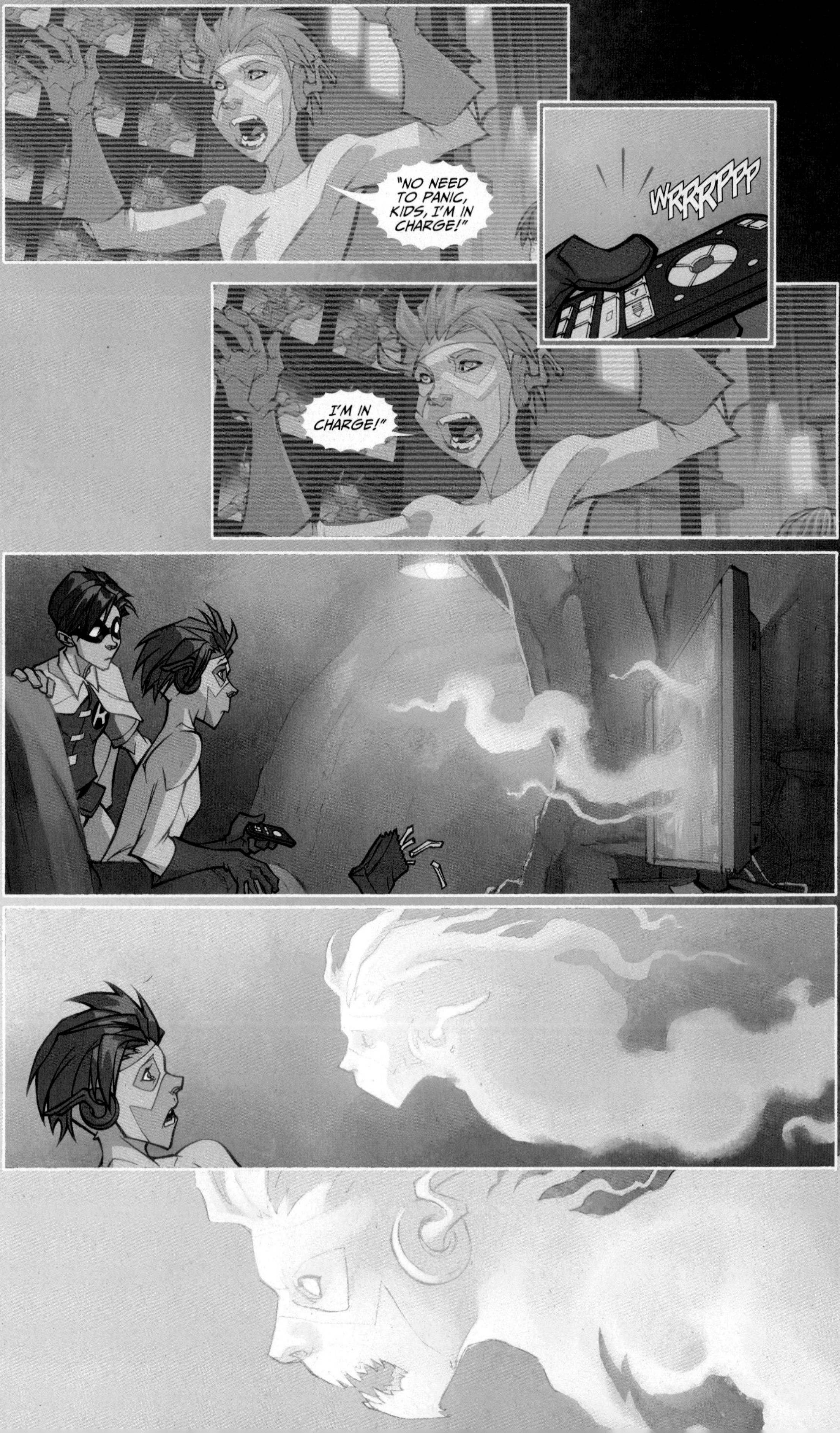
"NO NEED TO PANIC, KIDS, I'M IN CHARGE!"
WRRRPPP
I'M IN CHARGE!"

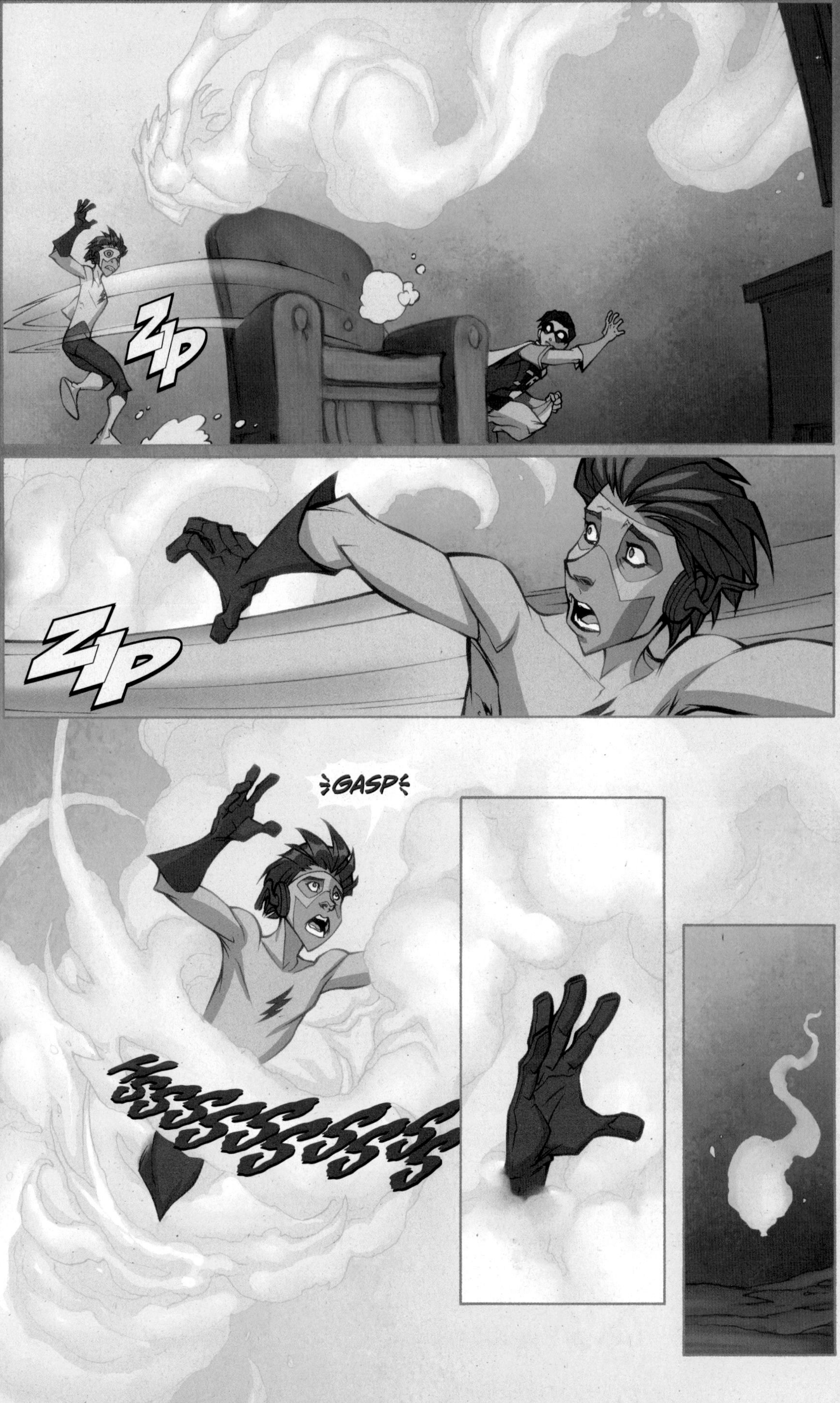
ZIP
ZIP
GASP
HSSSSSSSSSS

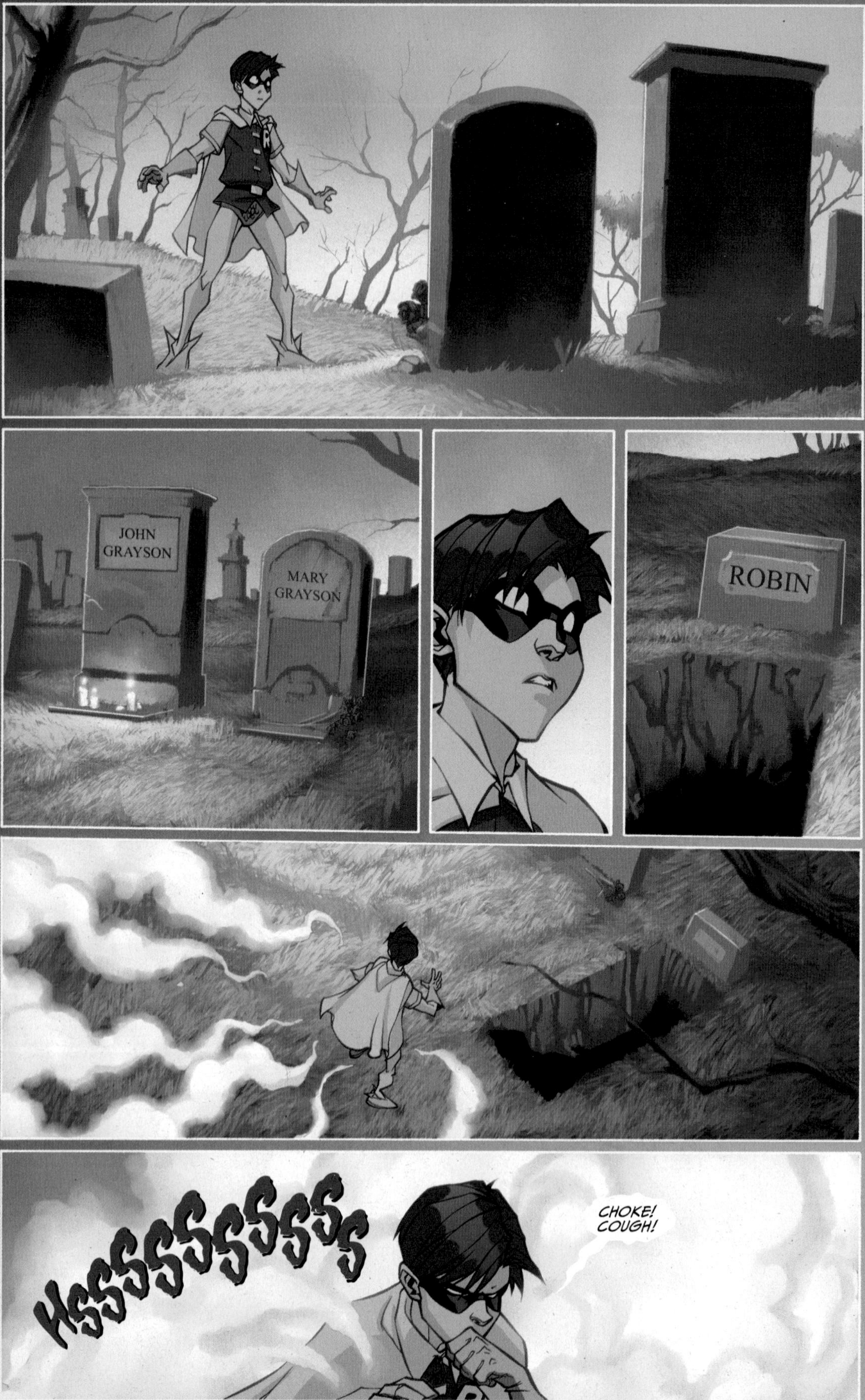
JOHN
GRAYSON
MARY
GRAYSON
ROBIN
HSSSSSSSSSSS
CHOKE!
COUGH!

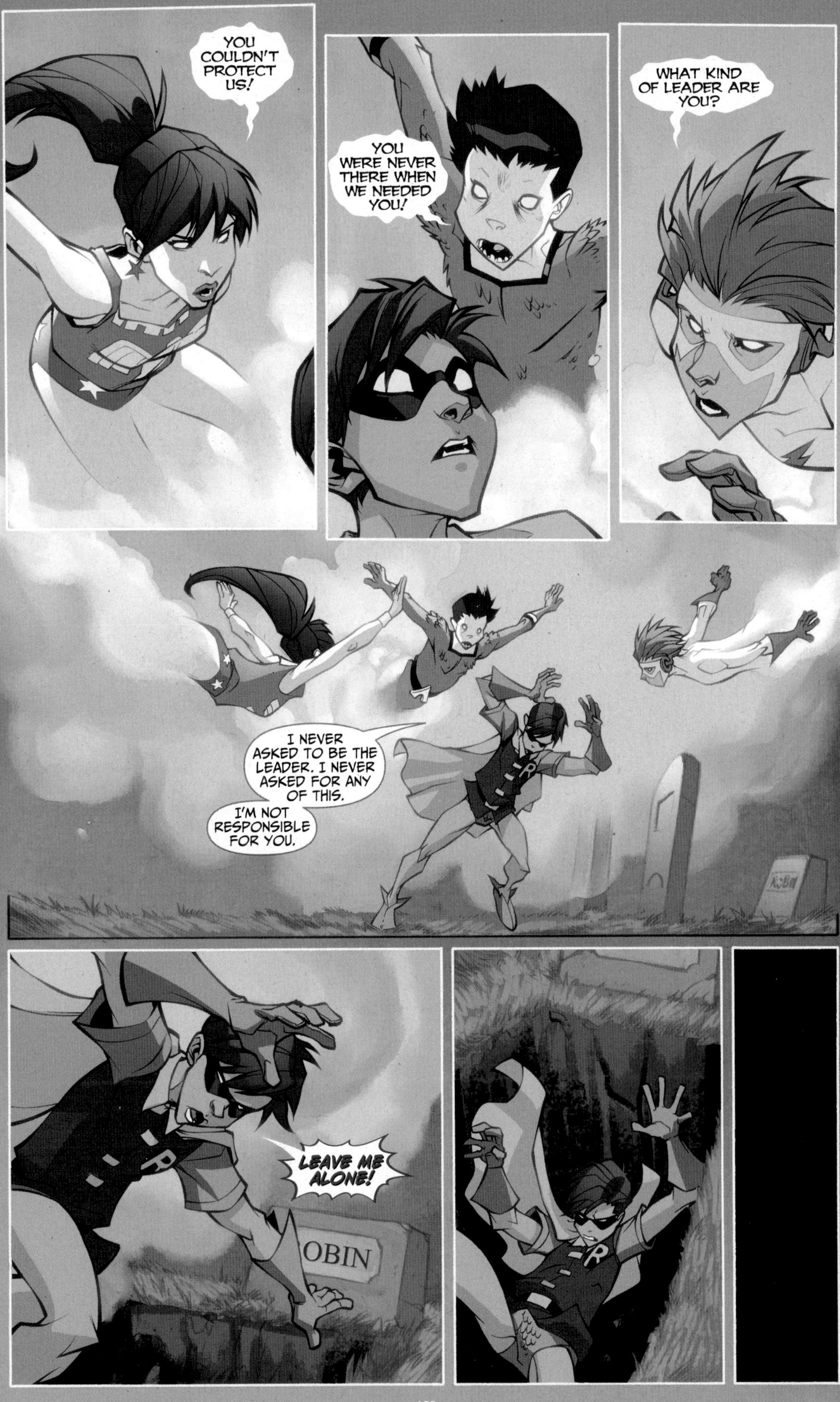
YOU COULDN'T PROTECT US!
YOU WERE NEVER THERE WHEN WE NEEDED YOU!
WHAT KIND OF LEADER ARE YOU?
I NEVER ASKED TO BE THE LEADER. I NEVER ASKED FOR ANY OF THIS.
I'M NOT RESPONSIBLE FOR YOU.
LEAVE ME ALONE!
OBIN

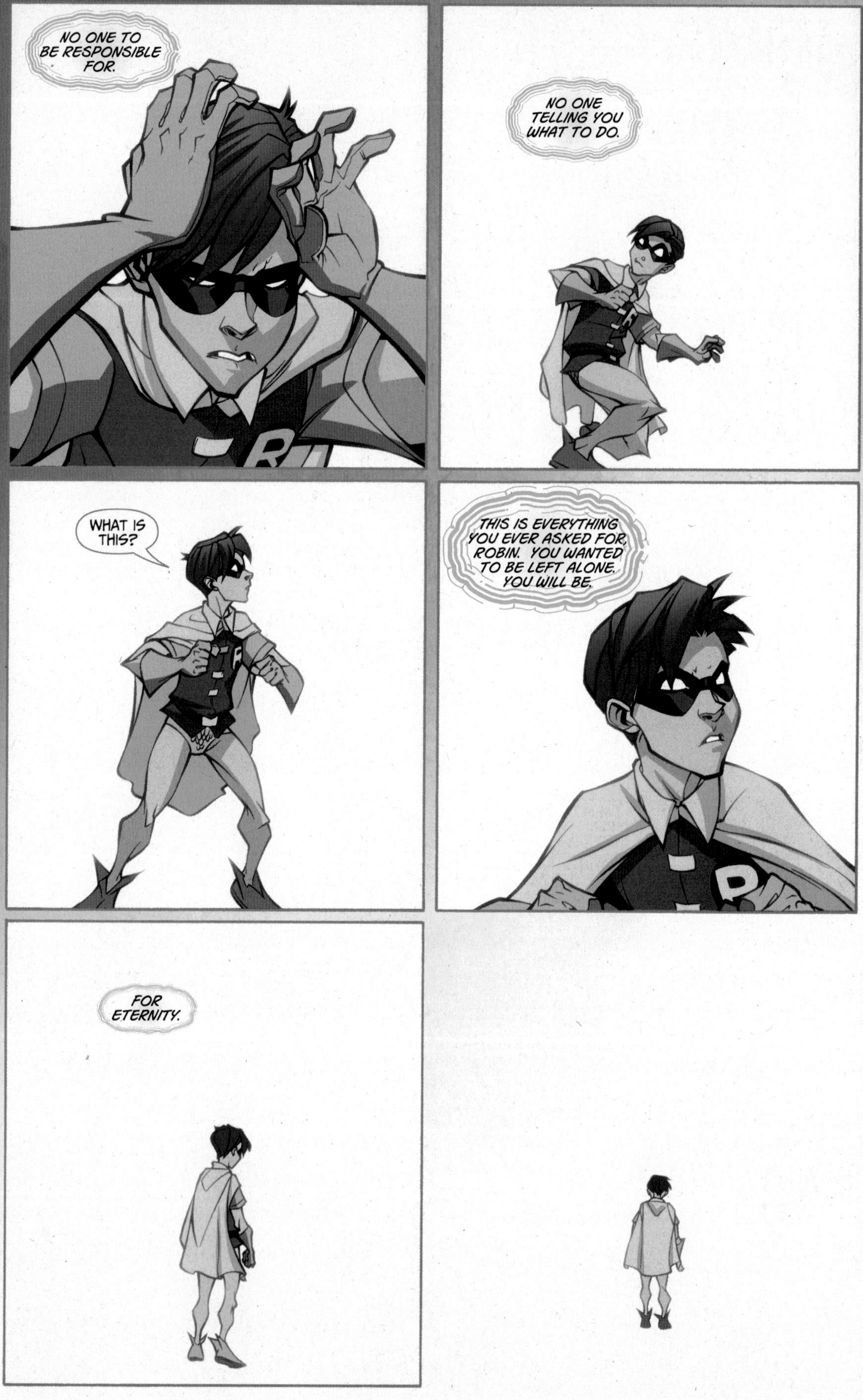
NO ONE TO BE RESPONSIBLE FOR.
NO ONE TELLING YOU WHAT TO DO.
WHAT IS THIS?
THIS IS EVERYTHING YOU EVER ASKED FOR, ROBIN. YOU WANTED TO BE LEFT ALONE. YOU WILL BE.
FOR ETERNITY.

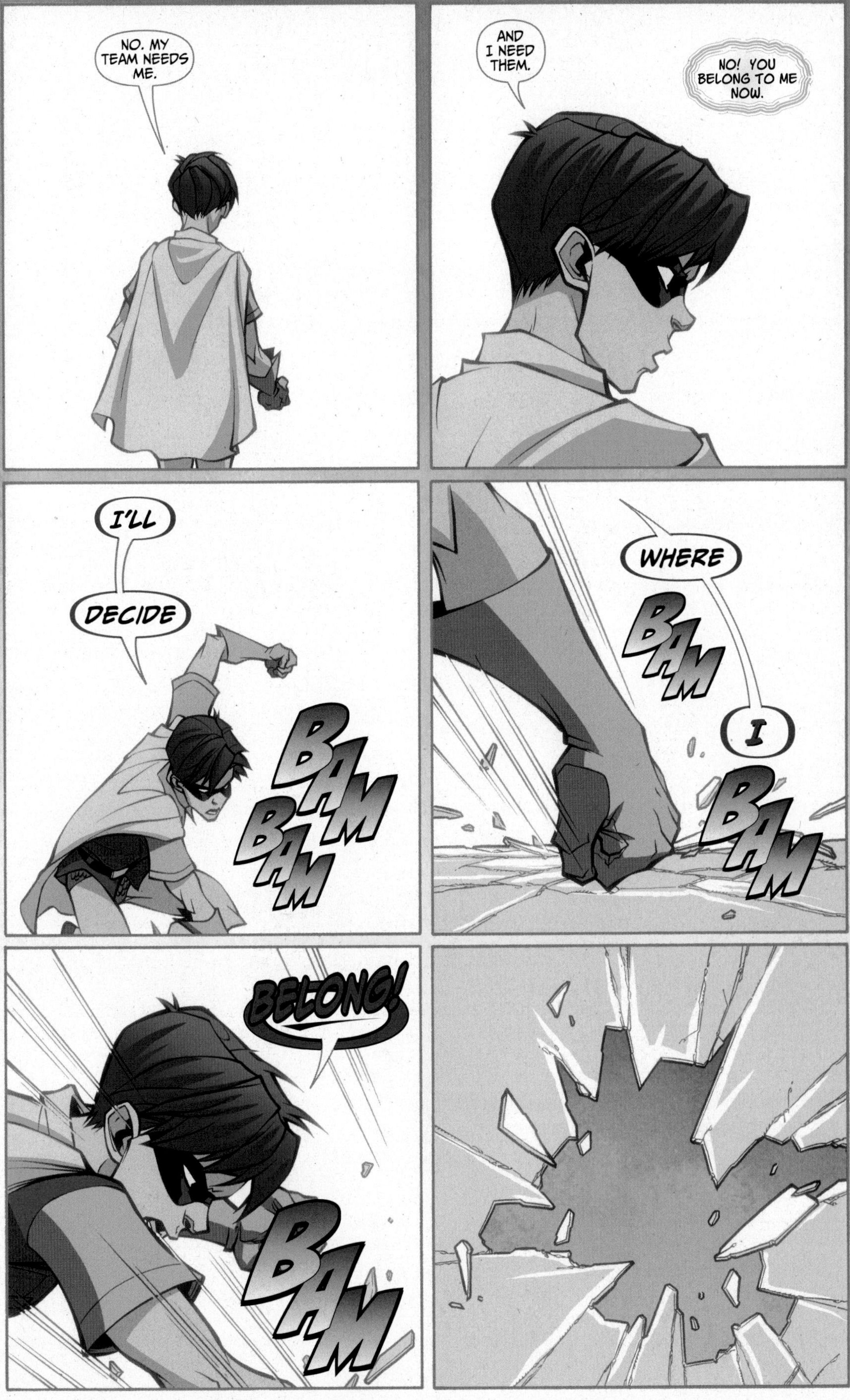
NO. MY TEAM NEEDS ME.
AND I NEED THEM.
NO! YOU BELONG TO ME NOW.
I'LL
DECIDE
BAM
BAM
WHERE
BAM
I
BAM
BELONG!
BAM

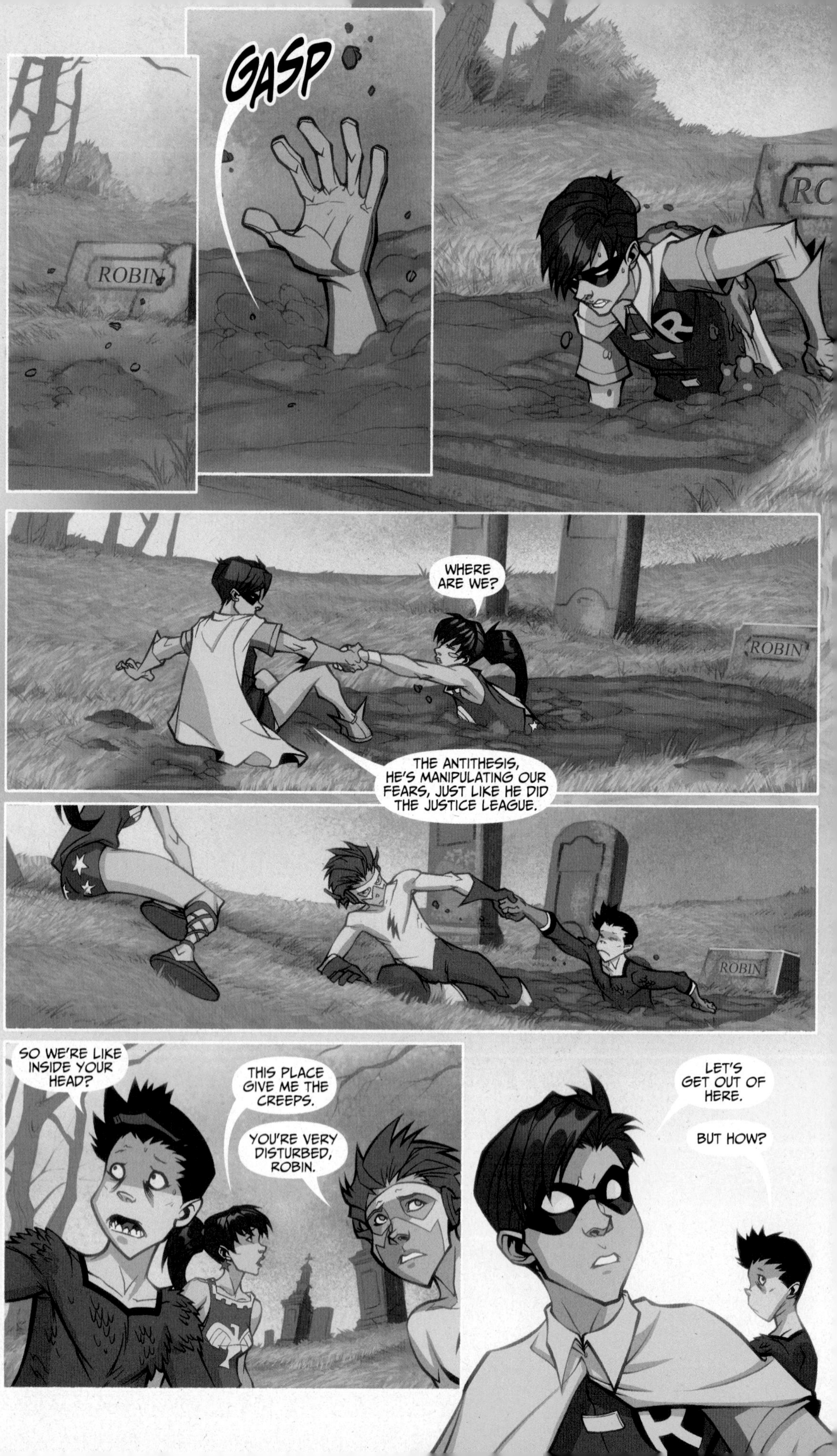
GASP
ROBIN
RO
ROBIN
WHERE ARE WE?
THE ANTITHESIS, HE'S MANIPULATING OUR FEARS, JUST LIKE HE DID THE JUSTICE LEAGUE.
ROBIN
SO WE'RE LIKE INSIDE YOUR HEAD?
THIS PLACE GIVE ME THE CREEPS.
YOU'RE VERY DISTURBED, ROBIN.
LET'S GET OUT OF HERE.
BUT HOW?

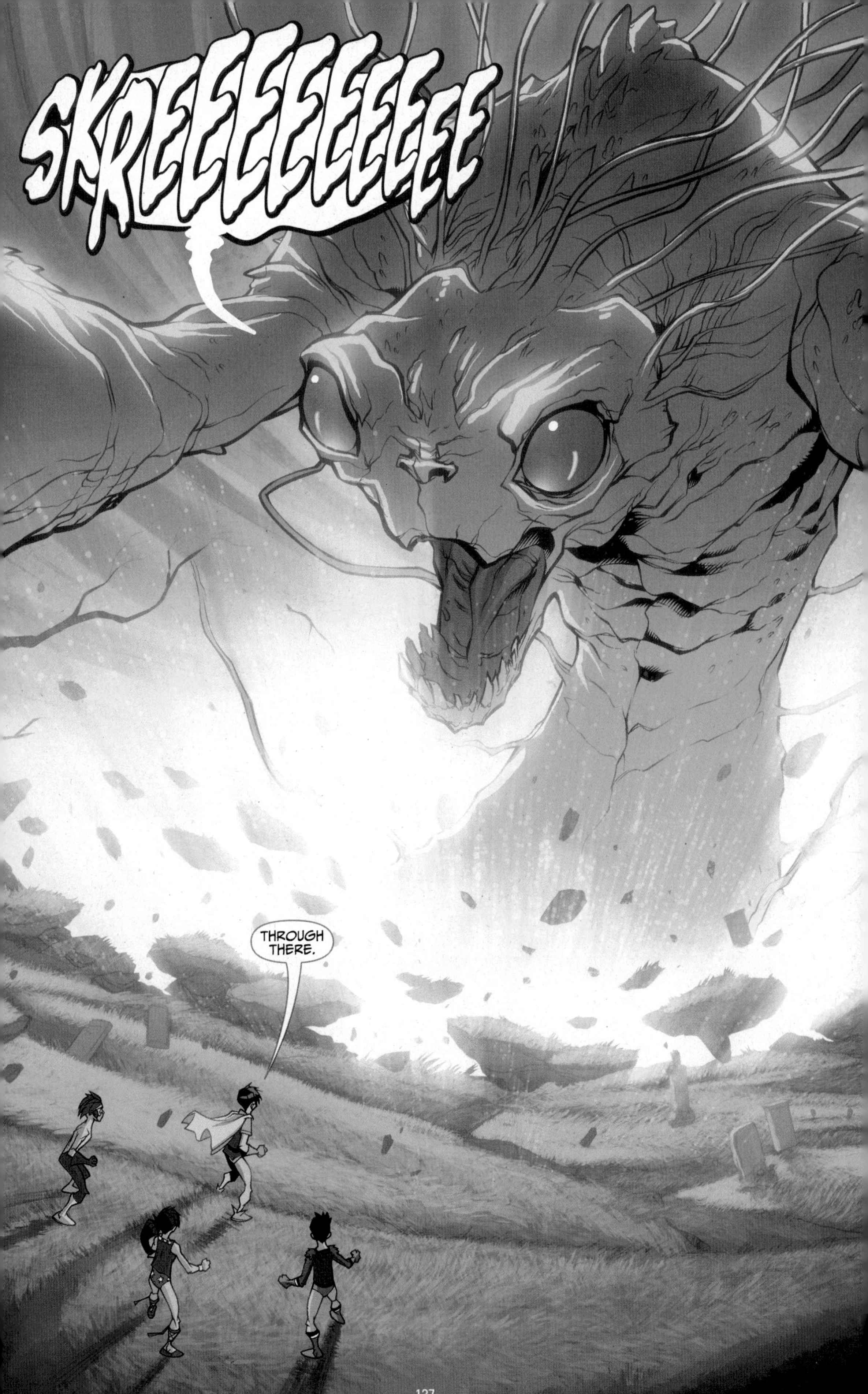
SKREEEEEEEEE
THROUGH THERE.

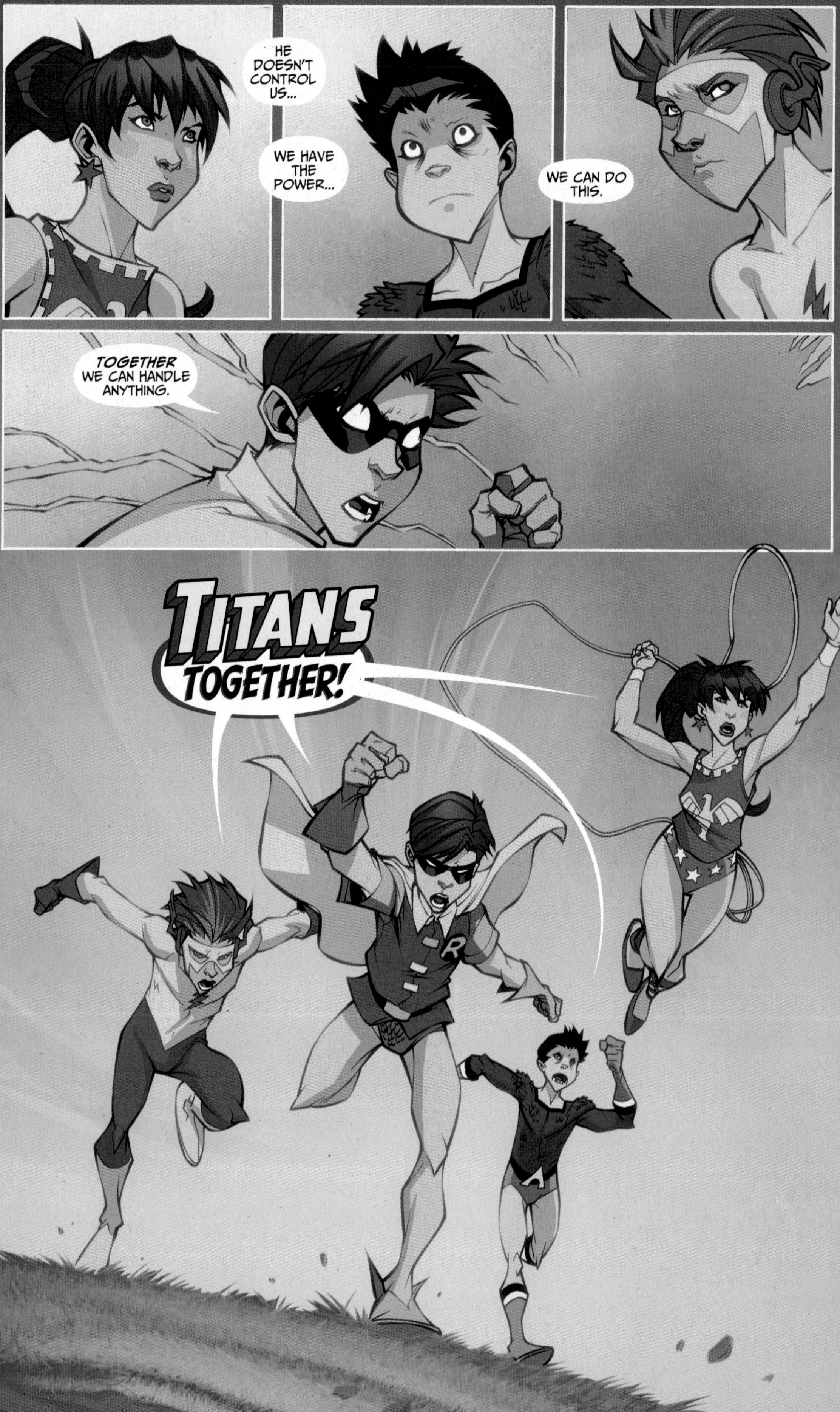
HE DOESN'T CONTROL US...
WE HAVE THE POWER...
WE CAN DO THIS.
TOGETHER WE CAN HANDLE ANYTHING.
TITANS TOGETHER!

ROBIN.

ROBIN. I WANT YOU TO KNOW...

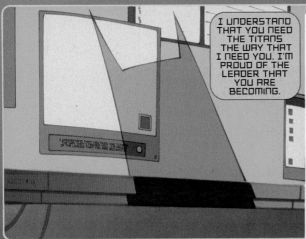

I UNDERSTAND THAT YOU NEED THE TITANS THE WAY THAT I NEED YOU. I'M PROUD OF THE LEADER THAT YOU ARE BECOMING.

HRM...DAMN IMS.

BLINK

ROBIN, COME HOME...

THE VERY END

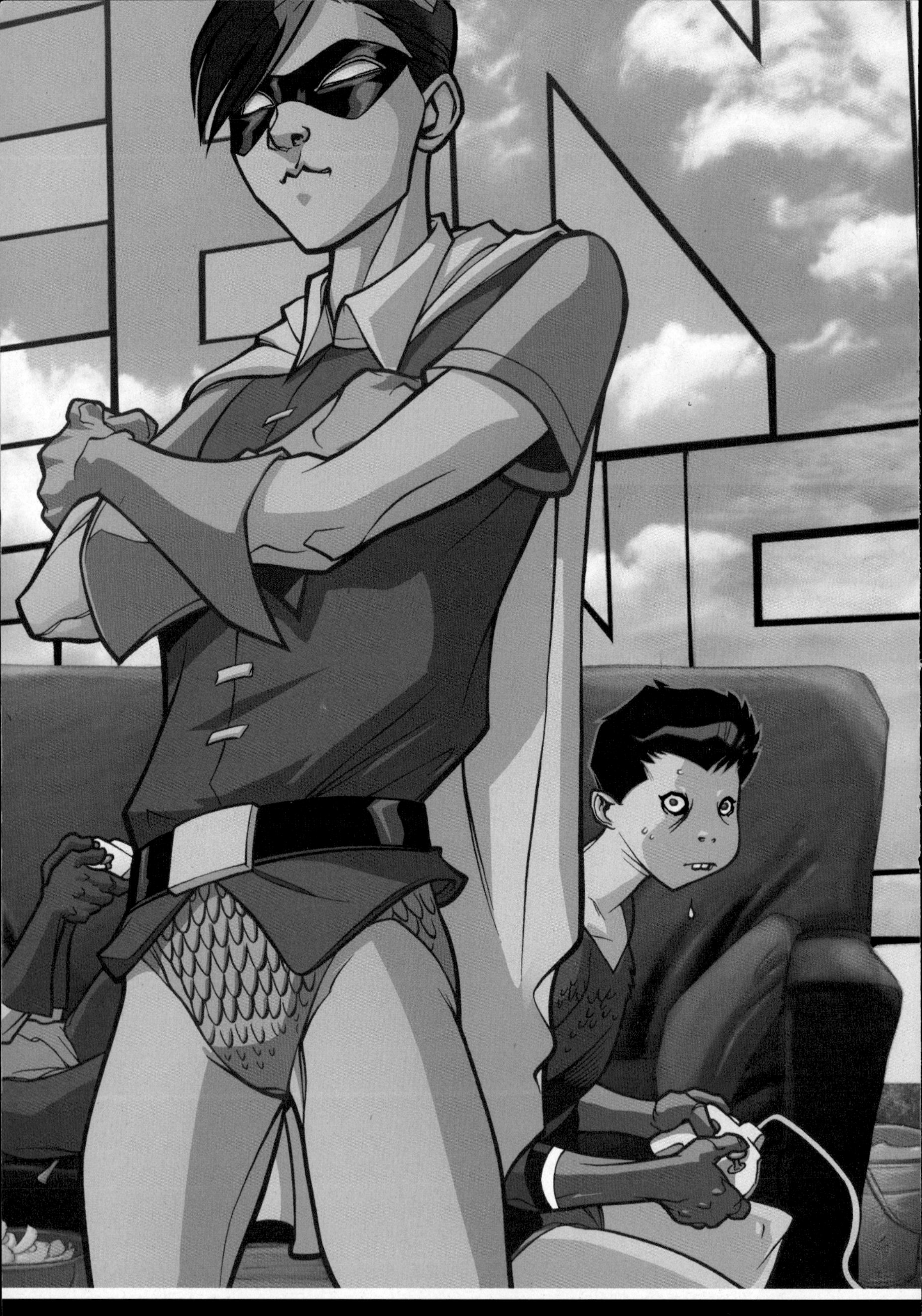

BONUS PINUP!

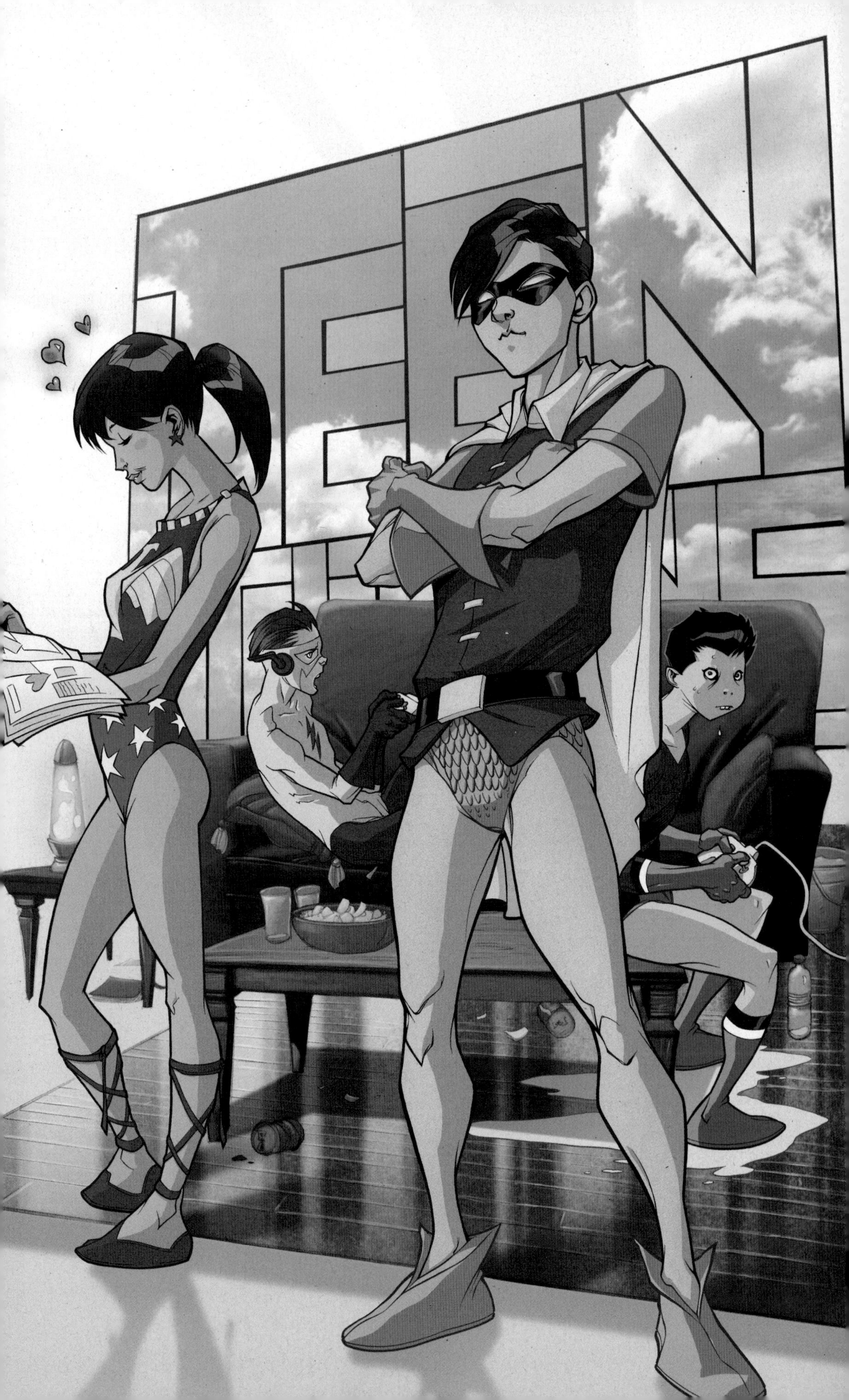

"Drips with energy."—IGN

"Grade A."—USA TODAY

START AT THE BEGINNING!

TEEN TITANS
VOLUME 1: IT'S OUR RIGHT TO FIGHT

TEEN TITANS
VOL. 2: THE CULLING

TEEN TITANS VOL. 3:
DEATH OF THE FAMILY

THE CULLING: RISE OF
THE RAVAGERS

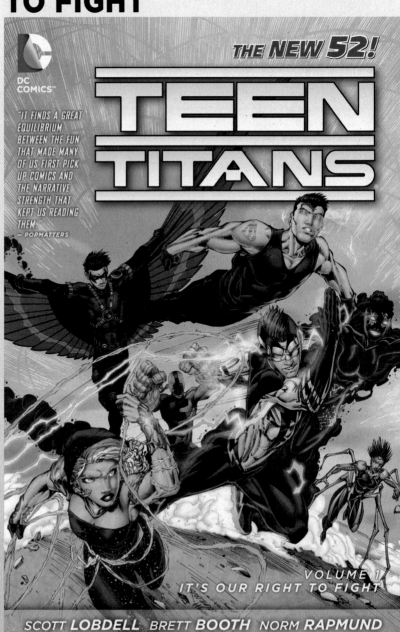

"Stellar. A solid yarn that roots itself in Grayson's past, with gorgeous artwork by artist Eddy Barrows."—IGN

"Dynamic."—The New York Times

"A new generation is going to fall in love with Nightwing."
—MTV Geek

START AT THE BEGINNING!

NIGHTWING
VOLUME 1: TRAPS AND TRAPEZES

NIGHTWING VOL. 2:
NIGHT OF THE OWLS

NIGHTWING VOL. 3:
DEATH OF THE FAMILY

BATMAN:
NIGHT OF THE OWLS

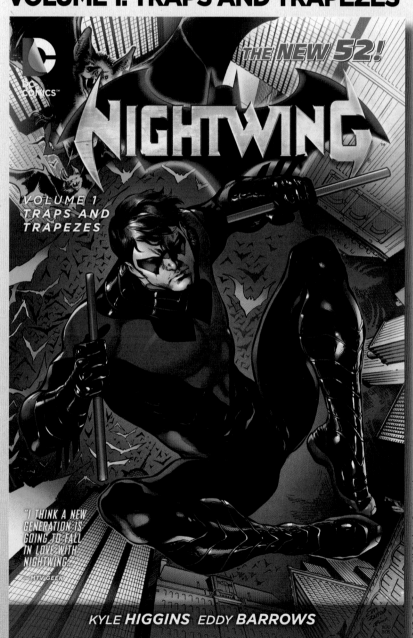

KYLE **HIGGINS** EDDY **BARROWS**

DC COMICS™

"Impressive."
—MTV SPLASH PAGE

"The Flash couldn't be in better hands."
—NEWSARAMA

"Geoff Johns on THE FLASH has been a true boon for the Scarlet Speedster, putting him right up there in popularity with the likes of Batman, Superman and Green Lantern."
—USA TODAY

FROM THE WRITER OF *JUSTICE LEAGUE* AND *GREEN LANTERN*

GEOFF JOHNS

with ETHAN VAN SCIVER

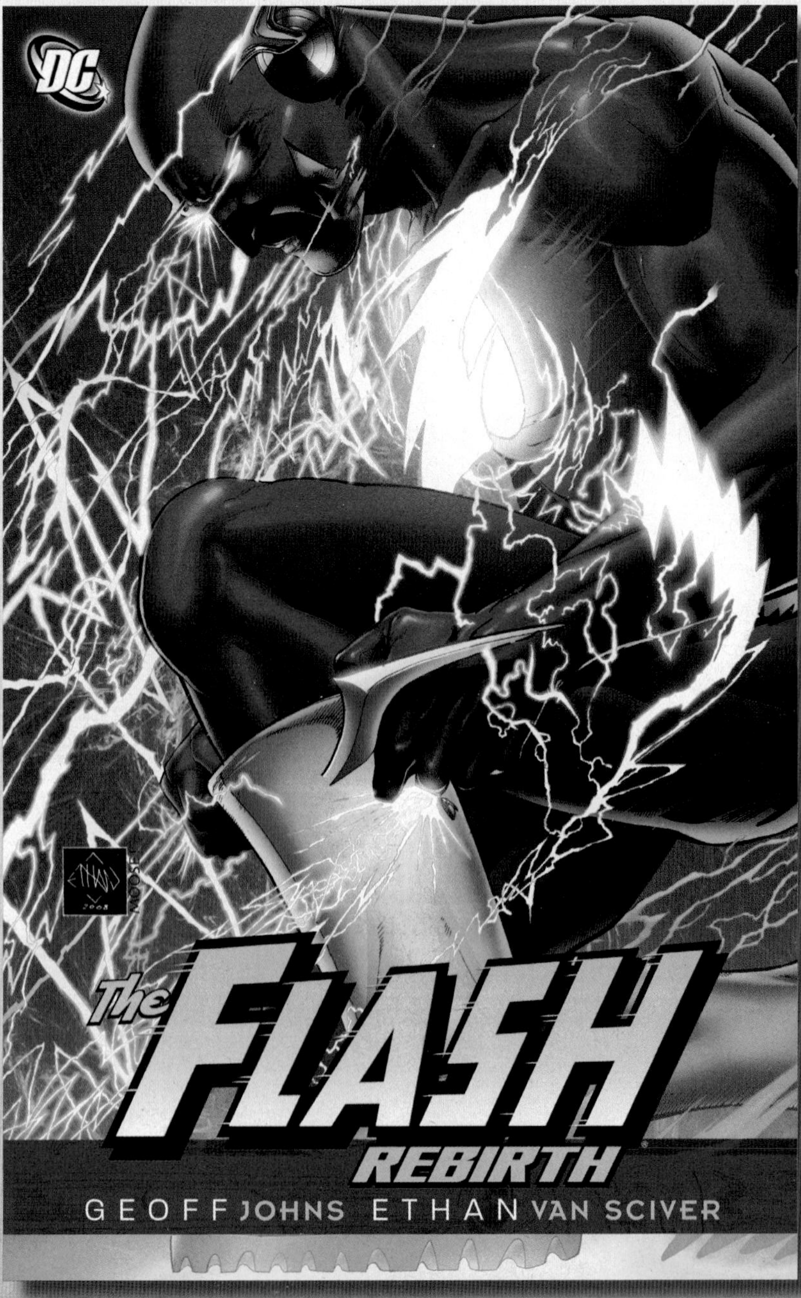

The FLASH
REBIRTH
GEOFF JOHNS ETHAN VAN SCIVER

THE FLASH: THE DASTARDLY DEATH OF THE ROGUES!

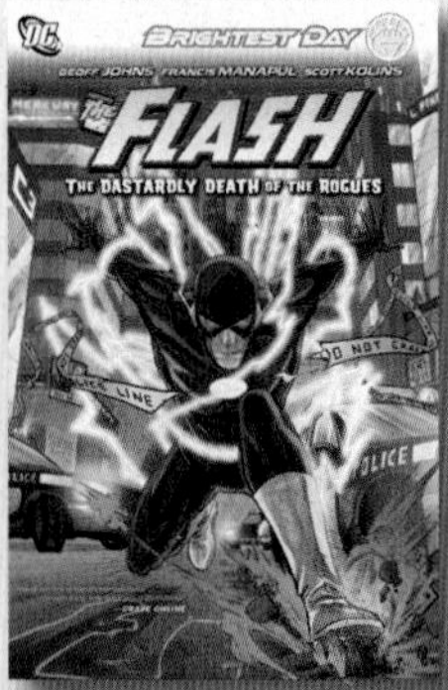

BRIGHTEST DAY
GEOFF JOHNS FRANCIS MANAPUL SCOTT KOLINS
The FLASH
THE DASTARDLY DEATH OF THE ROGUES

with FRANCIS MANAPUL

THE FLASH: THE ROAD TO FLASHPOINT

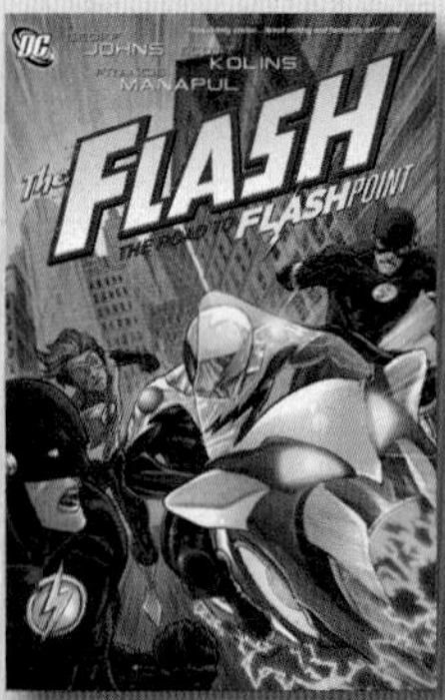

JOHNS
KOLINS
MANAPUL
The FLASH
THE ROAD TO FLASHPOINT

with FRANCIS MANAPUL and SCOTT KOLINS

FLASHPOINT

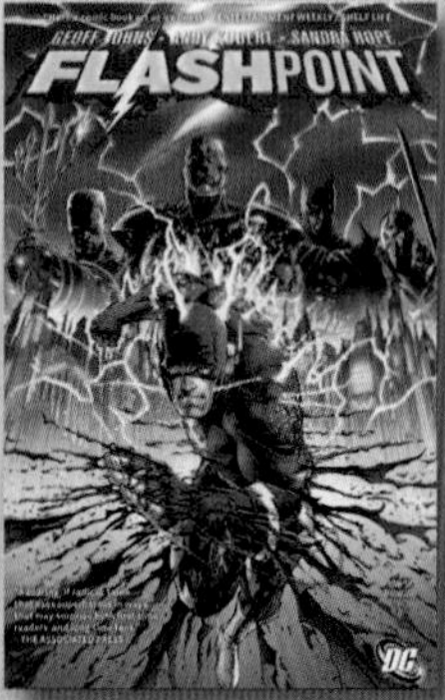

FLASHPOINT

with ANDY KUBERT